Compleat Traveler's Guide

ALSO AVAILABLE IN THE COMPLEAT TRAVELER SERIES

- ☐ *George Ferguson's* Europe by Eurail
- ☐ *George Ferguson's* Britain by Britrail
- ☐ The Total Traveler by Ship *(Ethel Blum)*

- ☐ Country Inns & Historic Hotels of Great Britain
- ☐ Country Inns & Historic Hotels of Canada
- ☐ Country Inns & Historic Hotels of Ireland

- ☐ Country New England Inns
- ☐ Country Inns & Historic Hotels of the Middle Atlantic States
- ☐ Country Inns & Historic Hotels of the South
- ☐ Country Inns & Historic Hotels of the Midwest & Rocky Mountain States
- ☐ Country Inns & Historic Hotels of California and the West

- ☐ Country New England Historical & Sightseeing Guide
- ☐ Country New England Antiques, Crafts, & Factory Outlets
- ☐ Guide to California and the Pacific Northwest
- ☐ Guide to the Southwest
- ☐ Guide to the South

If your local bookseller, gift shop, or country inn does not stock a particular title, ask them to order directly from Burt Franklin & Co., Inc., 235 East 44th Street, New York, New York 10017, U.S.A. Telephone orders are accepted from recognized retailers and credit card holders. In the United States, call 212-687-5250 during regular business hours.

THE COMPLEAT TRAVELER'S COMPANION

Guide to TEXAS and the SOUTHWEST

by

Anthony Hitchcock

and

Jean Lindgren

BURT FRANKLIN & CO.

PHOTO CREDITS

Pp. 22 bottom, 48 top, 127 top, 129 top: National Park Service photos. P. 49 bottom: courtesy Amon Carter Museum, Fort Worth, Texas. P. 74 top left: photo by June M. Secrist. P. 102 bottom: Oklahoma City Chamber of Commerce.

Published by Burt Franklin & Company
235 East Forty-fourth Street
New York, New York 10017

The volume has been published in two separate editions:
Guide to the Southwest
L.C. # 81-355 ISBN: 0-89102-209-0
and
Guide to Texas and the Southwest
L.C. # 79-27766 ISBN: 0-89102-200-7

Manufactured in the United States of America
3 4 2

Contents

Introduction vii

TEXAS 1

OKLAHOMA 89

NEW MEXICO 115

ARIZONA 143

Index 171

Introduction

TEXAS AND THE SOUTHWEST are vast areas that are home territory both for most American Indians and for an increasing number of industrial corporations drawn to the rapidly growing sun-belt cities. This is a land influenced by many cultures, rich in resources and diverse attractions both natural and man-made that appeal to tourists from all parts of the world. Whether in the bayou country of East Texas, the Grand Canyon, the Spanish missions of Arizona, or the Taos pueblos, visitors can expect to find both variety and grandeur in the Southwest. You are certain not to be disappointed here.

Before planning a trip to this region, you would be wise to arm yourself with the helpful free literature available from the separate states. Addresses of important travel departments and chambers of commerce are given in the introduction to each state and key city. It is important to remember that many of the most renowned attractions are within the boundaries of national parks and monuments. Visitors planning to go to several parks should consider obaining a Golden Eagle Passport, which costs $10 and admits the holder and a carful of passengers to all national parks, monuments, and recreation areas. People without such passports pay individual fees ranging from 50¢ to $3 at each area. Those sixty-two or older may obtain a Golden Age Passport free of charge. Both passports are available from the National Park Service Headquarters, Room 1013, U.S. Department of the Interior, Eighteenth and C Streets, N.W., Washington DC 20240. The passports are also available at all regional offices and at any fee-charging tourist area.

Because fees are often subject to change, we have not attempted to list specific charges. Instead, fees are listed as "free" or "nominal charge" or "fee charged." "Nominal charge" means adults pay fees of less than $2 per person. "Fee charged" means adult charges are more than $2 per person. Children's rates are almost always less, and young children are often admitted free.

The attractions included in these pages were chosen to represent a wide range. Although most are scenic or historic points of interest, we have included a number of more commercial activities because of their popularity with travelers. We have made every effort to provide accurate information but we remind readers that all rates and schedules are subject to change. Finally, we have neither solicited nor accepted any fees or gratuities for inclusion in this book or any other books in the Compleat Traveler's Companion series.

Because it is very important to us that the book continue to grow in usefulness in succeeding editions, we are eager to hear of your experiences using this travel guide. We will make every effort to answer all letters personally. Please write to us in care of our publishers, Burt Franklin & Co., 235 East Forty-fourth Street, New York, NY 10017.

Texas

SEVERAL EARLY SPANISH explorations reached Texas soil, but the most important was inadvertent—the result of a shipwreck. The Spanish explorer Cabeza de Vaca and three shipmates swam ashore on the Texas coast and walked all the way to the Mexican Pacific coast, bringing with them tales of cities of gold. For years afterward, Spain mounted expeditions to the Southwest searching for the fabled "Seven Cities of Cibola." These were never found, although both Francisco de Coronado and Hernando de Soto made thorough explorations in the Texas–New Mexico area. French explorers were led by Sieur de La Salle, who established a short-lived settlement at Fort Saint Louis on the coast. The French failure left the region open to settlement by the Spanish, who soon established widespread missions, many of which were fortified against Indian attack. San Antonio emerged early as the seat of the Spanish colonial government.

When Mexico gained its independence from Spain in 1822, control passed to the Mexican government, which began to allow immigration by American settlers, but in 1830 Mexico began to worry about the large number of Americans living on Mexican soil and ended legal immigration. This damaged the already strained relations betweeen the two nations and resulted in the successful American attack on Mexican troops stationed at San Antonio. In retaliation, Mexicans laid siege to a band of Americans at the Alamo and finally overran it, killing its defenders, including Davy Crockett and Jim Bowie. Under the leadership of Sam Houston, the area's Mexican government was overthrown and the independent republic of Texas established, which

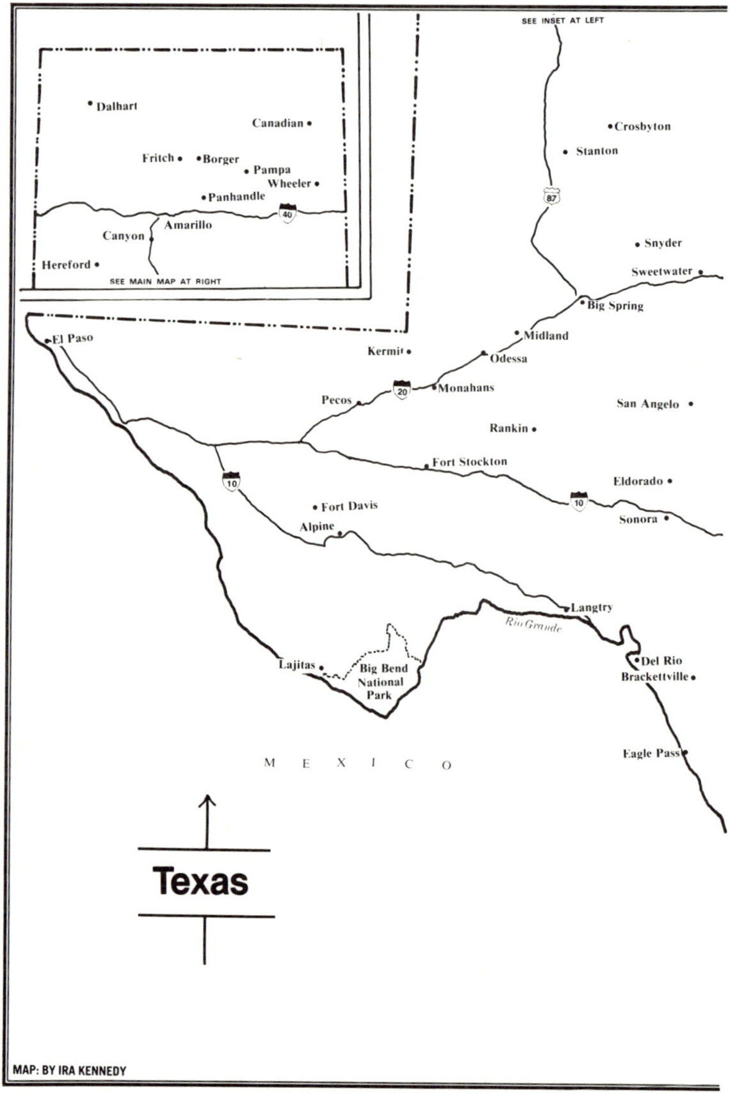
SEE INSET AT LEFT
Dalhart
Canadian
Fritch
Borger
Pampa
Wheeler
Panhandle
40
Amarillo
Canyon
Hereford
SEE MAIN MAP AT RIGHT
Crosbyton
Stanton
87
Snyder
Sweetwater
Big Spring
Midland
El Paso
Kermit
Odessa
20
Monahans
Pecos
San Angelo
Rankin
Fort Stockton
Eldorado
10
Fort Davis
Sonora
Alpine
Langtry
Rio Grande
Del Rio
Brackettville
Lajitas
Big Bend
National
Park
Eagle Pass
M E X I C O
Texas
MAP: BY IRA KENNEDY

OKLAHOMA
Crowell
Wichita Falls
Saint Jo
Denison
Gainesville
Sherman
Bonham
Texarkana
Windthorst
Sunset
Cooper
Decatur
Denton
McKinney
30
Jefferson
Karnack
Fort Worth
Dallas
Quitman
Albany
Weatherford
Grand Prairie
Marshall
Arlington
20
Abilene
Baird
Eastland
Tyler
Glen Rose
Corsicana
Hillsboro
Rusk
Coleman
Santa Anna
Mexia
Fairfield
Grapeland
Nacogdoches
Brownwood
Clifton
Waco
Lufkin
Gatesville
45
Marlin
Zavalla
Killeen
Temple
Madisonville
Menard
35
Woodville
Livingston
Burnet
Bryan
Junction
Saratoga
Washington
Orange
Fredericksburg
Stonewall
Johnson City
Austin
Beaumont
Liberty
Nederland
Bastrop
Round Top
Chappell Hill
Port Arthur
Wimberley
San Marcos
Columbus
Houston
Richmond
Bandera
Boerne
New Braunfels
10
Seguin
Galveston
San Antonio
West Columbia
Devine
Cuero
Bay City
Victoria
Goliad
Port Lavaca
Corpus Christi
G U L F
Laredo
Kingsville
O F
Falfurrias
M E X I C O
Edinburg
Rio Grande City
Pharr
Harlingen
Alamo
Port Isabel
Weslaco
Brownsville

continued until 1845, when Texas became the twenty-eighth state to be admitted to the Union.

Almost any schoolchild knows that Texas is the second largest state in the country, but few who have not been there can imagine the diversity of its geography. From the bayou and plantation country near Louisiana to the vast cattle ranches of the west and the waterfront cities on the Gulf, Texas beckons visitors. For a 150-page preview of many of its wonders, send for the full-color *Texas, Land of Contrasts* from the Department of Tourism. Write to it at Texas, Department CTC-9, Box 5064, Austin TX 78763, or call 512-475-4326. Also, a particularly helpful pamphlet is available from the Texas Historical Commission. Entitled "Texas Museum Directory," it can be ordered from the commission at P.O. Box 12276, Austin TX 78711; or by telephone, by calling 512-475-3092. We are indebted to the two above-mentioned publications and want to thank both the Department of Tourism and the Texas Historical Commission for their cooperation in the preparation of this chapter.

ABILENE The *Abilene Fine Arts Museum*, in Oscar Rose Park, deals mainly with twentieth-century American art but also has changing international and historical exhibits. Open all year Tuesday through Friday 9–5, weekends 1–5; closed mid-July to mid-August. Free. 915-673-4587.

Abilene Zoological Gardens is in Abilene's Nelson Park, Route 36 at Loop 322 off I-20. Covering 53.8 acres and housing more than four hundred animals from all over the world, the zoo has won national and state awards for its low-profile garden design. It has been honored as "best small zoo in the country" by a national zoo organization, and it won an award of merit from the American Institute of Architects. There are few cages here at Nelson Park; the animals are separated from visitors by a large moat. Several different habitats, which allow animals from different regions to roam in more natural settings, include those of the Texas Plains, the African veldt, and Australian and South American settings. Open the year around, weather permitting, winter and summer weekdays 10–5, weekends and summer holidays 10–7. Nominal charge. 915-672-9771.

The frontier is recaptured at *Old Abilene Town*—on I-10 at Loop 322—a Western-style amusement park depicting early Abilene and the West Texas frontier days. Street-front recreations include pioneer stores, the Golden Stage Restaurant, the Last Chance Saloon, and various antique and historical exhibits. Open daily 11–7, except Christmas; in summer, 8 A.M. to 9 P.M. Nominal charge. 915-677-2611.

ALAMO The *Santa Ana National Wildlife Refuge,* off U.S. 83, about 8 miles south and east on U.S. 281, is a Federal Registered Natural Landmark, one of more than four hundred such National Wildlife refuges administered by the U.S. Fish and Wildlife Service. In 1903, President Theodore Roosevelt established the first refuge, a 3-acre island along the eastern Florida coastline. Today, several million acres are managed for wildlife preservation and the enjoyment and education of the public. Santa Ana, a 2,000-acre native brush tract containing elm, ebony, blackberry, mesquite, and many other species, is the habitat for some 322 species of birds and 2 rare mammals, the ocelot and jaguarundi. The wildlife drive open all year 8–6; foot access dawn to dusk. Free. 512-787-3079.

The town of Alamo was named for the Alamo Land and Sugar Company. The region continues to be a major center for citrus and truck farming. The *Live Steam Museum,* about 2 miles north of U.S. 83 on F.M. 907, has collected a wide assortment of early engines and pumps that provided the power to run frontier farms as well as ships, and for other purposes. All the steam engines are fully restored and in working order. A good time to visit is on Sundays from December through April—"Live Steam Days"—when a number of engines can be seen in operation. Open daily 8–5. Donation. 512-787-1941.

ALBANY An early supply point for the trail to Dodge City, Albany remains an important beef-farming and oil-producing center. The *Ledbetter Picket House Museum,* in Webb Park at 1010 Railroad Street, contains relics from the Ledbetter Salt works, founded in 1860. In a frontier "dog-run" cabin composed of slender, upright pickets, the museum building is furnished with antiques and items from the frontier period. Open daily 8–5. Free. 817-762-3087.

ALPINE Man has occupied the Big Bend region since about 10,000 B.C., and its cultural influences may be grouped into four main categories: Indian, Spanish, Mexican, and Anglo-American. The *Museum of the Big Bend,* on the campus of Sul Ross State University, displays these diverse past cultures side by side. Exhibits give the progressive history of the Big Bend from the stone tools of the prehistoric inhabitants to the artifacts of the permanent settlements of the nineteenth century. Themes include early transportation, ranching, mining, and town-building, and period-room displays show pioneer life, early stores, and elaborate Victorian furniture. American folk arts are seen in displays of early quilt patterns, woodworking tools, and implements used in the home before the present electrical age. Open Tuesday through Saturday from 9–5, Sunday 1–5; closed Monday and school holidays. Free. 915-837-3461, ext. 212.

The *Woodward Agate Ranch,* on Route 118, 14 miles south of Alpine, offers visitors a chance to hunt and collect the world-famous Texas red plume and pom-pom agate. Material collected is paid for at the rate of about 35 cents a pound (subject to change) and also includes jasper, labradorite feldspar, calcite, opal, and other mineral specimens. Grading of material found is provided by ranch experts at no additional charge. Open daily all year. No charge to enter the ranch and lapidary shop. Fee charged for camping on the site.

AMARILLO Amarillo has been called the helium capital of the world because about 90 percent of the available helium in the free world is located within a 250-mile radius of the city. In 1968, about four thousand items were placed in the *Helium Time Column,* at 2701 I-40, a six-story monument that will be opened in the year 2968. They range from common office supplies to movie projectors and include the history of a Texas Panhandle county, a dehydrated apple pie, and U.S. currency. A savings passbook for an account opened for $10 (payable to the U.S. Treasury) is gathering 4 percent interest and is expected to yield over one quintillion dollars when the capsule is opened. The site also contains a museum of history and science as well as a tourist information center. Monument and museum open daily 10–6, April to October 1; 9–5 the rest of the year. Free. 806-373-1122.

The *Amarillo Art Center,* on the campus of Amarillo College at 2200 Van Buren Street, is a complex of three buildings designed by Edward Durell Stone—who also designed the Kennedy Center in Washington D.C. It is devoted to the graphic arts, music, and drama and includes exhibition and teaching areas. It has a permanent collection of painting and sculpture, and there are regular performances of dance and drama. Open Tuesday through Friday 10–5, weekends 1–5, Wednesday evenings 7–9:30. Closed Mondays. Free. 806-372-8356.

The *Don Harrington Discovery Center,* at 1200 Streit Drive in the medical center, was one of the first computer-operated planetariums in the country. Shows are offered Friday and Saturday evenings at 8, Sunday afternoons at 3. The center also has a limited number of special exhibits on loan from the American Medical Association and NASA, which may be seen weekdays 9–4:30. Exhibits free; nominal charge for planetarium shows. 806-355-9547.

ARLINGTON The *Six Flags over Texas* amusement park, between Dallas and Fort Worth, off I-30, is the state's most popular tourist spot, attracting almost 3 million visitors each year. Six Flags over Texas, the first regional theme park in the country, started a new trend in family-oriented entertainment. It consists of 200 lavishly landscaped acres devoted to the historic themes of the six flags that have governed Texas since its discovery by the Spanish. With more than 2,500 employees, 100 rides and attractions, and more than six hours of special shows, there is something for every member of the family. Among the more famous rides is the Texas Chute-Out (a parachute drop), the Shock Wave (the park's spectacular double-loop roller-coaster), the original Log Flume, and the Runaway Mine Train. Under construction is a new wooden roller-coaster designed to satisfy a growing number of roller-coaster nostalgia fans. Park open daily in summer, on weekends in spring and fall. Hours vary according to season. One-price-for-all-rides admission policy. 817-461-1200.

AUSTIN The *Texas Capitol,* built over a six-year period starting in 1882, was constructed from 15,000 carloads of Texas pink granite. The capitol dome rises 7 feet higher than that of the Capitol in Washington. The interior wainscoting is of oak, pine, cherry, cedar, walnut, ash, and mahogany and the floor is of local rock terrazzo. When it was completed, the Texas Capitol was the seventh largest building in the world. Visitors are welcome in many parts of the building, including the entrance foyer, rotunda, the Governor's Reception Room in the south wing, the House of Representatives (except during sessions), the Senate (except during sessions), and the legislative Reference Library. When in session, the House and the Senate may be seen from chamber balconies on the third floor. Open twenty-four hours. Guided tours daily from 8:15–4:30. Free. 512-475-2323.

The 1856 *Governor's Mansion* is the oldest building in the Capitol complex. Typical of fine homes of this period, the mansion is an example of Neoclassic or Greek Revival style. Most of its rooms are furnished with antiques of historical significance and are viewed by thousands of visitors each year. The governor and his family have a private apartment on the mansion's second floor. Open for tours Monday, Wednesday, and Friday 10–11:40 A.M. Closed state holidays and other weekdays as well as during certain official functions. Visitors are urged to check tour schedules in advance by telephone (512-475-2121). Free. Tourist parking available in the State Visitor Parking lots at the southeast corner of Eleventh and Congress Avenue (south of the Capitol) and at the mid-1500 block of Congress Avenue (north of the Capitol). Two-hour parking limit. Free.

The *Old Land Office Building Museum,* at 112 East Eleventh Street, was built in 1857 and is two museums in one. The Daughters of the Confederacy museum on the ground floor contains Confederate relics and records. The Daughters of the Republic of Texas Museum on the second floor shows records, exhibits of Texas Republic days, and material about famous early Texans. Open Monday through Friday 9–12 and 1–5.

The *Natural Science Center,* off Lake Austin Boulevard, on the northwest shore of Town Lake, features live exhibits of native mammals, reptiles, amphibians, birds, and insects. There is a "Wisdom Woods" nature trail and the Nature Center itself, which is in a one-story limestone structure built in 1915 as an arcade in a commercial amusement park featuring, among other things, a diving horse. The property is now owned by the city, and the spring-fed pool used by the horse has been renamed Deep Eddy Pool. Inside the center are a number of participatory exhibits in the "Discovery Room" with hands-on displays and a "touch table." There are stereoscopic microscopes; mounted specimens of poisonous snakes and dangerous animals; and a large walk-around aquarium. Open daily 1–5; closed holidays. Free to individuals; guided group tours are charged. 512-472-4523.

The sculptress Elisabet Ney was born in Westphalia, Germany, in 1833. The daughter of a successful stonecutter and cabinetmaker, she received early training in his studio. Overcoming great social pressure, she became the first woman accepted to the Munich Art Academy. Working under the master sculptor Christian Rauch, she was introduced to the intellectual life of the capital. Ney's first career, in mid-nineteenth-century Europe, ended in 1870 when she and her husband moved to Georgia following the outbreak of the Franco-Prussian War. Soon thereafter they moved to Texas, but she did not resume her career until the 1890's. Commissioned to model General Sam Houston and Stephen F. Austin for the Columbian Exhibit in Chicago, she showed that a lapse of twenty years had not diminished her mastery of the medium. The statues may be seen in both the Texas and national capitols. The first unit of her Austin studio, "Formosa," was started in 1892, and work on it continued sporadically until her death in 1907. The *Elisabet Ney Studio* at 304 East Forty-fourth Street, is a memorial to the woman and her work.

Listed on the National Registry of Historic Sites, it was designed to resemble a Romanesque German castle and survives with its contents and furnishings intact. Open Tuesday through Friday 11–4:30, weekends 2–4:30; closed Monday and major holidays. Free. 512-477-6511, ext. 2611.

The *Neill-Cochran Museum House,* at 2310 San Gabriel, is the home of the National Society of the Colonial Dames of the United States in Texas. A blend of Greek Revival and native Texas materials, the elegant 1855 building was constructed of native Austin limestone and Texas pine; it is most unusual in that the foundation of each room goes right to the ground, forming a box. Antique furnishings and memorabilia from the sixteenth to the early twentieth century have been assembled here, and many rooms have been set up to reflect eclectic Victorian tastes. A prized possession of the museum is the *Bluebonnet* painting by Miss Mode Walker, which helped convince state legislators to choose the bluebonnet as the state flower. There are also extensive collections of cookbooks, fans, and pioneer artifacts housed in the Rock House Dependency. Open Wednesday through Sunday 2–4; closed major holidays. Nominal charge. 512-478-2335.

The *Jourdan-Bachman Pioneer Settlers Memorial Park and Pioneer Farm,* 11418 Sprinkle Cut-Off Road, features assorted farm animals on a 77-acre operating replica of a central Texas family homestead of 1860-80. The reconstructed and authentically reproduced farm structures include a "dog-trot" cabin, barn, bunkhouse, root cellar, forge, granary, and smokehouse, all typical of the period. The land was donated to the Austin Heritage Society by the grandchildren of the farm's original settlers. The Pioneer Farm is operated by the Outdoor Nature Programs Section of Austin's Parks and Recreation Department. Open for special programs abut six times a year. Fees charged. For information, call 512-837-1215.

The *Laguna Gloria Art Museum,* at 3809 West Thirty-fifth Street, features changing exhibitions of twentieth-century American art. Open Monday through Saturday 10–5, Thursday to 9, Sunday 1–5. Free. 512-458-8191.

The *O. Henry Home,* at 409 East Fifth Street, was the residence of William Sydney Porter, the eminent short-story writer who signed his works "O. Henry," and who lived in Austin from 1885–95. The cottage contains his desk, writing materials, and other furnishings of the period. Open Monday through Saturday 11–4:30, Sunday 2–4:30. Donation.

The *Lyndon B. Johnson Library and Museum,* at 2313 Red River, contains archives of manuscripts and audio-visual records relating to the president's life, as well as historical materials from the Johnson years. Slides, motion pictures, closed-circuit television, and mobile techniques are all used in the presentation. Exhibits include gifts from foreign heads of state, classical Western art, a moon rock, and a replica of the Oval Office of the White House. Open daily 9–5. Free. 512-397-5137.

The *Michener Galleries,* at the Harry Ransom Center at Twenty-first and Guadalupe, feature rotating exhibits from the permanent University of Texas "Art of the Americas" collections. Other collections include photography, theater arts, and literary iconography. Open Monday through Saturday 9–5, Sunday 1–5. Free. 512-471-7324.

The *Texas Memorial Museum,* at 2400 Trinity, contains exhibits on Texas history from the Spanish Mission era to post–Civil War days. The story of man's habitation of the region emphasizes the story of the American Indian. There are displays of dinosaur tracks as well as dioramas dealing with history and petroleum. Open Monday through Saturday 9–5, and Sunday 2–5. Free. 512-471-1604.

The *36th Infantry Division War Museum,* in Camp Mabry, at 2500 West Thirty-fifth Street displays military artifacts and mementos of the famed "T-Patch" Infantry Division and includes items from both World Wars I and II. Open daily 8–5.

The *University Art Museum,* at Twenty-third and San Jacinto, is a teaching gallery with rotating exhibits directed toward instruction. Exhibits change approximately monthly, and gallery tours are available. Open Monday through Saturday 9–6, Sunday 1–5. 512-471-7324.

BAIRD The *Callahan County Pioneer Museum,* in the basement of the Callahan County Courthouse at Market and Fourth streets, contains pioneer farm and ranch implements, household items, clothing, barbed wire and county documents. Open Monday through Friday 9–5. Free. 915-854-1718.

BANDERA The *Frontier Times Museum,* one block north of the Bandera courthouse, offers a collection of relics from Texas frontier days. The native-fieldstone building with beamed ceilings has exterior walls containing curious formations of stone, stalactites and stalagmites, fossils, and pieces of petrified wood. Inside the museum are old-time spinning wheels, music boxes, ox-yokes, sidesaddles, garden tools, branding irons, spurs, lariats, and other horsemanship articles. There are mounted animals and historical photographs, and a collection of South

American items includes the shrunken heads of a wild dog and a human. The Cordon collection contains five hundred bells from all parts of the world. Included in the bottle collection are many said to have come from Judge Roy Bean's saloon in Langtry. The museum also has many anthropological items from the local Indian populations and a Frontier Gallery of art of the old West, including watercolor studies by Warren Hunter for his paintings now at the Alamo. Open daily 10–12 and 1–4:30, Sunday 1–4:30. Closed Monday. Nominal charge. 512-796-3864.

BASTROP One of the state's oldest settlements, Bastrop is a pleasant town, filled with many historic homes. Of interest is the *C. Erhard and Sons Drug Store,* at 921 Main Street, the oldest in the state (1847), which displays early furnishings and patent medicines.

The *Bastrop County Historical Museum,* 702 Main Street, is in the Cornelson-Fehr House, built in 1850 and enlarged four years later. The museum features manuscripts and miscellaneous pioneer and Indian artifacts. Open Saturday 9:30–5, Sunday 1–5. Nominal charge. 512-321-5031.

BAY CITY The *Matagorda County Historical Museum,* 1824 Sixth Street, contains early pioneer exhibits and collections. On display are early clothing, books, Texas maps, furniture, paintings, carpenter's tools, rare books, and a collection of early issues of the *Matagorda Gazette.* Open Tuesday through Friday 3–5, Sunday 2–5. Free. 713-245-7502.

BEAUMONT By the late nineteenth century, the first commercial oil fields had been developed in Pennsylvania, and Russia claimed to have discovered the first oil gushers. However, the oil age was really ushered in with the massive oil discovery at Spindletop Heights, Texas. The belief that there was oil at Spindletop had been firmly held by a local man, Pattillo Higgins. (So great was his conviction that he outlined a proposed model industrial city to be called "Gladys City," in honor of Gladys Bingham, a seven-year-old member of his Sunday-school class.) Higgins and his partners started the search for oil in the Spindletop area, but dissension soon arose and the project was abandoned, against Higgins's will. In 1900 the drilling rights were leased to the Pittsburg wildcatting team of James Guffey and John Galey, who encountered serious problems and almost gave up several times. On January 10, 1901, their drill became stuck in a crevice at 1,006 feet below ground. While they tried to dislodge it, the Lucas Gusher blew in. Oil spewed 100 feet over the tops of the derricks for nine days until the gusher could be capped, and the well went on to yield between 80,000 and 100,000 barrels per day. Overnight a boom town arose, and more than six hundred oil companies were chartered in the next few years. Most disappeared as quickly, but the Guffey Petroleum Co. went on to become Gulf Oil, and other local companies evolved into Texaco, Mobil, and Sun Oil. The *Gladys City Boomtown Museum,* at 950 East Florida, is a fourteen-building reconstruction of the oil-field boom town that ushered in the fuel age. Artifacts and archival material depict the early days in the oil fields and the boom towns. The original Spindletop oil field is about 1½ miles south of the museum site. Museum open Tuesday through Friday 1–5, Saturday 9–5, Sunday 1–5. Closed Monday. Nominal charge. 713-866-5058.

A Regency-style mansion set on 5 landscaped acres houses the *Beaumont Art Museum,* at 1111 Ninth Street. Included in its collection are twentieth-century Texas and American painting, sculpture, graphics, photography, and archaeological items. Open Tuesday through Friday 10–5, weekends 2–5. Closed Monday, New Year's, Easter, July 4, Thanksgiving, and December 24, 25, and 31. Free. 713-832-3432.

The *John Jay French Trading Post Museum,* 2985 French Road, is reached by taking Route 69 to the Lucas Exit and following the access road to French Road. The historic site features the French family home furnished as it had been in the 1840s, including some of the possessions they brought from Connecticut and New York to take up life on the frontier. John French built the house in 1845, and the site illustrates a typical mercantile community of the nineteenth century. He was a tanner and merchant and opened the nearby tannery and began trading goods in 1845. Today, the house and outbuildings are completely restored and clearly depict the life and times of a typical east-Texas settler of the period. Interpreters guide visitors through the house and grounds, and a small gift shop offers items typical of the mid-nineteenth century. Open daily 1–4, except Monday and holidays. Nominal charge. 713-898-0348.

The *Babe Didrickson Zaharias Memorial Museum,* at the Gulf Street exit of I-10 East, honors Beaumont's "Babe" Didrickson, one of the world's foremost athletes. On display are trophies, artifacts, and memorabilia. Open daily 10–5. Free. 713-833-4622.

BIG BEND NATIONAL PARK *Big Bend National Park* encompasses more than 700,000 acres from the canyons of the Rio Grande to the Chihuahuan Desert. A wide variety of plant and animal life reflects the park's many ecological settings. Like all national parks, Big Bend has a full range of ranger-naturalist activities. Visitors should stop first at the Big Bend Park Visitors' Center at Panther Junction before exploring the hundreds of miles of hiking trails and paved and dirt roads. Center open all year 8–5, in summer to 8 P.M. Free. 915-477-2251.

BIG SPRING The *Heritage Museum* is at 610 Scurry Street, just off Route 87, in the 1909 home of the late Mrs. Dora Roberts. Several rooms exhibit displays portraying the life of a frontier woman, the American Indian, early forms of local transportation, and the cowboy. An important part of the collection are the many works of cowboy artist H.W. Caylor. Open weekdays 9–5, weekends 1–5. Free. 915-267-8255.

BOERNE *Cascade Caverns,* on Cascade Caverns Road, just off I-10, about 5 miles south of Boerne and 25 miles north of San Antonio, has been known for generations and was once occupied by a hermit. In 1930, the full length of the mazelike interior was explored, and the caverns were found to have huge rooms and crystal pools laced by a profusion of cave growth. There is a 90-foot underground waterfall. Fee charged. 512-755-9285.

Another underground cavern, *Cave Without a Name,* is 11 miles northeast of Boerne on R.M. 474. The cave, which can be visited by appointment, displays vast corridors and grottoes sheathed with sparkling cave growth, the icelike scenes suggesting a bizarre winter on another planet. Fee charged. 512-537-4212.

BONHAM Speaker of the House Sam Rayburn served for more years than any other House speaker before or since. His personal papers and books are preserved in the *Sam Rayburn Library* on West Sam Rayburn Drive. As a visitor enters the main lobby, which is faced with Italian marble, he looks ahead through double doors leading to the replica of the speaker's office in the nation's Capitol. Many artifacts once housed in Washington have been brought to the library, including a crystal chandelier that hung in the White House until 1907 and a fireplace from the House of Representatives. The speaker's office furniture and many of the decorations from his Washington office are now in place in the replica. A special display room traces through mementos of Speaker Rayburn's life and career. Trained librarians assist visitors in the use of the reference material housed in the library and index. Museum open Monday through Friday 10–5, Saturday 1–5, Sunday 2–5. Free. 214-583-2455.

The *Sam Rayburn House Museum,* ½ mile west of the city of Bonham on Route 82, contains personal artifacts of the late speaker of the

House. Built in 1916 by Sam Rayburn for his parents and himself, the building is considered a symbol of the better life Rayburn wanted for rural folk. Its interior and furnishings are maintained as they were in his lifetime, and the grounds include six outbuildings and three Rayburn vehicles. More than three thousand items, including linens, china, and clothing, are in the unostentatious collection that is in keeping with Speaker Rayburn's preference for the simple life on his working ranch. Open Tuesday through Friday 10–5, Saturday 1–5, Sunday 2–5. Closed Monday, Thanksgiving, and Christmas but open 1–5 other Federal holidays. Free. 214-583-5558.

BORGER The *Hutchinson County Museum (Boom Town Revisited),* on Main Street, is in the old 1927 hardware store that boasted a hotel on its top floor. The museum depicts the county's history from its days as Indian territory in 1875 to the oil strike and boom of 1926. The existing town literally sprang up after 1926; Borger was the famous *Boom Town* of Thomas Hart Benton's 1927, painting which is on display here. Of interest in the museum is a blowup of Borger's Main Street when it was just ninety days old. Open daily 1–5, except Tuesday. Free. 806-273-2181.

BRACKETTVILLE *Alamo Village* is a family amusement park set within the movie set for the John Wayne movie *The Alamo*. The Alamo replica, built by adobe craftsmen from Mexico, overlooks a complete nineteenth-century frontier village. Within the amusement center are a cantina-restaurant, trading post, Indian store, authentic stage depot, old-time jail, bank, saddle shop, and many other Western shops. In summer there are stagecoach rides, country Western shows, and "shoot outs" between Texas lawmen and desperados. Open all year 9–6; in summer to 8 P.M. Fee charged. 512-563-2580.

BRAZOSPORT The *Brazosport Museum of Natural Science*, 400 College Drive off Route 288, is devoted to the natural history of this area of the Gulf Coast from prehistoric times to the present. There is an extensive collection of shells from the Gulf and around the world. Exhibits include rocks and minerals; a unique ivory and jade collection; fossils; wildlife; and aquariums; and in the archaeology section Indian tools. Open Tuesday through Saturday 10–5, Sunday 2–5. Closed Monday and major winter holidays. Free. 713-265-7831.

BROWNSVILLE The *Gladys Porter Zoo*, at 500 Ringgold Street (exit at Sixth Street on Expressway 77-83), covers 31 acres and offers many species of rare and endangered animals all in natural, barless settings. This outstanding zoo is the first to have been built, stocked, staffed, and equipped by a private foundation and then given to a community. Mrs. Gladys C. Porter is its founder and president of the Earl C. Sams Foundation, which gave the zoo to Brownsville. The successful program of breeding rare species has won the zoo many awards and much national recognition. Some of the animals found here are in no other zoos in the entire world. Established to conserve our vanishing wildlife and to foster interest in education about and preservation of that wildlife, the zoo is laid out in five major areas, four of them zoogeographically into Tropical America, Indo-Australia, Asia, and Africa. The other section brings together many compatible animals for viewing and care. Some favorite areas are the Free-flight Aviary, the Children's Zoo, and the Herpetarium, the only enclosed building on the grounds, housing a fine collection of reptiles and amphibians. Open daily 10 A.M. to dusk. Fee charged; children under 2 free. 512-546-7187.

The *Stillman House Museum*, at 1305 East Washington, is the 1850 home of Charles Stillman, the founder of Brownsville. It contains his possessions, mementos of early Brownsville, furnishings, heirlooms, books, coins, and pictures. Open Monday through Friday 10–12 and 2–5, Sunday 3–5. Nominal charge.

The *Neale House and Brownsville Art League's Museum* is at 230 Neale Drive near the Gateway Bridge—left just short of the bridge, and then right onto Neale Drive. The Neale House, given to the museum by the city, was built in 1836 and is used now to display a fine collection of local painters' works in a variety of media. Nearby on the property is a small museum housing more art, which will be opened to visitors who visit the Neale House first. Open all year Monday through Friday 9:30–3. Free. 512-542-4001.

BROWNWOOD The *Douglas MacArthur Academy of Freedom* is in the exact middle of Texas, in the triangle between Abilene, Fort Worth, and Waco. The museum is on the campus of Howard Payne University in the 1890 former administrative building, a distinctive structure built of native stone with unique turrets. It contains spectacular environmental and educational replica halls filled with murals, documents, and reproductions depicting the western civilizations that contributed to America's development. One-hour conducted tours of the halls include a three-story Hall of Christian Civilization complete with an enormous mural representing man's relationship with God; a Mediterranean Hall with Egyptian statuary, a facsimile of the Rosetta

Stone, and a replica of the Parthenon; Magna Carta Hall with a re-creation of a medieval European castle great hall containing seventeenth-century weapons and armor; and Independence Hall, a copy of the original, with peg floor, twin marble fireplaces, and period furnishings. The museum also houses memorabilia of Douglas MacArthur. Open during the normal academic year, including summer terms. Tours conducted daily at 11, 1:30, 2:30, and 3:30, including Saturday. Sunday tours conducted in the afternoon only; closed for national holidays. Free. 915-646-2502.

BRYAN The *Brazos Valley Museum,* at 3232 Briarcrest Drive, is a history and science museum. Its collections include mammals, birds, amphibians, reptiles, fish, marine invertebrates, fossils, rocks, minerals, Indian artifacts, insects, and shells. There is also a 36-acre wilderness area for hiking and nature study. Open Tuesday through Saturday 9–5, Sunday 1–5; closed Monday and federal holidays. Free. 713-779-2195.

BURNET In 1848–49, the U.S. Army set up a series of frontier forts arranged in a string stretching from the Rio Grande northeast to the upper Trinity River. Designed to protect the eastern settlements against Indian attack from the west, the forts were gradually abandoned in the seven years that followed. *Fort Croghan* was in the middle of the cordon of forts. Currently owned by the Burnet County Historical Society, the property consists of one restored original stone building and four historic buildings that were moved onto the site in the 1950s. Hundreds of historic items were donated to the resulting museum complex by local families. Site now open May 1 through November 1. Nominal charge.

Longhorn Cavern State Park, reached by U.S. 281 11 miles southwest of town to park road 4, has the third-longest cavern in the world. The home of prehistoric cavemen, the cavern was once used as a secret gunpowder factory by the Confederate Army. Tours conducted daily all year. Fee charged. The park museum displays Indian artifacts, frontier and Civil War items, and mineralogy exhibits. Open daily 9–5, March through October 1, daily except Monday and Tuesday the rest of the year. Free. 512-756-4680.

CANADIAN The town of Canadian takes its name from the Spanish word *canada,* meaning canyon or narrow valley. The *Hemphill County Pioneer Museum,* on Main Street, contains a country store, an old barber shop, and a sheriff's office, as well as collections of old guns, pictures, clothing, covered wagons, and cowboy gear. Open Monday through Saturday 9–5, Sunday 1–5. Donation. 806-323-6392.

CANYON The *Panhandle-Plains Historical Museum,* one block east of U.S. 287 on Fourth Avenue, dates from 1932 and is the oldest state museum in Texas. The Hall of Texas History traces diverse Texas subjects ranging from Paleozoic fossils, early man, the Spanish conquistadors, and the Plains Indians to early ranching and industrial development. The Hall of the Southern Plains Indians examines the culture of the Comanche, Arapaho, Kiowa, Apache, and Cheyenne tribes. The Hall of the Cattlemen contains the Nicholson Gun Collection and ranch artifacts. Pioneer Village is a reconstruction of a 1900 Panhandle town, with a country store, print shop, bank, saloon, school, hotel, dress shop, blacksmith shop, jail, stable, and home furnished as they were at the turn of the century. Other exhibits include art galleries, antique furniture, historic fashions, early transportation and communication devices, natural history displays, and a historic research center. The oldest intact ranch house in the Panhandle is preserved outdoors and open to the public in summer, by appointment. Museum open daily 9–5, Sunday 2–6. In summer, weekday hours to 6. Free. 806-655-7191.

The *Pioneer Amphitheatre*, in the heart of the Palo Duro Canyon State Park, uses the canyon walls as a backdrop as a cast of eighty perform nightly (except Sundays) during the summer in Pulitzer Prize–winner Paul Green's production of *Texas.* The musical tells the story of the lives of the early Texas Panhandle pioneers who fought Indians, stampedes, nesters, sheepmen, droughts, sickness, and each other. *Texas* is an award-winning production, for which admission is charged. In the fall a sound-and-light show *Palo Duro* is put on in conjunction with a dance presentation. Show time in the summer is 8:30 P.M. Tickets may be ordered from P.O. Box 268, Canyon, TX 79015, or at the *Texas* Information Center, 2010 Fourth Avenue, Route 217 in Canyon. 806-655-2182.

CHAPPELL HILL The *Stagecoach Inn,* at Main and Chestnut Streets, was built in 1850 by Jacob and Mary Haller and was a popular stopping place along the Houston to Waco or Austin stagecoach lines in the mid- to late nineteenth century. The Greek Revival building includes an ornamental Greek-key frieze worked into the cornice encircling the building. The cedar used for construction was reputedly sawed at nearby Jacksonville Mill, one of the first mills in the Republic of Texas. The Inn's entry has an unusual oak stairway. With each of its risers, the height of the balusters is increased, resulting in one continuous graceful curve in the handrail where the stairs turn. The present owners, Harvin

C. and Elizabeth Moore, of Houston, are responsible for the research and restoration of the old inn. Open Monday through Saturday 10–4. Nominal charge to tour the building. 713-523-6616.

Just behind the inn is the historic *Asenath Weems House,* also owned by the Moores. Built in 1886 by Mrs. Weems on a lot on Church Street, it was later moved to its present site on Chestnut Street behind the Stagecoach Inn. Mrs. Weems was the widow of Dr. Mason Locke Weems, whose grandfather, Parson Weems, wrote the original story of George Washington and the cherry tree. After restoring the Greek Revival home, Mr. and Mrs. Moore filled it with a collection of fine antiques and furnishings and now operate it as a quality antique shop. Open 10–4. Free. 713-523-6616.

CLIFTON Clifton was settled in 1854 by Norwegians, and many Scandinavian traditions are still carried on by their descendants. Norwegian artifacts abound in the collections of the *Bosque Memorial Museum,* on South Avenue Q, west of Route 6, which also displays Texas minerals and fossils, guns, coins, sailing ship models, pioneer kitchen equipment, farm tools, and Indian artifacts. It has a rocking chair made by the Norwegian trailblazer Cling Peirson, who led the immigrants to America beginning in 1825. Open Thursday through Saturday 9–5, Sunday 2–5. Nominal charge. 817-675-8733.

COLEMAN The *Coleman County Museum* is in a replica of Camp Colorado, built in 1936 and now part of the city park. It includes pioneer memorabilia, clothes, dishes, farming equipment, saddles, barbed wire, pictures, and a famous horse statue, larger than life-size, brought to Coleman in 1884 to display saddles. Open weekends all year 1–6, daily except Thursdays 1–6, in June, July, and August. Free. 915-625-4128.

COLUMBUS The *Koliba Home Museum Complex*'s special feeling has come about because of the museum's origin. Koliba Home, at 1124 Front Street, was first, and still is, the home of Mr. and Mrs. Homer Koliba, a former State Representative. The 1840 home is on the State Register of Historic Places and is filled with many antiques and memorabilia, among them hand-crank telephones, livestock bells, lanterns, guns, bottles, old postcards, canes, old typewriters, a pump organ, a large collection of hand irons, and a complete blacksmith shop, toolshed, and old barber shop. Mrs. Koliba has designed the three-room Storybook Land Cottage with children especially in mind. Much of Mr. Koliba's political memorabilia is contained in his legislative room. Museum open daily 10–6. Nominal charge. 713-732-2916.

COOPER In the Texas Midland Railway Station built in 1903, the *Patterson Memorial County Library and Museum* features exhibits relating to "Home Life in Yesteryears in Delta County," displaying furniture, implements, tools, and other memorabilia of early settlers. Open Monday through Thursday 1–5, Friday and Saturday 8–5. Hours vary, and visitors should check first. Free. 214-395-2264.

CORPUS CHRISTI The *Japanese Art Museum,* 426 South Staples Street, is devoted to the art and culture of Japan. On display are Hataka dolls, models of famous pagodas, shrines, and temples, Japanese sculptures, distinctive furniture, paintings and other decorative Oriental artifacts. Open Monday through Friday 10–12 and 1–4, Sunday 2–5. Nominal charge. 512-883-1303.

The *Art Museum of South Texas,* at 1902 North Shoreline, is in a striking contemporary building designed by architect Philip Johnson. The building is of reinforced concrete formed and cast in place. The openings are enclosed with bronze-tinted glass that will not distort color and that shut out heat from the sun. The vast expanses of glass offer natural daylight for the works of art and, at the same time, offer breathtaking views of the bay. The museum grew out of the intense interest generated by an art sale sponsored by the Corpus Christi *Caller Times* in 1944. Over the years it has grown to its present size and offers each year approximately twenty changing exhibitions that cover a broad range of periods and media. The permanent collection reflects this cross section of interest in art technique and periods and includes a collection of drawings done by living American artists. Open Tuesday through Saturday 10–5, Sunday 1–5. Closed Monday, New Year's, Memorial Day, Labor Day, Thanksgiving, and Christmas. Free. 512-884-3844.

The *Corpus Christi Museum,* 1919 North Water, is in the bayfront science section of the north end of Shoreline Drive. A lively place, it offers objects to touch, multimedia shows, films, games for children, weekend performances of all sorts, and features the history and natural history of the Gulf Coast. The area's colorful and varied past is brought to life with exhibits and displays of weapons, memorabilia, and anthropology. Open Tuesday through Saturday 10–5, Sunday 2–5; closed Monday. Free.

CORSICANA *Pioneer Village,* at 912 West Park Avenue, is owned and maintained by the Navarro County Historical Society. The village is composed of a cluster of pioneer buildings, some 142 years old. The buildings have been reconstructed from historically correct materials removed from the county's earliest settlements. The village park is a repository of Navarro County's heritage, with displays and exhibits of prehistory and Indian Times, the days of the Confederacy, and modern culture and industry all housed in century-old landmark structures. The village's authentically furnished buildings include an 1838 Indian trading post, a frontier home, a blacksmith shop, and a general store from the mid-nineteenth century, old barns, and a grist mill. Open Monday through Saturday 9–5, Sunday 1–5. Nominal charge. 214-872-1468.

CROSBYTON The *Pioneer Memorial Museum,* at 101 Main Street and U.S. 82, is in the Crosby County Pioneer Memorial Building, a replica of the Hank Smith rock house, the first home in the county. On display are Indian artifacts and a cross section of pioneer memorabilia. There are five period rooms and a reconstructed half-dugout. Across the street is an early barn with a display of agricultural implements. Open Tuesday through Saturday 9–12 and 2–5, Sunday 2–4, May through September. Free. 806-675-2331.

CROWELL The *Firehall Museum,* at 116 North Main Street, contains re-creations of a pioneer schoolroom and old-fashioned family settings in an ambience that preserves the rustic accents of the county's heritage. In addition to the household and farm implements, there is a detailed scale model of a country Texas town of the 1900s. Open daily 9–5. Free. 817-684-3391.

CUERO The old F. W. Bates–H. D. Sheppard home, 312 East Broadway, was designated as the *Dewitt County Historical Museum* in 1973 and is maintained as a museum by the County Historical Commission. Except for special exhibits, three rooms are furnished in the style of the late-Victorian era when the house was built. The Bates-Sheppard house was constructed in 1886, partially with lumber salvaged from the ruins of the family home in Indianola, which was destroyed by the hurricane that year. It was family-owned until 1968. Open Thursday and Friday 9–5, Sunday 2–5. Free. 512-275-6322.

DALHART The XIT ranch in the 1880s was the largest range in the world under fence. Its 3 million acres sprawled from the old Yellow House headquarters, near what is now Lubbock, Texas, northward to the Oklahoma Panhandle in an irregular strip roughly 30 miles wide. (Although many have said that the XIT brand represented the phrase "Ten in Texas," it was, in fact, designed to thwart rustlers.) In 1881, when it was necessary to replace the original capitol in Austin, the legislature agreed to pay the builders of the new building with the XIT acreage in lieu of a cash payment of $3 million. The *XIT Museum,* at 108 East Fifth Street, one block off Route 54, exhibits a 1900 parlor, bedroom, kitchen, and pioneer chapel. There is an antique-gun collection and a fine revolving Indian-artifacts exhibit. One of the displays in the Kitchen of the Prairie shows a chuckbox and cook's wagon used by ranchers when working cattle, building fence, and doing other ranch work. Open Tuesday through Saturday 2–5 and the afternoon of the first Sunday of each month. Free. 806-249-5390.

DALLAS *State Fair Park* is the home of the nation's largest annual exposition. The grounds host millions for sixteen days each October. The rest of the year the area serves as a city park and is home to the several museums listed below. The Park is at 2nd and Parry Streets, approximately 2 miles east of downtown Dallas, just off Route I-30.

The *Dallas Health and Science Museum,* at First and Forest Avenue in Fair Park, includes exhibits on the human body, health, human diseases, mineralogy, astronomy, and other scientific topics. Included in the human section are life-size models of the "transparent" man and woman. There are regular shows in the museum planetarium. Open Monday through Saturday 9–5, Sunday and holidays 1–5. Free, except for nominal charge for planetarium shows. 214-428-8351.

The *Dallas Aquarium*, at First and Fourth Streets in the Fair Park, entertains more than a million visitors each year. More than two thousand different specimens are on display, including native freshwater species, cold-freshwater species, tropical freshwater species, marine fish, reptiles, and amphibians as well as aquatic mammals. Open Monday through Saturday 8–5, Sunday 1–5. Free. 214-428-3587.

The *Texas Hall of State*, in the Fair Park, off I-30 (Thornton Freeway) between Grand Avenue and Nimitz Drive, is operated by the Dallas Historical Society. The Hall of State building was constructed for the Texas Centennial of 1936 as a memorial to the state. It cost $1 million and took half a year to build. It is a wonderful example of the Art Deco of the period; its lofty marble halls are filled with gigantic murals and heroic statuary. The main floor contains the Hall of Heroes, Hall of the Six Flags, and four halls, each dedicated to a geographic section of Texas: East, West, North, and South. The museum's collections and exhibits pertain to the state, the city of Dallas, and the Southwest. Open Monday through Saturday 9–5, Sunday 1–5; closed major holidays. Free. 214-421-5136.

The *Age of Steam Railroad Museum*, at Fair Park, ten minutes from downtown Dallas, is operated by the Southwest Railroad Historical Society and is one of the finest railroad collections anywhere. Dedicated to the preservation and display of trains, railroad buildings, and related items, it displays five steam locomotives and other rolling stock, as well as a sizable collection of railroad antiques and artifacts. The Baggage Car has been converted to a souvenir and gift shop offering railroad-oriented items not ordinarily found in regular stores. All restoration here is done by Society volunteers, as is the routine maintenance of the big machines. All the cars—parlor, club, dining, Pullmans, cabooses, and so on—are open to the public, who are invited to walk through them. Outstanding in the exhibit is the 1903 railroad station, the only one of its kind left standing in Texas. Open Sunday 11–5. Field tours available at other times by advance appointment. Fee charged. 214-361-6936.

The *Dallas Museum of Fine Arts,* in the original 1936 Texas Centennial Building located in Fair Park, features a large permanent collection of art, including African sculpture, outstanding pre-Columbian art, and Impressionist, classical, nineteenth- and twentieth-century American, contemporary, Japanese, and Baroque art. Open Tuesday through Saturday 10–5, Sunday 1–5. 214-421-4187.

The *Garden Center*, in City Park, is considered one of the most notable in the country. The 7-acre site is planted with specimens representative of the Southwest. The Garden for the Blind is planted with raised beds of herbs and flowering plants noted for their scent.

The *Dallas Museum of Natural History*, in Fair Park, southeast of downtown Dallas off I-30, Second Avenue, Fair Park exit, offers an excellent and comprehensive introduction to Texas's wildlife and varying habitats. A tour through the museum takes visitors to the seashores, prairies, mountains, swamps, and the deserts of this vast state. Texas flora and fauna are the museum's primary focuses, and, reflecting that interest, major exhibits include fifty habitat groups representing the plants and animals in their natural surroundings, as well as a fossil hall and a bird hall. Other exhibits are the procelain-bird collections of Edward Marshall Boehm and Dorothy Doughty, a fine game-trophy head collection, geological items, poisonous snakes, and small mammals of Dallas County. On weekends, volunteers provide rolling carts, called "Touch Carts," loaded with specimens of mammals, reptiles, rocks, fossils, and birds to feel and ask questions about. The museum is one of six museums and cultural institutions that reflect the Art Deco style of

The old West and the new. *Above:* Old Abilene Town. *Below:* The Amarillo Art Center.

Top left: A 90-foot waterfall in Cascade Cavern, Boerne. *Top right:* The Spinnaker thrill ride at Six Flags over Texas, a theme park in Arlington. *Below:* A volcanic peak in Big Bend National Park.

Above: A performance in the Pioneer Amphitheatre of Palo Duro Canyon State Park. *Below:* The Art Museum of South Texas in Corpus Christi.

Above: A diorama of reddish egrets in the Dallas Museum of Natural History. *Below left:* The Wise County Heritage Museum in Decatur. *Below right:* A Mexican Franciscan at the Ysleta Mission near El Paso.

Places to go near El Paso. *Above left:* The Juarez Race Track. *Above right:* McKelligon Canyon Park. *Below:* The Sun Bowl stadium, with downtown El Paso in the background.

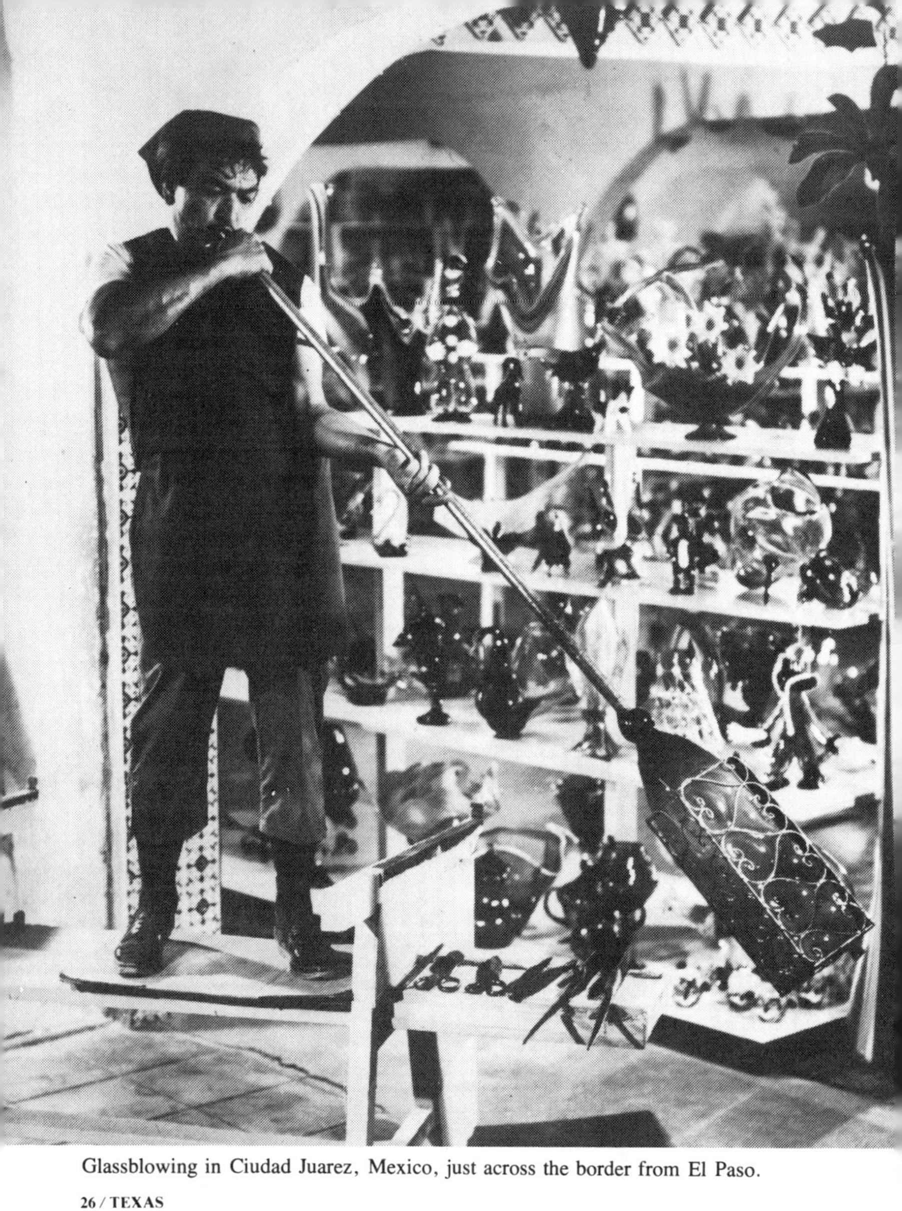

Glassblowing in Ciudad Juarez, Mexico, just across the border from El Paso.

exposition architecture of the 1920s and 1930s. Open daily Monday through Saturday 9–5, Sunday and holidays, 1–5. Closed Christmas. Free. 214-421-2169.

The *Biblical Arts Center*, on Boedeker at Park Lane, across from Northpark Shopping Center, has received national acclaim for its unique 124-foot mural depicting the Miracle at Pentecost. Painted over a three-year period by artist Torger G. Thompson, the mural is in a specially constructed three-dimensional theater setting at which a special narration is presented. The Biblical Arts Center is undergoing a major rebuilding and expansion program that will close the exhibit to the public until the fall of 1980. At that time, information on the new schedule of presentations and the special new museum exhibits may be obtained by calling 214-691-4661.

The *Meadows Museum*, on the campus of Southern Methodist University, includes more than a hundred paintings covering four hundred years of Spanish art, including works by Goya, el Greco, and Velazquez. Tours are available for school and community groups, in several languages, including Spanish, French, and German. Open Monday through Saturday 10–5, Sunday 1–5. Free. 214-692-2516.

The *Museum of African-American Life and Culture* sponsors five special exhibitions each year, September through May, including their annual Black Art Competition and Black Texas Art Exhibition. 214-372-8140.

John Neely Bryan was the founder and first settler of Dallas. The *John Neely Bryan Cabin* is a restored, one-room, 14- by 15-foot cabin located in the Dallas County Historical Plaza (bounded by Elm, Main, and Market streets). The cabin is close to its original site and may be viewed at any time from the outside only, although the interior is visible through two windows. Nearby are the 1890 Richardsonian Romanesque courthouse known as "Old Red" and the recent John F. Kennedy Memorial designed by Philip Johnson, as well as the Texas School Book Depository Building from which the fatal shots were fired in 1963. Free.

Old City Park, at 1717 Gano Street, just off route I-30, is an outdoor cultural history museum consisting of twenty-two restored buildings that show the cultural and architectural past of north Texas. Representing the period from 1840 to 1910, they are maintained by the Dallas County Heritage Society and feature a fine museum store and a luncheon facility. Museum complex open all year Tuesday through Friday 10–4, weekends 1:30–4:30. Closed major holidays. Nominal charge. 214-421-5141.

The site of the tragic assassination of President John F. Kennedy on November 22, 1963, Dallas has several monuments and museums that have been erected in memory of the event. The *John F. Kennedy Museum*, at 501 Elm Street, across from the assassination site, contains oversize reproductions of assassination stories from newspapers of fifty states, a detailed model of the city tracing the route of the motorcade, and films and narrations. Nominal charge for some museum areas. 214-742-8582.

DECATUR The *Wise County Heritage Museum*, 1602 South College, is housed in the administration building of Decatur Baptist College, the oldest planned junior college in the world. The building, a fine old towering Gothic stone structure, is listed in the National Registry of Historic Places. It features a number of collections devoted to Wise County history. There are an Art and Furniture Room; pioneer collections; the Decatur Baptist College Collection; the Wise County Historical Commission Archive; a little theater where various kinds of theatrical productions are put on by a local theater group; doll collections; and a scale model of the old town of Audubon. Open Monday through Friday 9–4:30, Saturday and Sunday 1–4:30; closed major winter holidays. Nominal charge. 817-627-3921 or 3732.

The *Wise County Courthouse*, constructed of bright pink limestone, is on the town square. Built in 1895, it is considered one of the finest examples of architecture of its time and type.

DEL RIO The *Whitehead Memorial Museum*, at 1308 South Main Street, is in the old Perry Mercantile, at one time the largest store between San Antonio and El Paso. The museum is dedicated to the life and legends of the frontier Southwest. Judge Roy Bean is buried on its grounds. Open daily 9–5. Free. 512-775-6911.

DENISON Dwight David Eisenhower was born in the two-story frame house at 208 East Day Street, the son of a worker in the nearby railway shops. Displays at the *Eisenhower Birthplace* include a quilt made by Eisenhower's mother, an old-fashioned crank telephone with recorded greetings from "Ike," and household furnishings of the period. Open daily 10–12 and 1–5; June through Labor Day, daily 8–6. Nominal charge. 214-465-8908.

DENTON The *Historic Costumes and Furnishings Collection of the DAR Museum*, Texas Woman's University, on Bell Avenue at Texas Street, features the gowns of the first ladies of Texas. There are gowns belonging to the wives of the governors of Texas and the presidents of the

Republic of Texas, as well as dresses worn by wives of two presidents of the United States and a wife of a vice-president of the United States. The collection also includes pieces of silver, books, jewelry, personal mementos, and pictures that have been associated with these women. Open daily Monday through Friday 8–5 during normal university operating calendar. Free. 817-382-8821.

There has been a *Historical Collection at North Texas University*, at Avenue A and Mulberry, since 1925. Displayed are weapons, ceramics, uniforms, baskets, dolls, music boxes, diaries, *penitentes*, pioneer tools, military items, Indian artifacts, and other items of local history and archaeology. Open Monday through Saturday 1–5; closed during university holidays. Free. 817-788-2386.

DEVINE The *Bigfoot Wallace Museum*, on Main Street (F.M. 472) in the town of Bigfoot, 6 miles southwest of Devine via Route 173, is in an old school building and in a three-room log cabin that is a replica of the home of the famous Indian fighter and Texas Ranger. On display are old machinery and memorabilia of Wallace's activities in the Texas War of Independence, the Mexican war, and the Indian campaigns. Nominal charge. 512-663-2495.

EAGLE PASS *Fort Duncan*, established in 1849, was occupied by three companies of the First U.S. Infantry Regiment. During the Confederacy, it was occupied by Confederate Army troops, then by Federal troops until 1916. The restored fort includes the post headquarters, powder magazine and six other restored stone buildings. The museum, in Fort Duncan Park, is in the fort headquarters and features exhibits of archaeological interest as well as displays on local and pioneer history. Open all year; in summer, daily except Sunday 10–5; the rest of the year, weekends 2–5. Nominal charge.

EASTLAND *Old Rip* reposes peacefully in his plush casket in the lobby of Eastland's county courthouse on Courthouse Square. He is Eastland's famed horned toad who was imprisoned alive in the cornerstone of the then new courthouse in 1897. In 1928 the old courthouse was being demolished to make way for the new. More than three thousand people gathered and watched with bated breath to see if the toad might still be alive. A Bible and other objects were removed from the cornerstone hole, then the toad was pulled out and held up for all to see. A leg twitched, the crowd roared, and Old Rip awakened after his 31-year snooze to capture the hearts of the nation. He even visited President Calvin Coolidge. Old Rip died of pneumonia in 1929 and can be seen today in his glass enclosure, which may be viewed from outside the courthouse. Courthouse open Monday through Friday 8–5, except state holidays. Free.

EDINBURG The *Hidalgo County Historical Museum*, at 121 East McIntyre Street, contains mementos of the early life in Hidalgo County and the Rio Grande Valley, with special emphasis on pioneer, farm, and home items from this Latin-accented area. Open Tuesday through Friday 9–5, Sunday 1–5. Donation. 512-383-6911.

EGYPT The *Northington-Heard Memorial Museum,* at the Egypt Plantation Headquarters, has artifacts pertaining to the history of local Texans during the nineteenth century. Included in the regional memorabilia are photographs, furniture, manuscripts, and displays of mineralogy and natural history. Open weekdays 8–5, Saturday 8–12.

EL PASO A fine way to see El Paso and more is to ride to the top of Ranger Peak in the *Aerial Tramway*. The glass-sided gondola rises to 5,632 feet, where occupants may step out to a viewing platform to see vast areas of Texas, New Mexico, and Mexico. The tramway operates daily noon to 9 P.M. in summer; the rest of the year, noon to 9 P.M. on weekends and holidays, to 6 P.M. on weekdays; closed Tuesdays. Nominal charge for the round trip. 915-566-6622.

The *Fort Bliss Replica Museum*, in the U.S. Army Defense Center at Fort Bliss, consists of four adobe buildings containing items relating to the history of the U.S. Army, Fort Bliss, and the city and county of El Paso. Included are military and Western-style small arms from 1808 to the present, uniforms, and other military artifacts. Open daily 9–4:30, except holidays. Free. 915-568-2804 or 4518.

The *Magoffin Home*, at 1120 Magoffin Avenue, was built in 1875 by pioneer El Pasoan Joseph Magoffin, who rose from being a bookkeeper to being one of the major landholders in El Paso, one of its incorporators, and, finally, its mayor (serving four terms). The home displays a regional architectural style developed in the Southwest between 1865 and 1880. A combination of native building techniques and materials and of popular building motifs in the eastern United States, the Territorial Style was one of the first signs of the Americanizing of the Southwest. The Magoffin Home is built of sun-dried adobe (mud bricks) with Greek Revival details. The original six rooms were enlarged with an east ell and three south wings sometime after 1875. Purchased by the state and city in 1976, the home contains many of the family furnishings including the 13-foot-high canopied bed, full-length pier-glass-mirrored wardrobe, marble-topped chest, and washstand in Mrs. Magoffin's bedroom. Open daily 9–4 with tours available. Closed Christmas. Nominal charge. 915-533-5147.

The *Tigua Indian Reservation*, reached by taking I-10 to the Avenue of the Americas exit and proceeding to 119 Old Pueblo Road, is the oldest community within the present boundaries of Texas. Established in 1681 by Spanish missionaries and loyal Tigua Indians, the mission church is still the religious focal point of the Indian community. Although only part of it is of original construction, the structure has been faithfully reconstructed and restored. Several acres of the mission lands have been under constant cultivation since 1682. At one time the mission was on the Mexican side of the Rio Grande, but changes in the river's course have since placed it on Texas soil. Visitors to the Tigua Reservation may see the typical adobe pueblo-style buildings that include an arts-and-crafts center and a restaurant featuring authentic Tigua Indian foods, among them Indian chili, *gorditas* (Indian-style tacos), and freshly baked Indian bread. Among the crafts offered are silver and turquoise jewelry, blankets, beadwork, and pottery. Pueblo open all year; in winter, tours are offered on weekends only. Nominal charge for tours, Indian exhibits, and dancing. For complete information about activities at the reservation, call 915-859-3916.

Chamizal National Memorial, at 800 South San Marcial just off Paisan Drive, commemorates the history of the U.S.–Mexican border, its disputes and cooperation. The site of a long-standing border dispute, the monument stands on the Rio Grande where a new channel marks the adjusted international boundary in a peaceful settlement of the disagreement. The building houses material pertaining to the border history, and there are art exhibits encompassing fine art and folk art in the Culture Center, as well as films in Spanish and English. The Siglo de Oro Drama Festival is held here annually in March, and the El Paso–Chamizal Fiesta of the Arts takes place daily from the last week in June through the first week in July on the monument grounds. Open all year daily 9–5. For information about times of evening programs of the performing arts, call 915-543-7780. Free.

The *El Paso Museum of Art*, 1211 Montana Avenue, is a municipal art museum in the 1908 former home of Senator and Mrs. W. W. Turney. As originally constructed, the site covered an entire city block. It was an imposing classic structure of cream-colored brick and two-story Corinthian columns. A roof balustrade completely encircles the building. In the rear, a coach house now serves as the restoration center. During the Pancho Villa episode in Juarez, Mexico, many friends of the Turneys stayed with them, as their basement was well stocked with ammunition and food. In 1940, following the death of Senator Turney, the home was dedicated to use as a museum and as a center for the wartime "Bundles for Britain" effort. In 1958, plans were laid for the addition of two wings to the museum to hold one of the Samuel H. Kress regional art collections. At present the museum specializes in European art, with special collections from the Italian Renaissance, as well as Italian, French, and Spanish Rococo seventeenth- and eighteenth-century oils. Open Tuesday through Sunday 10–5. Free. 915-543-3800.

The *El Paso Centennial Museum* is on the campus of the University of Texas at El Paso, at University Avenue and Wiggins Road. Its diverse collections include archaeology, anthropology, plants, animals, and geology. Open Monday through Friday 10–5, weekends and holidays 1–5. 915-747-5565.

The *Wilderness Park Museum*, at 2000 Trans-Mountain Road, off I-10, contains five important dioramas that reflect the region's anthropology and archaeology. The Cave Valley diorama consists of a replica of Olla Cave, a Mogollon cliffhouse dwelling in the mountains west of the Casas Grandes in Chihuahua, Mexico. The Paleo diorama depicts a typical hunt that would have occurred in the Southwest between 20,000 and 7000 B.C. The Hueco Tanks diorama reflects the natural desert countryside and the natural caves that sheltered many primitive peoples in the Hueco Tanks region to the northeast of El Paso. Other museum displays include a typical Pit House pueblo and replicas of rock-art designs from the Tularosa Basin and Gila Wilderness regions. There are also several displays of pottery, baskets, and other artifacts. Open Tuesday through Saturday 9–5, Sunday 1–5. Free. 915-543-3819.

The *El Paso Cavalry Museum*, at 12901 Gateway West, has collections of saddles, guns, horse gear, and historic photographs pertaining to the cavalry. Open Tuesday through Saturday 9–5, Sunday 1–5. Free. 915-543-3828.

ELDORADO The *Schleicher County Museum*, on the corner of San Angelo and Menard highways, houses relics and mementos of county history. The collections of household articles and other belongings of the early pioneers are in an old 1924 hardware store. Open most afternoons except Saturdays, June to September. Free. 915-853-2709.

FAIRFIELD The *Freestone County Museum,* at 203 Main Street, is in the old Freestone county jail, constructed of handmade brick in 1857. Museum exhibits contain articles relating to early life, education, history, and development of Freestone and the surrounding counties. Collections include uniforms, documents, and other items from the seven wars in which Freestone men have participated. Adjacent to the museum are two restored log cabins. The *Potter-Watson Cabin,* built by Daniel Potter, a farmer who tamed wild horses, has a cedar floor, walls of hewn logs, and a board roof joined by pegs. It houses tools used during the early days of the county. In the *Carter Log House*, built in 1845 on a site 3 miles east of Kirvin, tongue-and-groove logs were joined with wooden pins. These and other wood members were hauled to the construction from Rusk, more than 70 miles away. The house contains a number of the original pieces of furniture and others typical of the period. Museum and cabins open Wednesday and Saturday 10–4, Sunday 1:30–4. Closed Christmas and July 4. Nominal charge. 214-389-3738.

The *Moody-Bradley House*, at 318 Moody Street, near the junction of U.S. 84 and I-45, was the home of two illustrious Freestone County families. The antebellum Greek Revival house was built in 1860 by William Lewis Moody, Sr., for his bride, Elizabeth Bradley, and W. L. Moody, Jr., founder of the Moody Foundation in Galveston, was born here in 1865. His father, a Civil War hero, organized the first company of Freestone County soldiers to see action. After the war, Moody moved to Galveston, where he became a leader in financial, business, philanthropic, and civic affairs. Open Sunday 1–5, at other times by appointment. Nominal charge. 214-389-3229.

FALFURRIAS A century ago the Texas Ranger was a shield between the pioneer settler and a hostile land. As recently as thirty-six years ago, Falfurrias still wore that shield with the Company D, Texas Rangers stationed there as the area headquarters. Today, visitors may glimpse into the Rangers' past at the *Texas Ranger Museum*, in the Chamber of Commerce building on U.S. 281. The first Texas Ranger museum in the state, it is dedicated to preserving the frontier heritage in artifacts, guns, relics, records, pictures, transcripts, and personal papers of the men whose deeds are so much a part of Texas history. Open all year. Tuesday through Friday 11–5, Saturday 1–5. Free. 512-325-2907.

FORT DAVIS *Fort Davis* was ordered established in 1854 by Jefferson Davis, the U.S. Secretary of War. Erected during a period of intense conflict with local hostile Indians, the fort was initially used as a watering stop and protective stronghold for gold seekers, settlers, traders, and troops on their way west. In 1867 a series of substantial rock and adobe buildings were constructed, and the fort continued to be used until 1891. It slowly deteriorated in the years that followed, until it was named a National Historic Site in 1961. It was restored by the national Park Service and is considered today to be one of the most extensive and impressive of the Southwestern frontier forts. The Fort Davis Museum is located in the reconstructed barracks. Open daily during daylight hours. Nominal charge for entrance to the site. 915-426-3225.

The *Neill Museum*, in the historic Truehart House, seven blocks west of the courthouse, contains antique toys made in Texas, dolls, bottles, and furniture. Open June through September 9–5. Nominal charge. Call first. 915-426-3969.

The *McDonald Observatory*, northwest of Fort Davis on route 118 (turn right on Spur 78), is on scenic Mount Locke, a 6,791-foot peak selected because of its clear air, high ratio of cloudless nights, distance from concentrations of artificial lights, and the relatively dust-and-radiation-free atmosphere. McDonald Observatory, operated jointly by the University of Texas and the University of Chicago, has a 2.7-m telescope, one of the largest in the world. The observatory offers a visitors' center with a bookstore. Daily lectures acquaint the general public with the origins of the observatory and with the work that it does. It was made possible by a wealthy Texas banker, W. J. Mcdonald, who left the bulk of his estate to "aid in erecting and equipping an astronomical observatory for the promotion and study of the science of astronomy." Visitors' center open Monday through Saturday 9–7, Sunday 1–7, June through August. Lectures scheduled approximately every hour on the hour. Center open Monday through Saturday 9–5, Sunday 1–5, September through May. Lectures every hour on the hour on weekends, 9, 11, 1:30, 3, and 4 on weekdays. Closed major winter holidays. Free. 915-426-3263.

FORT STOCKTON The original *Fort Stockton* was constructed of adobe in 1859 and abandoned twenty-seven years later. Many original buildings of adobe and hand-hewn limestone remain today, including Officer's Row and the old guardhouse on Williams Street between Fourth and Fifth streets.

The *Annie Riggs Hotel Museum* is in an adobe hotel built in 1890. Once a popular stop on the Butterfield stage route, the hotel now contains area-related displays of life at the turn of the century. Open daily, except Wednesdays; hours vary though usually closed at lunch hour. Check first. Donation. 915-336-7106.

FORT WORTH The prominence of Fort Worth can be traced to the tremendous early influence of the cattle barons who made their vast fortunes in the region. One such family were the W. T. Waggoners. In 1903, Electra Waggoner wed the Philadelphia socialite A. B. Wharton. In honor of her wedding, her family built *Thistle Hill*, at 1509 Pennsylvania Avenue, designed by a prominent architect in a manner suited to the needs of the East Coast elite. Facing Pennsylvania Avenue at the peak of what was then called "Quality Hill," the house certainly was dominant among the homes of those who dominated. In 1910, a second cattle baron, Winfield Scott, bought the house for $90,000 and spent another $100,000 furnishing and landscaping it to perfection. Thistle Hill is listed on the National Register. Open all year Monday through Friday 9–4, Sunday 1–5. Tours are available weekdays 10–3:15. Nominal charge. 817-336-1212.

The *Fort Worth Art Museum*, 1309 Montgomery, off I-20 Montgomery Street exit, features contemporary twentieth-century art, and its permanent collection contains fine examples of all aspects of the period. Traveling exhibits and an active performing arts program are offered by the museum, which also provides an up-to-date glimpse into current art trends. The artists themselves often work in the galleries, and visitors have the opportunity to meet them and discuss the work. Open Tuesday 10–9, Wednesday through Saturday 10–5, Sunday 1–5. Closed Monday and major holidays. Donation. 817-738-9215.

The *Fort Worth Museum of Science and History*, at 1501 Montgomery Street, was founded in 1941 as the Children's Museum. It has progressed from its original two rooms to its present 88,000-square-foot structure, which includes anthropology, geology, natural sciences, medical, and Texas history halls. It also exhibits pre-Columbian and North American Indian artifacts, dinosaur scenes, lasers, antique calculators, and computers. Its planetarium shows are weekends, September to June. In summer, there are an additional four shows daily. Open Monday through Saturday 9–5, Sunday 2–5; closed major holidays. Free to county residents; nominal charge to all others. Separate nominal charge for planetarium shows. 817-732-1631.

Amon Carter Museum is within walking distance of three other museums on the west side of Fort Worth: the Kimbell Art Museum, the

Fort Worth Museum of Art, and the Fort Worth Museum of Science and History. Devoted to depicting Western America, its exhibitions include Western art, publications, and special exhibitions of various facets of American art and history that change about every six weeks. The museum's extensive permanent collections of paintings, sculpture, prints, and photography include works by such American masters as Winslow Homer, Albert Bierstadt, George Caleb Bingham, Frederic Remington, Charles Russell, Georgia O'Keeffe, John Marin, Ben Shahn, and Ansel Adams. The nucleus of the museum's holdings is the large collection of Remingtons and Russells owned by the founder, Amon Carter, Sr. The museum is in a building designed by internationally known architect Philip Johnson, who also designed the latest wing and originally placed the museum on a hill facing east to emulate the Indian tradition of facing the rising sun. Open all year Tuesday through Saturday 10–5, Sunday 1–5:30. Closed Monday and winter holidays, other holidays 1–5:30. Free. 817-738-1933.

The *Fort Worth Public Library*, 300 Taylor Street, can be reached by taking I-20 to Henderson Street north to Trinity River, then parking in the adjacent Tandy Center lot and riding free (on the world's only free private subway) to the library. It has extensive collections of information on genealogy, including books, manuscripts, photographs, and audio-visual material. The first library to be built underground, it is a fine example of innovative architecture, design, and construction. When the library was founded in 1892, the founding committee asked for donations toward the building fund by requesting the price of a good cigar. Mrs. D. B. Keeler happened to ask a Mr. Carnegie for that price and ended up with the whole library. Teddy Roosevelt planted a tree on the grounds during a visit in 1905. Open all year Monday through Thursday 10–9, Friday and Saturday 10–6. Closed holidays. Free. 817-870-7740.

The *Kimbell Art Museum,* on Will Rogers Road West, between West Lancaster and Camp Bowie Boulevard, contains the Kay Kimbell Collection of eighteenth-century portraits and old masters. The multimillion-dollar collection, now including works from prehistoric times to Picasso, is displayed in an impressive building designed by architect Louis I. Kahn that uses cycloid vaulting to provide optimum lighting and display possibilities. Open Tuesday through Saturday 10–5, Sunday 1–5. Free. 817-332-8451.

Fort Worth's *Log Cabin Village*, at University Drive and Colonial Parkway in Forest Park, contains six log cabins, all more than a century old and furnished in keeping with their nineteenth-century construction. Also on the site are a restored well and working grist mill. Open Monday through Friday 8–4:30 and weekend afternoons. Nominal charge. 817-926-5881.

The *Fort Worth Botanic Gardens*, 3220 Botanic Garden Drive, are a showcase for 150,000 specimens of live plants representing 2,500 species, displayed in both formal and natural settings. Special gardens and collections include more than 4,000 rose bushes, native plants, and a scented garden for the blind. Gardens open during daylight hours; free. Of particular interest is the Japanese Garden. An enchanting 6-acre plot, it includes exotic plants, lotus pools, quaint arched footbridges, delicate waterfalls, and teahouses. Open Tuesday through Friday 10–4, Saturday 10–5, Sunday 1–5. Nominal charge. 817-870-7686.

Forest Park Zoo, at 2727 Zoological Park Drive in Forest Park, is devoted to mammals, birds, and reptiles from throughout the world. Special features include the Rain Forest, Great Apes House, Herpetarium, Seal Pool, and Children's Zoo. Open daily to 9:30 in summer, to dusk in other seasons. Nominal charge. 817-870-7050.

The *Pate Museum of Transportation*, on Route 377, 14 miles southwest of Fort Worth, is on 180 acres and features a vast array of classic, antique, and special-interest cars, a large exhibit of aircraft, and an antique 1914 private railroad car paneled in rich mahogany and completely furnished. A minesweeper sits high and dry beside a U.S. Navy F-9F jet, the kind used on aircraft carriers. The automobiles range from an elegant, exotic 1933 Studebaker commissioned by a rich Argentinian to a 1904 Schact "Tin Lizzie" to a Russian-built 1950 ZIM, a gift from Nikita Khrushchev to the premier of Norway. There are also examples of customized cars from the 1940s and 1950s, and much more. Open daily 9–5, except Monday. Free. 817-332-1161.

FREDERICKSBURG The *Admiral Nimitz Center*, 328 East Main Street, consists of three main units. The Admiral Nimitz Steamboat Hotel, a famous Southwest frontier hostelry, is now being restored to its original steamboat shape and pre-1900 appearance. It will house an exhibit on World War II and Fleet Admiral Chester Nimitz. The Garden of Peace was built as a symbol of friendship between America and Japan, using funds raised by the people of Japan. Designed by Taketora Saita of Tokyo, the garden incorporates the beautiful features of the classic Japanese garden and includes a replica of Admiral Togo's study that was built in Japan and brought to Fredericksburg, where it was reassembled.

The History Walk of the Pacific War consists of an outdoor stroll past a vast collection of World War II relics, including Japanese and American aircraft, weaponry and other military articles. The walk traces events from the sinking of the fleet at Pearl Harbor to Admiral Nimitz signing the surrender in Tokyo Harbor. Center open seven days a week 8–5, except Thanksgiving, Christmas, and New Year's. Nominal charge for persons over 6 years, except those in military uniform. 512-997-4379.

FRITCH The *Lake Meredith Aquatic and Wildlife Museum*, on Route 136, contains living specimens of fish found in the lake, as well as several wildlife dioramas depicting American eagles, wild turkeys, pronghorn antelopes, coyotes, deer, and raccoons. Open Wednesday through Saturday 10–6, Tuesday and Sunday 2–6. Closed Monday. Free.

The *Alibates Flint Quarries National Monument* can be reached from Fritch by going south 6 miles to Alibates Road and taking the right-hand fork to the Alibates Contact Station. It preserves the site where prehistoric Indians quarried flint for some twelve thousand years. They dug a few feet into the ground to expose the flint layer, which was then broken up and removed for use in tool and weapon making. Plans are underway for a visitors' center showing the main features of life of the more recent quarry users (1200–1400). Tours of the site consist of a 3-mile drive, then a 1-mile round-trip walk up a hill to the quarry. Sturdy shoes are recommended; during the summer, visitors may want to bring a canteen of water. Tours daily Memorial Day to Labor Day 10 and 2. Off-season tours may be arranged by calling in advance. Free at present. For information, contact the Superintendent, Lake Meredith Recreation Area. 806-857-3151.

GAINESVILLE The *Morton Museum of Cooke County*, at the corner of Dixon and Pecan streets, is maintained by the Cooke County Historical Society and contains items reflecting the history of the county and its environs. The museum is in Gainesville's oldest civic building, erected in 1884 as a city hall, fire station, and calaboose (jail). Renovation for use as a museum involved using a stained-glass skylight from the home of the late U.S. Senator Joseph Weldon Bailey. Other items from the Bailey home have been incorporated into the architecture, including three stained-glass windows, wrought-iron gates, and three wood-panel doors at the rear of the exhibit area. Museum visitors may obtain a handsome brochure which will direct them on a self-guided tour of Gainesville's Victorian homes, many of which are of brick. Open Friday, Saturday, and Sunday 2–5. Free. 817-668-8900.

GALVESTON Tours of the city are available on the *Treasure Isle Tour Train*, which may be boarded at 2106 Seawall Boulevard. The sixty-four-passenger open-sided train covers old and new Galveston, historic old homes, churches, the shrimp fleet, yacht basin, medical school, remains of old Fort Crockett, and many other places of interest. Two to five departures daily, except December through February and on Monday, September 1 to December 1. Fee charged. For schedule information, call 713-765-9564.

The Greek Revival *Sydnor Powhatan House*, at 3427 Avenue O, was built in 1847 by John Seabrook Sydnor not as a residence but as a hotel. When it became unprofitable, the 24-room hotel was used as a school, a military academy, and, finally, as the city orphanage. It was later purchased, divided into three smaller buildings, and moved to its present location. The larger, central portion of the original building became the home of Mrs. Caroline Ladd. After many years the building was purchased to be garden club headquarters. One room has been developed into a John Seabrook Sydnor Museum honoring the original builder, who was a noted amateur architect, patriot, and civic leader. In addition to its restored interior, the home boasts lovely gardens designed and maintained by the garden club. Open Tuesday through Saturday 1–5, June through August. Other months, open Tuesday, Friday, and Saturday 1–5. Nominal charge. 713-763-8604.

The *Galveston County Historical Museum*, at 2219 Market Street, contains artifacts and displays relating to county history from Indian times to 1950. Included are materials from the Karaukwa Indians, reflectors from the South Jetty Light House, and items relating to Jean Laffite, Cabeza de Vaca, the Austin colonists, the Texas navy, Gail Borden, Ashby Smith, and Nicholas Clayton. The museum is in the 1910 Moody National Bank building, noted for its painted, arched ceiling. Open all year Monday through Saturday 8–4:30, Sunday 2–5. Free. 713-766-2340.

The *Bishop's Palace* stands majestically on the northwest corner of Fourteenth and Broadway amid Galveston's most famous ancestral homes. Built over a seven-year period ending in 1893, it was occupied from 1923 to 1950 by Bishop Christopher E. Byrne, who called it his "palace in the sky" (hence its popular appellation). Before that time it was known as Gresham's Castle in honor of its builder and occupant for more than twenty-five years. During its construction, ships brought Texas granite, limestone and sandstone, Siena and Numidian marble from Italy, onyx and silver from Mexico, crystal chandeliers from Venice, damask from England, and fine woods from forests around the world. The oak staircase alone took sixty-six craftsmen seven years to build and was so massive it had to be floated down the Mississippi by barge from Cincinnati, where it had been built. The edifice survives today with all its original ornate woodwork, stained glass, and fine furnishings intact, open to the public as a museum and testimony to the period of its construction. Open daily all year, except Tuesdays in winter. Nominal charge. 713-762-2475.

Since 1859, *Ashton Villa*, at 2328 Broadway, has serenely withstood onslaughts of man and nature. The grand Italianate mansion, one of the first brick houses in Texas, was built by James Moreau Brown, a wealthy businessman and civic leader, as a home for his lively family and a setting for their lavish entertaining of Galveston society. Elegantly restored and furnished, it still stands on Galveston Island's oleander-lined Broadway Boulevard. During the Union blockade of the port of Galveston, women and children left the island; but James Brown stayed in Ashton Villa, which became the site of many important meetings and planning sessions during the Civil War. The house was untouched in those years, even though battles raged just a few blocks away. As it survived the war, so it survived the Great Fire of 1885, the Great Storm of 1900, and the threat of demolition in 1968. Ashton Villa features a slide presentation as well as a guided tour of the mansion. The slide show, called *The 1900 Storm*, tells the story of that terrifying hurricane, Galveston before the storm, and the remarkable building of the seawall and grade-raising of the island afterward. Extraordinary architecture and furnishings are visible on the tour, and the mansion includes collections of photography, oil paintings (many by a female artist who was a family member), a restored nineteenth-century dollhouse, and a collection of old toys. Open weekdays 10–4, weekends 12–5. Closed Tuesday, September through May. Fee charged. 713-762-3933.

The *Galveston Arts Center on the Strand*, 202 Kempner, is in the fine old 1867 First National Bank Building. With the ornate ironwork on its cornice, the two-story structure is in keeping with the Strand's Victorian character. The art center features rotating exhibits of contemporary artists in all media. About twelve to sixteen shows a year present work by relatively unknown or younger artists. Open all year Monday through

Friday 8–5, Saturday 11–4, Sunday 1–4. Free. 713-763-2403.

The *Sea-Arama Marineworld*, at Seawall Boulevard at Ninety-first Street, is a multimillion-dollar showcase for native Gulf Coast and exotic marine specimens. Trained-animal shows regularly feature performing porpoises, kangaroos, bears, birds, penguins, seals, and many other specialty acts. Underground portholes offer excellent observation and photographic points for visitors. Pool open daily from 9 A.M., with shows held continuously until dusk. Fee charged. 713-744-4501.

Seawolf Park, on Pelican Island, offers tours of several vessels and is a fine location for observing seagoing vessels entering and departing the port of Galveston. There are also tours of the World War II submarine U.S.S. *Cavalla*, the destroyer escort U.S.S. *Stewart*, a navy jet, and military vehicles. Open all year, tours daily 10–dusk. Nominal charge. 713-744-5738.

GATESVILLE Gatesville grew up around the U.S. Army's Fort Gates, which was established in 1849. The *Buckhorn Museum*, at 612 Leon Street, was designed to resemble an early-West barroom. It displays Indian artifacts, branding irons, settlers' household items, guns, mounted animal-horns, photographs, and barbed wire. Open Monday through Saturday 8 A.M.—10 P.M. Free.

The *Lee County Museum*, in the old jail building on Route 77 South, has collections of photographs, books, clothing, household items, and farm implements. Much of the material relates to the Wendish community (an early German religious sect) founded a few miles south of Giddings. Free. 713-542-2102.

GEORGETOWN The *Inner Space Cavern* on I-35 offers underground tours of the stalagmite-filled chambers where dinosaur bones may be seen. Wear a coat as it is chilly. 512-863-5545.

GLEN ROSE Some of the best-preserved dinosaur tracks in the state are in *Dinosaur Valley State Park*, 5 miles west of town via U.S. 67 and F.M. 205. Here, the first tracks of the sauropods, 30-ton plant-eating reptiles, were found. Other tracks include those of duckbilled dinosaurs and of the meat-eating theropods. Nominal charge for each car entering park. 817-897-4588.

The *Somervell County Museum*, at Elm and Vernon streets, offers an excellent introduction to local anthropology and archaeology (Dinosaur Valley State Park is nearby) as well as items of local history. Displays include pioneer memorabilia, household tools and furnishings, and agricultural items, as well as archives, geological displays, and paintings by local artists. Open Sunday through Friday 1–5, Saturday 10–5, June to Labor Day. Rest of the year, open by appointment. Free. 817-879-6613.

GOLIAD *Goliad State Park*, on Routes 183 and 77A, south of Goliad, contains the *Mission Espiritu Santo*, established in 1749 and subsequently rebuilt on the same site and restored. The park also has a museum with memorabilia, documents, and artifacts of the Texas Revolutionary War, as well as Spanish and Indian artifacts. Nominal charge to enter park. 512-645-3405.

Near the mission is the restored *Presidio La Bahia*, a mile south of town on Refugio Highway. The Spanish fort, built to protect the mission, is the finest example of a complete Spanish presidio in Texas. Its chapel is still in regular use. A museum contains relics found during restoration, as well as memorabilia of the Texas Revolution and evidence of nine levels of civilization in the history of the site's habitation, starting with the pre-Spanish Indian period. Nominal charge. 512-645-3752.

GRAND PRAIRIE *International Wildlife*, 601 Lion Country Parkway, at the Beltline Road exit from I-30 between Dallas and Fort Worth, is a drive-through game preserve featuring wild animals from Africa. Included are lions, rhinos, elephants, zebras, giraffes, ostriches, cheetahs, and other exotic species. A free entertainment area has a petting zoo, picnic area, lion and tiger shows, elephant rides, paddle boats, and a snack bar. Park open daily April 30 to September 30; drive-through available 9–6, entertainment to 7:30. Fee charged. 214-263-2201.

The *Southwestern Historical Wax Museum*, at 601 East Safari Parkway, contains 80 displays with more than 180 wax figures. It emphasizes scenes from the Southwest, with such characters as Calamity Jane, Billy the Kid, the James boys, "Doc" Holliday, and Judge Roy Bean; other scenes depict such entertainers as Elvis Presley, Johnny Cash, and Joan Crawford. One scene is of the Last Supper. An important part of the museum collection is the Harrison H. Schwend frontier gun-collection, which comprises more than three hundred weapons and is considered one of the finest of its kind. Additional displays include pre-Columbian art, Indian artifacts, Western art, and early modes of transportation. Open 9–9 Memorial Day through Labor Day; weekdays 10–5 and weekends 10–6 the rest of the year. Fee charged. 214-263-2391.

GRAPELAND *Mission Tejas State Park*, on Route 21, is dedicated to preserving the Spanish heritage in Texas and to portraying pioneer construction methods. In it are a replica of the 1690 Mission San Francisco de los Tejas, the first Spanish mission in Texas, and the Rice Family Log Home. Now fully restored, the home was constructed in three phases, starting in 1828, using three different types of log notching. In addition to its historical displays, the park has full camping, hiking, and picnicking facilities. Open daily 8 A.M.—10 P.M. Nominal charge for each car entering the park. 713-687-2394.

GREAT PRAIRIE The *Fire Museum of Texas*, at 702 Safari Parkway—take I-30 (the old Dallas–Fort Worth Turnpike) to Beltline Road—is dedicated to preserving artifacts and fire apparatus of Texas volunteer, professional, and industrial firemen. It features more than twenty-three antique fire trucks and all types of fire equipment. A highlight is a fire-engine ride on a 1940 Mack. Fire-safety education programs include: films that are entertaining and informative; a forestry diorama with a life-sized, animated Smokey the Bear; and safety displays. The gift shop offers many fire-company-related items and souvenirs. Museum open daily 10–6. Closed Thanksgiving and Christmas. Fee charged for admission; discounts to firemen and their families, service men and their families, and to senior citizens. 214-263-1042.

HARLINGEN *Six Shooter Junction*, on South F Street via U.S. 77/83 South, is a re-created-frontier-village family amusement park that features stagecoach rides, a steam train, street-front "shoot-outs," kiddie rides, can-can shows, and authentic frontier shops with practicing craftsmen. Open Thursday through Sunday 11–7. Nominal charge. 512-423-1100.

The *Confederate Air Force Flying Museum*, at Harlingen International Airport, is dedicated to keeping obsolete military aircraft in flying condition. The organization maintains an impressive array of functioning World War II planes that occasionally stage flying demonstrations, the biggest of which is held on a weekend in early October. The museum's planes represent the finest flying machines of the United States, Britain, Germany, and Japan. Open Monday through Saturday 9–5, Sunday and holidays 1–6. Nominal charge. 512-425-1057.

HEREFORD Hereford is fewer than 60 miles from the Alibates National Monument, where for thousands of years Indians mined the great alibates flint outcroppings along the breaks of the Canadian River. The *Deaf Smith County Museum*, at 400 Sampson, displays arrow points, pottery, tools, and other Indian artifacts from the collection of Dennis Lomas. Other exhibits include a half-dugout (typical of the first homes built by many Plains settlers), a country store with many items from early Hereford businesses, and an interdenominational chapel filled with historical items surviving from the county's first churches. Open Tuesday through Saturday 10–5, Sunday 2–5. Free. 806-364-4338.

The *National Cowgirl Hall of Fame*, temporarily in the Deaf Smith County Library, pays tribute to all the women who contributed to the development of the West and to the pioneer spirit of women everywhere. Paintings, sculptures, and displays trace the careers of the honorees. Open Monday through Saturday 10–5. Free.

HILLSBORO The *Confederate Research Center and Audie Murphy Gun Museum* is on the campus of Hill Junior College, on I-35 at Route 22 in Hillsboro. The museum features firearms and edged weapons, and informative changing exhibits are set up by the Texas Gun Collectors Association. On display are articles belonging to Audie Murphy, World War II war hero and screen personality. The research center is dedicated to history of the Civil War and primarily to the role of Hood's Texas Brigades in the conflict. Dioramas, paintings, bronzes, and commemorative dinner plates are among the educational displays and exhibits, and extensive library collections of books on the Civil War and on firearms, ammunition, edged weapons, and artillery are available for public use. Museum and center open daily 8–4. Free. 817-582-2555.

HOUSTON The *Lyndon B. Johnson Space Center*, 2101 NASA Road #1, contains a collection of spacecraft and flight articles as well as exhibits about America's space-flight program. NASA films are shown throughout the day in the auditorium, and visitors may take self-guided tours of other designated facilities, including the Mission Simulation and Training Facility. The Mission Control Center is generally included on the guided tour on weekdays only; visitors should inquire about visiting it on weekends. Open daily 9–4, except Christmas. Free. 713-483-4241.

The *Museum of Fine Arts*, 1001 Bissonnet (at Main), is the largest art museum in the Southwest. Its permanent collections of both historic and contemporary works include ancient art from Egypt, Greece, and Rome; primitive art from Africa, Oceania, and North and South America; American paintings and decorative arts—including the Hogg Brothers Collection of Frederick Remingtons—as well as modern, Renaissance, and Baroque paintings and sculpture. A new wing has doubled the size of the museum and was designed by Mies Van Der Rohe. Open Tuesday through Saturday 10–5, Sunday 12–6. Free. 713-526-1361.

The *Bayou Bend Museum*, at 1 Wescott Street, is a branch of the

Museum of Fine Arts. In a twenty-four-room Latin Colonial structure, the former home of Ima Hogg—daughter of James Stephen Hogg, the first native-born governor of Texas—it is dedicated to American decorative arts from 1650 to 1850. Open the second Sunday of each month. Two-hour tours, by reservation only, Tuesday through Saturday. For reservations, contact the curator, P.O. Box 13157, Houston, TX 77019, or 713-529-8773.

The *Hermann Park Zoo*, at Zoo Circle Drive in Hermann Park, is a full zoological park with reptile, mammal, primate, and gorilla houses. The Tropical Bird House has been made to resemble an Asian jungle and has more than two hundred exotic birds flying freely through the aviary "rain forest." The Children's Zoo has wildlife from remote parts of the world as well as more familiar animals. Open daily in summer 9:30–8, the rest of the year to 6. Free. 713-523-0149.

The *Houston Museum of Natural Science*, 5800 Caroline Street in Hermann Park, contains space-science exhibits as well as those relating to geology, archaeology, prehistoric life, and natural history. Within the museum is the Burke Baker Planetarium, considered by many to have one of the finest and most sophisticated science-teaching devices in the world: a projector capable of reproducing any sky scene at any time of night at any point on earth. Burke Baker also has other scientific displays. Shows go on all year, at varying hours. Nominal charge. (For current schedule, call the number below.) Science museum open Tuesday through Saturday 9–5, Sunday and Monday 12–5. Open Friday and Saturday evenings 7:30–9 P.M. Free. 713-526-4273.

HOUSTON The *Houston Astrodome* at I-610 and Kirby Drive is the second largest enclosed stadium in the country. The 280-foot-high stadium is the home of the Houston Oilers, the Houston Astros, the Houston Hurricanes (soccer) and the University of Houston Cougers. The stadium seats between 45,000 and 66,000 persons, depending on the sport being played.

Astroworld, Loop 610 at Kirby Drive, is part of the Six Flags family of amusement parks and features more than a hundred shows, rides, and attractions for the entire family. There are miniature trains and autos, a sky ride, giant roller coaster, and a total of eleven differently themed areas within the park. The Astroneedle lifts visitors high above the park for a view of surrounding Houston. Open weekends in April and May, and from Labor Day through November. Open daily in summer. One-price-for-all-rides admission policy. 713-748-1234.

The *Rice Museum*, University Boulevard at Stockton Street, is on the Rice University campus and offers a program of changing temporary exhibits of art, ranging from primitive to the most contemporary. These include shows organized by the Rice Institute for the Arts and many traveling exhibitions from other institutions. A wheelchair ramp provides easy access to the building. Open Tuesday through Saturday 10–5, Sunday noon–6. Closed major holidays and during exhibit installation. Free. 713-522-0886.

The *Aline McAshan Botanical Hall and Arboretum*, at 4501 Woodway Street, offers many opportunities for nature study by young and old alike. The hall, with an exhibit and orientation room and a reference library, adjoins the greenhouse. The 260-acre arboretum has hundreds of species of trees, shrubs, ferns, wild flowers, and native small animals. Arboretum trails open Monday through Saturday 8:30–5:30. Free. 713-681-8433.

The *Museum of Medical Science*, at 5800 Caroline C. Hermann Park, is dedicated to improving the lives of others through better health standards. Permanent exhibits deal with the anatomy and physiology of the human body. Specific exhibits include ones on cell mitosis, bones and muscles, the kidney and urinary system, heart and lungs, a transparent woman, birth models, egg-to-embryo, the five senses, the chemical engineers of life, genetics, the brain and nervous system, variations on the theme of life, and the teeth. Open Sunday and Monday noon–4:45 and other weekdays 9–4:45. Free. 713-529-3766.

The *Museum of American Architecture and Decorative Arts*, in the Moody Library at Houston Baptist University, 7502 Fondren, displays a permanent exhibit of early Texas furniture, household utensils, and tools. There are also usually about four special exhibits drawn from the museum's collections of antique dolls, pre-Columbian pottery, and African wood-carvings. Many exhibits are specially directed to younger children. Open Tuesday, Wednesday, and Thursday 10–4, Sunday 1–4. Closed August and some school holidays. Free. For current schedule, call 713-774-7661, ext. 311.

The *Contemporary Arts Museum*, 5216 Montrose Boulevard, displays changing exhibitions of art by living artists presently working in virtually all media. Recent exhibitions have included examples of video art, conceptual art, and process art. Open Tuesday through Saturday 10–5, Sunday 12–6. Closed Monday, Christmas, New Year's, July 4, and Thanksgiving. Free. 713-526-3129.

El Paso's many attractions include ballet and theater, golf, and shopping on the Mexican side of the border.

Fort Davis National Historic Site.

McDonald Observatory near Fort Davis.

Two Fort Worth museums. *Above:* A 1929 Packard in the Pate Museum of Transportation. *Below:* A hall in the Amon Carter Museum.

Galveston has much to offer. *Above:* The Treasure Isle Tour Train takes sightseers through the city. *Below left:* Ashton villa, a nineteenth-century mansion. *Below right:* A diver feeds a sting ray at Sea-Arama Marineworld.

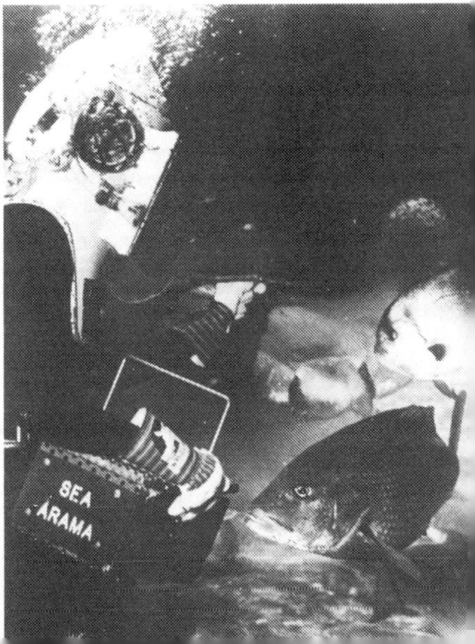

The *San Jacinto Museum of History* is in the base of the San Jacinto Monument on the San Jacinto Battlefield, 21 miles east of Houston. Said to be the tallest masonry monument in the world, it rises 570 feet above ground. At the site of the battle that won independence for Texas, the museum traces regional and Texas history from the Indian civilizations Cortez encountered to the formation of the State of Texas. Open weekdays and Saturday 9:30–5:30, Sunday 10–6. Free (nominal charge for the elevator to top of monument). 713-479-2421.

Also at the battleground is the battleship *Texas*, moored in a permanent slip, which may be toured. The *Texas*, the only survivor of the dreadnought class, was presented to the State of Texas by the U.S. Navy. Commissioned just before World War I, the ship was a flagship in the 1944 D-day invasion of Europe commanded by General Dwight D. Eisenhower, a native of Denison, Texas. Open 10–7 May through Labor Day; 11–5 (closed Monday and major holidays) September to May. Nominal charge.

To get to the battlefield, museum, and battleship from downtown Houston, take I-45 6 miles to I-610; take I-610 1½ miles east to Route 225, then drive 10 miles southeast to Route 134 and 3 miles to the battleground. 713-479-2421.

The *Art League of Houston*, 1953 Montrose, is a showcase of artwork produced by local artists, many of whom are professionals. There are juried exhibits of members' works shown all year, and a "Dimension Houston" show in late September and early October for all area artists. Open all year Monday through Friday 10–4; closed national holidays. Open Saturday noon–4 when an exhibit is hanging (most of the time). Free. 713-523-9530.

Sam Houston Park at 1100 Bagby is a collection of historic homes maintained by the Harris County Heritage Society who give guided tours.

INDEPENDENCE The small town of Independence, 12 miles northeast of Brenham, Texas, was once the site of Baylor College (for women) and Baylor University (for men). Both were moved (to Belton and Waco, respectively) in 1886, and the small town entered a decline. However, in recent years many tourists have been drawn to Independence. It has many early nineteenth-century homes still extant and is the site of the *Texas Baptist Historical Center and Museum*, which contains pictures and relics of Baylor University,gSam Houston's church pew, dining table, and wardrobe, and other early furniture and furnishings. The old stone church on the property, erected in 1872, is still in use and contains twelve pieces of furniture dating from 1840, including eight church pews made by slaves. Church services Sunday at 11 A.M. Museum open Wednesday through Saturday 10–4, Sunday 1–5; closed Christmas to New Year's. Free. 713-836-5117.

JEFFERSON One of Texas's most historic towns, Jefferson was settled about 1840 and grew up around a river landing on Big Cypress Bayou. It is proud of a number of Texas "firsts," including the first brewery, first ammonia-refrigerant ice plant, and the first use of artificial gas for street-lighting. By the end of the Civil War its population had peaked at 30,000. With a population today of about 2,500, Jefferson is a popular spot for tourists who come to see the many restored early homes and to enjoy the peaceful quiet of the bayou country of east Texas.

One of the best ways to be introduced to days gone by is a visit to the *Excelsior House Hotel*, 211 West Austin Street, a superb restoration with period furnishings of maple, cherry, and mahogany, including many of the original furnishings of the 1850 structure. Owned by the Jefferson Garden Club, which runs it as a working hotel, Excelsior House is fully described in *Country Inns, Lodges, and Historic Hotels of the South*, a companion volume to this book. The Excelsior House offers tours daily 1–4. Nominal charge. 214-665-2513.

Railroad tycoon Jay Gould was responsible for much of the development of the Texas rail system. He offered, late in the nineteenth century, to build a rail system to Jefferson, but the townspeople decided they preferred grass to the iron rails, and told Gould so. He angrily predicted the end of the city and took his offer elsewhere. Indeed, the city's population did decline in the years that followed, accounting for its lovely appearance today. *Jay Gould's Private Railroad Car*, the Atlanta, is on display on Austin Street, across from Excelsior House. The 88-foot stateroom, pulled across the state on Gould's lines, was a private palace on wheels, with a lounge, dining room, kitchen, butler's pantry, and bath. It is furnished with period antiques. Open daily 9:30–5. Nominal charge. 214-665-2513.

Built in 1850 by Williamson Freeman, the *Freeman Plantation*, at 212 Vale Street, is a Greek Revival–style antebellum home with a Louisiana influence. It was built with slave-made bricks and brick columns and with local pine and cypress. The home, in the National Register of Historic Places, is furnished with Victorian antiques. Open all year Thursday through Monday 1–5, and by appointment. Nominal charge. 214-665-2606.

The *Jefferson Historical Society Museum*, at Lafayette and Vale streets, is in a handsome red-brick building that was formerly a post office and federal court. More than three thousand items are displayed on four floors and in the garret. Included are mementos of pioneer days, early steamboat commerce, and the antebellum society that marked the town's heyday. Also on display are paintings and sculpture from the D. D. Feldman Collection. Open daily 9:30–5. 214-665-2775.

The glory of the riverboat days is recaptured on the *Cypress Queen*, on U.S. 59, a replica of a paddlewheeler that is skippered by a certified riverboat captain. The 45-minute cruise down Big Cypress Bayou features narration during the ride. On the dock is a free playground and an antique-car ride. Cruise operated daily in summer 1–7, except Tuesday and Thursday. Fee charged.

JOHNSON CITY The *Lyndon Baines Johnson National Historic Site,* a block off Main Street (follow signs), is the boyhood home of the late president and is furnished with many of the Johnson family heirlooms and period furniture. The small white house sits behind a white picket fence. Open daily 9–5, longer in summer. Closed Christmas. Free.

"Old Ranch," also part of the site, is the settlement that belonged to President Johnson's grandfather and great-uncle. The original 1856 dog-run cabin and other farm buildings have been restored and are part of a "living history" program that offers demonstrations of ranching, spinning, and other aspects of pioneer life. Visitors to the boyhood home may either walk the footpath to the "Old Ranch" or ride on a horse-drawn wagon. Open daily 9–5 in summer, weekends in winter.

For information on other LBJ National Historic Sites, see **Stonewall.**

JUNCTION The *Kimble Historical Museum,* at the intersection of Fourth and College streets, preserves material related to Kimble county. The collection includes documents, photographs, settlers' tools, household items, guns, and a large collection of fire-branding items relating to county stock-brands. The museum is in a building built entirely by the labor of American Legion members. Open Sundays 2–5, June 1 to October 31; by appointment other times. Closed in winter. Free. 915-446-3356.

KARNACK *Caddo Lake State Park* occupies 478 acres on Lake Caddo and is 2 miles north of Route 48. A visitors' interpretative center explains the culture of the Caddo Indians, a highly advanced prehistoric tribe that once lived in this area. Hiking is permitted around the lake.

KERMIT Kermit, a tiny hamlet of some eighty people when oil was discovered in 1926, quickly became an oil boom town. *Pioneer Park,* four blocks north of Route 302 at the eastern end of town, is an outdoor museum featuring the area's oil history. The Moorhead derrick, a huge cable-derrick with walking beam, is on display; it was the last operating derrick of its kind. Included in the museum are the "nesters' shack" and the town's oldest house. Open daily.

KILLEEN *Fort Hood,* on Route 190, 1 mile west of town, is a 218,000-acre U.S. Army base with the nation's greatest concentration of armored power. The base is open to visitors, and passes are not required. It is home to the *Museums of the 1st Cavalry Division and the 2d Armored Division,* which exhibit combat gear and artifacts from the World War II campaigns in Europe and North Africa. Information and directions are available at military police posts throughout the base.

KINGSVILLE The *King Ranch,* west of Kingsville off Route 141, is the largest ranch in the United States, comprising more than 800,000 acres covering four counties. Descendants of the Kings and the Klebergs (Robert Kleberg, the ranch's attorney, married the youngest King daughter) still control the great ranch. It deals with many aspects of cattle- and thoroughbred horse-breeding, as well as research in husbandry, agriculture, and wildlife conservation. The ranch is too huge and complex an operation to accept visitors, but they have set up a 12-mile road through the headquarters, stables, and other points of interest. The public may use this road only.

A regional-history museum on the campus of Texas Arts and Industries University that emphasizes Texas's bicultural history, the *John E. Conner Museum*, 820 Santa Gertrudis, has exhibits and local-history archives preserving items from the past. Exhibits range from prehistoric natural science to the economic development of south Texas in the twentieth century. Included are areas devoted to pre-Columbian and Indian artifacts, farm and ranch equipment, nine hundred cattle-branding irons, a frontier household, weapons, business machines, and professional offices. Natural-science exhibits pertain to fossils, seashells, and the rocks and minerals of south Texas. An exhibit is being prepared on the La Paloma mammoth found 35 miles southwest of Kingsville. Open weekdays 10–5, Sunday 2:30–5. Reserved for group attendance (by appointment) on Saturday. Free. 512-595-2819.

LAJITAS *Rio Grande Float Trips* on the river as it winds through the Big Bend canyons are available at the *Lajitas Trading Post.* Trips are arranged from one day up to three days. Next door is the Cavalry Post, a modern adobe motel that can arrange wilderness mountain pack-trips on burros. The area surrounding Lajitas features some of the nation's most breathtaking scenery. The road from Lajitas to Presidio following the Rio Grande (F.M. 170, or El Camino del Rio) is probably the most spectacular river road of all. Lajitas Trading Post: 915-371-2234. Cavalry Post: 915-371-2474.

LANGTRY The *Judge Roy Bean Visitor Center* is in the original Jersey Lily Saloon operated by the frontier judge known as the "Law West of the Pecos." Dioramas tell the story of Judge Bean, and his original lawbook, pistol, notary seal and other memorabilia are displayed. An adjacent garden has specimens of most of the native plants, with signs that identify them and indicate their practical uses. Open daily 8–5, except December 24, 25, and 26. Free. 512-291-3340.

LAREDO On the banks of the Rio Grande, at the foot of Washington Street, is an old border fort established in 1848, *Fort McIntosh.* Today, it is part of the campuses of Laredo Junior College and Texas A & I University. The remaining chapel, guardhouse, commissary and warehouse are now incorporated into the *Nuevo Santander Museum* featuring displays of photos, artifacts, and documents pertaining to the fort's and local history. Open Monday through Friday 9–4, Saturday and Sunday 1–5. Free.

Nuevo Laredo, just across the border in Mexico, is a colorful, flourishing border city with great appeal to visitors and shoppers. There are festive market places and plenty of native-foods restaurants and night clubs.

The *Museum of the Republic of the Rio Grande,* in the Republic of the Rio Grande Building, 1000 Zaragoza, began life in the early nineteenth century as the home of a Laredo family. When this area was the Republic of Rio Grande, the house served as the capitol building. In all, seven flags have flown over the quaint, single-story building, whose whitewashed, plaster-covered walls of rock and adobe are more than 2 feet thick. It now serves as a museum displaying guns, saddles, and household goods emphasizing the period of the republic (1839–41). Open all year, except major holidays. Hours vary but are usually Tuesday through Sunday 10–2. Free. 512-723-1286.

LIBERTY Liberty is one of the oldest of the Texas settlements. The *Geraldine Humphreys Museum,* 1710 Sam Houston, features period rooms displaying the local pioneer history of this historic area. There are changing special displays and art exhibits. Open Monday through Friday 10–6, Saturday 10–4. Free.

The *Sam Houston Regional Library and Research Center,* Farm Road #1011, 3 miles north of Liberty off Main Street (Route 146), is a handsome, white-columned building in a 110-acre wooded area. The library features a large collection of books, maps, documents, and family records and papers on Texas. The Historical Display Room has an Indian arrowhead collection, a journal of Jean Laffite's, photographs, guns, knives, and steamboat artifacts. Upstairs there is furniture typical of early frontier Texas. Open Monday through Friday 8–5, Saturday 10–4. Closed all state holidays. Free. 713-336-7097.

LIVINGSTON Displays at the modern *Polk County Memorial Museum,* at the intersection of Route 190 and Drew Street, include Indian artifacts, rocks and minerals, Chinese artifacts, nineteenth-century clothing, guns, tools, toys, furniture, items of warfare, newspapers, and musical instruments. Open Monday through Friday 12:30–5. Free. 713-327-4786.

LUFKIN The *Ellen Trout Zoo,* in the city park at Loop 287 and Lake Street, has more than three hundred specimens representing a cross section of native and exotic wildlife. The zoo's main features are the hippopotamus, small mammal, bird, and reptile buildings. The Lufkin Lions Club operates a miniature train ride (nominal charge) in the park, and there is also a 50-acre lake with fishing. Open all year 10–5, to 6 in summer. Free. 713-634-6313.

The *Texas Forestry Museum,* 1905 Atkinson Drive, at Route 103 East, next to the Texas Forestry Association, is in the piney-woods region of eastern Texas. The museum, owned and operated by the Texas Forestry Association, is manned and maintained by members of the Retired Senior Volunteers. Lufkin is headquarters for the National Forests of Texas, and the museum preserves and records the history of forest-products industries and the Texas forestry profession through collections of relics, papers, photos, and forestry equipment in frequently changing exhibits. Included in the collections are early twentieth-century engines, a steam loader, a "high wheeled cart" used for dragging logs from the woods to a loading site, and an extensive group of fire-prevention paraphernalia used by the U.S. Forest Service. There is also a woodland nature trail designed by foresters that is similar to many throughout eastern Texas. Open daily 1–4:30. Free. 713-634-5523.

McKINNEY The *Heard Natural Science Museum and Wildlife*

Sanctuary, a mile east of Route 5 and south of McKinney, presents past and present natural history of north-central Texas through the use of habitat groups, interpretative exhibits, fossils, and Indian artifacts. The Seashell Room contains shell and other marine life. In the Rock and Mineral Hall are the several exhibits including the gemstone window; a cave; and many rock and mineral specimens. The Print Gallery's changing exhibits are of antique and contemporary nature prints; the Oriental Room has works of Eastern art. Memorabilia of the Heard Family is displayed in the Heard Heritage Room. The museum was founded by Bessie Heard, daughter of a Collins County pioneer, who wanted a place to preserve the land, foster a program of education and conservation, and allow others to enjoy her extensive collections. A 266-acre sanctuary has nature trails; visitors are permitted on the trails only when accompanied by guides. Museum and sanctuary open Tuesday through Saturday 9–5, Sunday 1–5. Closed Monday and major holidays. Free. 214-542-5012.

MADISONVILLE Joe and Pat Barrett set out to recreate an authentic turn-of-the-century, old-West town. To do this they salvaged fifteen original buildings from various locations and had them moved onto the site of what is now known as the *Yesteryear* ghost town, on Old San Antonio Road, just west of I-45, about 12 miles north of Madisonville. Among the many old buildings are a frontier jail, livery stable, blacksmith shop, stockade, general store, post office, saloon, doctor's office, and a log cabin. Transportation items on display include wagons, buggies, and a 1926 fire engine. There is a gift and antique shop in the ghost town, and a privately owned full-service campground nearby. Open daily May 1 to September 1, weekends the rest of the year, except January and February. Nominal charge. 214-344-2468.

MARLIN *Highlands Mansion,* 1 mile northeast of Marlin on F.M. 147 (Groesbeck Highway), is a nineteenth-century home built by a Civil War veteran, Basil C. Clark, who completed it in 1900. Its interior reflects the elegance of a gracious era. There are ceilings ornamented in gold leaf, leaded stained-glass windows and a stained-glass dome, oak and tufted-leather paneling, and period furnishings. Open weekdays 10–4, Sunday 1–4. Nominal charge. Children under 12 must be accompanied by an adult. 817-936-5234.

MARSHALL The *Harrison County Historical Museum* is in the remodeled courthouse on Peter Whetstone Square. Its exhibits on the Caddo Indians, area pioneers, and the old South depict the history of Harrison and Marshall counties. Special collections on display include one on the Civil War, a transportation and communication collection, the Governor Clark Collection, and Y. A. Tittle's pro-football memorabilia. Open Sunday through Friday 1:30–5. Nominal charge. 214-938-2680.

Ginocchio National Historic District covers 3 blocks in the heart of the old part of Marshall. Its centerpiece is the 1896 *Ginocchio Hotel,* a fine example of a Victorian hotel, with excellent interior work and decorative detailing. Open to guests for daily lunches and Tuesday through Saturday for dinner. The hotel's restored portions are open to the public for free tours.

The 1877 *Allen House Museum* is a white frame home near the hotel, at 610 North Washington Street. It is a fine example of early Texas architecture and features upstairs and downstairs verandas across the length of the house. Open Tuesday through Saturday 10–4, Sunday 1–4. Nominal charge for the tour.

Franks Antique Shop and Doll Museum, 211 West Grand Avenue and Route 80W, is in the Hockwald House built in 1895. The historic Texas house has been nominated to the National Registry of Historic Places. Mr. and Mrs. Franks have been in the doll-and-antique business for more than thirty-one years, and the house contains more than eight hundred rare and interesting dolls, doll furniture, toys, and related items. Open all year by chance or appointment, daily except Sunday. Nominal charge. 214-935-3065.

MENARD The *Menardville Museum,* in the 1910 Frisco Railway Depot, is a project of the Menard County Historical Society. The collection includes artifacts from Indian, Spanish, and pioneer settlements in the area. Among its prized possessions is a bar from an old-West saloon. Nearby are the ruins of the Spanish Presidio, built in 1757, and Fort McKavett, dating from 1852. Open all year 1:30–5. Free. 915-396-2562.

MEXIA The *Old Fort Parker State Historic Site,* near Fort Parker State Park, 8 miles southwest on Route 34, Park Road 35, was established by members of the Parker family to protect the eight families inside. In 1836 it was attacked and overrun by Comanches, who killed several Parker family members and carried off others, including Cynthia Ann Parker, a nine-year-old. She apparently lived happily with the Comanches and eventually married a Comanche chief. She and her daughter, Prairie Flower, were captured by white people and were returned to their kinfolk, much to her dismay. Cynthia tried many times to escape and return to the free life of her Comanches, to no avail. She and her daughter died four years later. Cynthia had spent twenty-four years with the Indians and was the mother of the last great Comanche chief, Quanah Parker. The old fort has been restored several times and houses pioneer articles in log blockhouses and the stockade. Open all year in daylight hours. Nominal charge.

MIDLAND The *Permian Basin Petroleum Museum* is 2 miles south of Midland on Route 349, or off exit 136 from I-20. The only major museum of its kind in the Southwest, it is designed to pay tribute to the area's largest industry, petroleum. The history of petroleum, its formation, discovery, and subsequent production, are brought to life in pictures, maps, and 3-D dioramas. Its enormous marine diorama, "Pana-Theatre," with 5 screens, shows visitors the sea floor from an ocean that disappeared more than 230 million years ago. Included in displays are a re-creation of a 1920s boom town, an animated drilling rig, and historic paintings. Exterior exhibits include nine full-sized antique drilling rigs. On forty-eight hours' notice, the museum can provide tours for the blind. It also provides Spanish-language tapes for interested visitors. Open Tuesday through Saturday 9–5, Sunday 2–5. Closed winter holidays. Nominal charge; preschool children free. 915-683-4403.

The *Nita Stewart Haley Memorial Library and J. Evetts Haley History Center,* 1805 West Indiana Avenue, two blocks south of Route 80, preserves and promotes the ideals and traditions of the cow country. Mr. Haley was a cowboy and cowman all his life, and he and his wife spent many years collecting the materials contained here. The theme of the library and history center is the life and times of the cowboy and the range-cattle industry. Unique to the collection are the manuscripts made up of nearly seven hundred interviews with frontier cowmen, trail drivers, Indian fighters, Texas Rangers, farming settlers, outlaws, and other early Southwestern characters. The history center exhibits a large selection of art and artifacts relating to the horseback tradition of the range country. The pride of the collection is the original Alamo mission bell, cast in 1722. The Library and History Center also offers special Western art exhibits and sales. Open all year Monday through Friday, 9–5. Free. 915-682-5785.

MONAHANS *Monahans Sandhills State Park,* 6 miles northeast of town on I-20, contains nearly 4,000 acres of sand dunes that have been called "the Sahara of the Southwest." Visitors to the beautiful park should plan a stop first at the park interpretative center, just inside the entrance. Within the center are displays related to the region's biology, geology, and archaeology. The dunes region was populated, on a temporary basis, by Indians as long ago as 10,000 B.C. The area was discovered by Spanish explorers four hundred years ago, but Indians continued to frequent the dunes until the 1880s, when the Texas and Pacific Railroad selected Monahans as a water stop between the Pecos River and Big Spring. The park concession stand is in the recently renovated railroad section-camp foreman's cottage. The interpretative center also contains botanical and herbarium materials, photographs, paintings of plant life, stuffed animals, explorer's maps, and a collection of insects of the sand dunes. It provides information for birders visiting the park. A self-guiding interpretative trail leads from the center and winds through the dunes. Park open every day 7 A.M.–10 P.M.; center open 8–5, in summer to 10, with special slide-program at 9. Charge for each car entering the park (except holders of special state passes). 915-943-2092.

NACOGDOCHES The *Hoya Memorial Library and Museum,* 211 South LaNana Street, offers visitors a glimpse of east Texas history. It occupies part of the old Adolphus Sterne house, built in 1826. Sterne owned the Nacogdoches general store, a successful endeavor that allowed him to build his bride a house just two years after the store opened. Active in early rebellions against the Mexican government, Sterne was captured in 1827 and condemned to death. Saved by the intervention of the Masonic Lodge, he pledged never to bear arms against Mexico again, and his home became a popular spot with both Mexicans and Texans. General Sam Houston was baptized in one of the home's rooms, more likely for self-serving reasons than for his commitment to the Roman Catholic Church. (A Mexican law at the time required that all persons who desired to own land in Texas also be members of the Church.) After Sterne's death in 1852, the house was purchased by the Hoya family, who lived there until 1896. The library and museum now contain many Sterne and Hoya family relics, including furniture, dishes, chests, deeds and other documents, and an early piano. Open from Monday through Saturday 9–12 and 2–5. Free. 713-569-8677.

Millard's Crossing, on Route 59 North, 6020 North Street, is a group of five restored nineteenth-century historic houses, completely furnished with pioneer articles and memorabilia and antiques. Open for guided tours daily Monday through Saturday 9:30 and 2, Sundays at 2 only. Fee charged. 713-564-6969.

The only remaining structure of *Old Nacogdoches University,* built in 1858, is the *Old University Building,* on the campus of Nacogdoches High School on Washington Square. The Greek Revival edifice was used during the Civil War as a Confederate hospital and, later, Union headquarters, a convent, a college, and more. It contains exhibits of antique furnishings, silver, and historical relics. Open in summer June through August 10–noon and 2–5, Sunday 2–5. Free. 713-564-7218.

Stone Fort Museum, Clark Drive and Griffith Boulevard, was built in 1779 as a trading post. It was rebuilt by the state and now houses artifacts and pottery found buried in Indian mounds in the area, General Houston's personal effects, and a copy of the first newspaper printed in Texas—the first two newspapers were actually printed in the historic old fort. It is famous as the place where "Three-legged Willie" held court with a pistol. Eight flags have flown over the fort, and it is now part of the campus of Stephen Austin State University. Other collections at the museum are dolls, coins, guns, and items of local area history. Open Monday through Saturday 9–5, Sunday 1–5. Free. 713-569-2408.

NEDERLAND *La Maison des Acadiens French Museum,* next to the Dutch Windmill Museum and part of Tex Ritter Park, is a replica of the houses built by the Acadians (Cajuns) in southern Louisiana during the late nineteenth century. It was built and dedicated to the preservation of the traditions and heritage of the French Acadian people who settled here. Most of the French Acadians had migrated to the Nederland area from Louisiana to work at the Texas Company Refinery (Texaco). The house contains late-nineteenth-century furnishings, including cooking equipment, a baby cradle, chairs, beds, and so on. There are firearms, musical instruments, a spinning wheel, and many farm tools. The curator, Joe LeBlanc, plays a guitar and sings Cajun songs on request. The Joe LeBlanc Leather Shop in the museum features handmade leather goods. Museum and shop open Tuesday through Sunday 2–6, March through August; Thursday through Sunday 1–5 the rest of the year. Free. 713-722-0947.

NEW BRAUNSFELS The *Ferdinand Lindheimer Home,* 491 Comal, was built around 1852 in the German colonial tradition called *Fachwerk,* which German settlers adapted to Texas cedar and limestone. The owner, Lindheimer, was an internationally reknowned botanist, the first to classify much of the native Texas flora; more than thirty varieties bear his name in their botanical titles. He led an adventurous life, and was considered by the Indians to be a medicine man and good friend. In 1844–47 he was one of the first to greet the more than seven thousand German emigrants arriving at Galveston. Prince Carl zu Solms-Braunsfels, one of the noblemen organizing the colonization, hired Lindheimer as a wilderness guide, and he led the colonists to the site of their first settlement, New Braunsfels. He was later selected to be the editor of the German-language newspaper. The house Lindheimer built has been restored by the New Braunsfels Conservation Society and is furnished with many of his possessions. Open daily 2–5, June through August, closed Monday. In winter, open only on weekends 2–5. Nominal charge. 512-625-5593.

Gruene, on the Guadaloupe River on Gruene Road off Loop 337, is a village established by the German immigrants before 1850 that is now a suburb of New Braunsfels. There are many historic old homes, stores, and ruins and restorations of other structures. Today the town has art galleries, a winery, an ice cream parlor, and an old-fahsioned beer hall from the 1880s.

Natural Bridge Caverns, just north of I-35 on F.M. 3009, are still in their formative stages. There are tours offered every half hour. Open in summer 10–6, in winter 10–4. Fee charged.

The *Sophienburg Memorial Museum,* at 401 West Coll Street at Academy Avenue, is on the hilltop spot where a log fortress was built by Prince Carl zu Solms-Braunsfels in 1845. The native-rock building exhibits memorabilia of the prince and the early German settlers, including furniture, the nobleman's personal effects, Indian artifacts, and pioneer items. Open Monday through Saturday 10–5, Sunday 1–5. Donation. 512-629-1572.

ODESSA The *Presidential Museum,* at 622 North Lee Street, can be reached by leaving I-20 at Grant Avenue (U.S. 385), then going left on Seventh Street to Lee. It displays and preserves items pertaining to the presidents of the United States. Its more than thirty thousand articles include campaign mementos, presidential china, also-rans items, presidential caricatures, and items relating to women candidates. There are several exhibits of presidential portraits and original cartoons and a First Lady Doll collection. This is probably the only museum dedicated solely to the office of the chief executive. Open Monday through Saturday 9–5, closed an hour at noon; opens Friday at 10. Closed Sunday and holidays. Free. 915-332-7123.

ORANGE The *Stark Museum of Art,* 713 Green Avenue, features exhibitions of art related to the land, wildlife, and people of the American West. The collections were assembled by the Stark family of Orange, primarily H. J. Lutcher Stark and his wife, Nelda Childers Stark. The Western Collection includes paintings, sculptures, prints, and rare books and manuscripts spanning the history of Western art from the 1820s to 1970. Of special interest are prints and books by James J. Audubon, sketches by Paul Kane, bronzes by Frederic Remington and Charles M. Russell, and the paintings by the twentieth-century artists of Taos, New Mexico. The American Indian Collection consists of objects crafted by tribes from the Great Plains and the Southwest. There are fine examples of Plains clothing, body ornaments, and beadwork; and from the Southwest there are baskets, Navajo rugs and blankets, pueblo pottery, and Hopi kachina dolls. Also on display are a series of porcelain birds by Dorothy Doughty and a collection of Steuben glass. The museum is in a handsome structure that has received the Tucker Award for excellence in concept, design, construction, and use of natural stone. Open Wednesday through Saturday 10–5, Sunday 1–5. Closed Monday, Tuesday, and major holidays. Free; children under 12 must be accompanied by an adult. 713-883-4147.

PAMPA The *White Deer Land Museum,* at 116 South Cuyler, is in a two-story red-brick Georgian building (1916) that once held the offices of the White Deer Land Company. That company, successors to the Francklyn Land and Cattle Company, once controlled more than 600,000 acres in the four surrounding counties. It is said they never repossessed land they sold, except on a few occasions when they were asked to do so by the purchasers. Among the display rooms are a Western Union office, the Pampa post office, a general store, a chapel, and an old-time school-room. The museum contains one of the largest arrowhead collections in the Southwest and has rooms that reflect the furnishings of the late 1800s and early 1900s, including a parlor, pioneer bedroom, and kitchen. Open daily except Monday 1:30–4. Closed holidays and some special occasions. Free. 806-665-5521.

PANHANDLE The *Square House Museum,* at Fifth and Elsie streets, is actually a complex of six buildings and a historic house. Square House itself has been associated with the history of the region since the mid-1880s, when it was used as a range headquarters of the N-N Cattle Company. Lumber for its construction was hauled by oxcart from Dodge City, Kansas. Artifacts in the museum relate to the West, from prehistoric times to the ranchers and cattle syndicates and to the discovery of oil and subsequent industrialization. Included in the museum displays is the Finch Farm and Ranch Display. Contributed by descendants of Panhandle settlers, Finch Farm includes a typical ranch-shed housing a chuck wagon, buggy, and cowboy gear. There is also a complete blacksmith shop, a restored 12-foot Eclipse windmill, and a dugout dwelling. Other items in the collection include a hand-hammered Spanish medallion found along Coronado's route, guns from buffalo hunters, pioneer tools, home furnishings, and a large group of prehistoric Indian artifacts. Within the Moody Wildlife Building are many displays of mounted birds, mammals, and local reptiles. Other exhibits include the Hall of the Plainsman and two art galleries. Open daily 8:30–5:30, Sunday 1:30–5:30. Closed Thanksgiving, Christmas, and New Year's. Free. 806-537-3118.

PARIS The *General Samuel Bell Maxey State Historic Structure,* built in 1867, is the restored home of the Confederate General and US Senator. The gravesite of *John Chisum,* for whom many cattle trails were named, is located in this town.

PECOS The *West of the Pecos Museum,* on the corner of Route 285 and First Street, is in the old historic Orient Hotel and Saloon. The ground floor, devoted to the restoration of the lobby, dining room, and saloon, contains restored ornate fixtures in what was the area's finest establishment in the late nineteenth century. The saloon was the site of a shoot-out in which two outlaws were gunned down by the bartender, Barney Riggs. There are period rooms, a rodeo room, rock and mineral exhibits, and general displays of local history and color. Open Monday through Saturday 9–6, Sunday 2–4. Nominal charge; children under 12 free. 915-445-5076.

The Chamber of Commerce and Tourist Center, on Cedar Street, are located in the *Old Pecos Town,* a re-created old-West town and park set up on two downtown blocks. Featured is Pecos's first building, moved to the spot and now housing a gift shop. Among the several attractions are a replica of Judge Roy Bean's Saloon and the grave of Clay Allison, the "Gentleman Gunfighter."

PHARR The *Old Clock Museum,* 929 Preston Street, a block off old Route 83, in East Pharr, is a private museum featuring clocks from all over the world, some dating back to the seventeenth century. The displays have many beautiful and exotic specimens. The owners live next door. Open daily all year. The museum, a nonprofit institution dedicated to horological research, does not charge admission but accepts contributions for charities such as the Boy Scouts and the local children's home.

PORT ARTHUR The *Port Arthur Historical Museum,* 441 Austin Avenue, features the history of Port Arthur as shown through exhibits of local articles and relics. There are artifacts from the Battle of Sabine Pass and a talking machine by Thomas A. Edison. Open Monday through Friday 9–4, Saturday 9–noon. Free. 713-736-1552.

PORT ISABEL The *Port Isabel Lighthouse* has been a dominant feature at the southern tip of the Texas Gulf Coast, the area long known to the coastal Barrado Indians, discovered by the Spanish in 1519, and settled by the year 1830. Port Isabel served as the supply depot for the American troops during the Mexican War in 1846. Construction on the lighthouse began in 1851 and was completed two years later. In the years that followed, the lighthouse at first played a major role in guiding shipping in the area. However, by 1905, traffic passing the point had declined drastically, and the light was extinguished permanently. The light, surrounding buildings, and land were donated to the state in 1950 for use as a park. From the top of the brick tower, there is a panoramic view of the surrounding Gulf and the Rio Grande Valley. Open all week 10–2 and 1–5. Nominal charge. 512-475-4848.

PORT LAVACA The *Calhoun County "Jail" Museum* is on 202 South Ann Street, next to the courthouse. The old jailhouse that once confined prisoners in Calhoun County now houses relics, artifacts, and mementos of Calhoun County's early days. Open Tuesday and Thursday 2–6, Saturday 9–1. Free.

QUITMAN The *Governor Hogg Shrine State Historical Park* encompasses almost 27 acres and includes the *Honeymoon Cottage, Miss Ima Hogg Museum, Stinson Home,* playground, and Old Settler's Tabernacle, all in beautiful wooded surroundings. The house-museums all belonged to various Hoggs, from one of Texas's most famed families. There are personal belongings of Governor and Mrs. James S. Hogg and their children, and the houses are furnished with period Victorian antiques. Open daily all year 8 A.M.–10 P.M. Park museums open Thursday through Monday for guided tours, 9–12 and 1–4. Miss Ima Hogg Museum free; nominal charge for guided tours. 214-763-2701.

RANKIN The *Rankin Museum,* just south of Route 67, is in the old Yates Hotel at 200 West Fifth Street. One of its important features is the Yates Hotel lobby, which has been restored to its original condition as a historical exhibit. The museum's collection consists mainly of memorabilia of the area, including churns, sadirons, early musical instruments (piano and organ), kerosene lamps, clothing, rocks and minerals of the area, and so on. The Yates Hotel was built as a showcase by Ira Yates to house the boom-time crowds drawn to Rankin to see his $15-million gusher of 1926. As the result of a swap-off of a general store he owned, Yates had been "stuck" with the land, which went on to yield the oil well. Open by appointment all year Monday through Friday, except some holidays. Free. 915-693-2309.

RICHMOND The *Fort Bend County Historical Museum,* 500 Houston Street, has been cited by the Historical Commission as one of the best small museums in the state. It depicts the history of the county, which was settled by Stephen F. Austin's colony, the Old Three Hundred, in 1822. Among the featured exhibits and artifacts are those relating to Austin's colonists; to Jane Long, the "Mother of Texas"; and to Carrie Nation, who began her nationwide campaign against Demon Rum here. There are also excellent collections of documents and photographs. Open Tuesday through Saturday 9–5, Sunday 1–5. Free. 713-342-6478.

RIO GRANDE CITY In October 1924, Father Gustavo Gollbach came to Rio Grande City and set out to re-create an exact replica of the Grotto of Lourdes, where the Virgin Mary is said to have appeared to Saint Bernadette. After four years of labor he completed the *Grotto of our Lady of Lourdes,* which is 90 feet wide and 33 feet high. Every year thousands of visitors of all faiths come to see it and the surrounding grounds at the Immaculate Conception Church at 101 East Third Street. There is a special Christmas pageant every year at the grotto, with productions in both Spanish and English. Grotto always open. Free. 512-487-2317.

ROUND TOP The *Winedale Historical Center,* on F.M. 2714, a mile north of F.M. 1457, consists of a "dog-run" farmhouse, built in 1848 of local eastern red cedar, and an 1861 Greek Revival house. Both buildings feature hand-painted decorations and collections of early Texas German furniture and decorative arts. Also on the property is a barn that is used as a theater and one housing an antique tool collection. Open to groups during the week (by appointment), to the public on Saturdays 10–5, Sundays 12–5. Nominal charge. 713-278-3530.

Henkel Square, a group of buildings constructed around 1820–70, sit behind a split-rail fence on the town square. A project of the Texas Pioneer Arts Foundation, its dwellings are filled with an excellent collection of Anglo- and German-American furnishings, utensils, and decorative arts of the period. Open 10–6. Nominal charge.

RUSK The *Texas State Railroad,* a state historical park following a rail route begun in 1896, offers a 3-hour, 50-mile round trip through the heart of east Texas. The rail system was originally constructed to serve an iron smelter at the state penitentiary in North Rusk. By 1917 the penitentiary and its smelter had closed, and the railroad was only occasionally used. In 1969 much of the original Texas State Railroad and surrounding land was conveyed to the Parks and Wildlife Department for the establishment of a state park dedicated to the preservation of steam locomotives and the golden age of railroading. The trains travel over thousand-foot-long trestles crossing the Neches River and numerous creeks and pass through dense forests where a variety of wildlife may be seen. They may be boarded either at the Rusk Depot in Rusk Park on Route 84 or at the Palestine Depot off Route 84 in Anderson County. Scheduled runs include full and short round-trips from each depot. Trains operate weekends only in March-May and September-October, and daily in June, July, and August. Closed November through February. Reservations recommended. Fee charged. 214-683-5126.

SAINT JO The *Stonewall Saloon Museum,* Main and Howell streets, on the north corner of the town square, was built as a saloon in 1873. It is the town's oldest building and now houses a museum containing many samples of cattle brands, pioneer farming and ranching items, and guns and household articles of the local settlers. Open daily 8–6. Free. 817-995-2758.

SALADO The *Central Texas Area Museum* is across from the *Stagecoach Inn,* a Texas Historic Landmark, which was once host to such notables as Robert E. Lee and Jesse James. The restored Stagecoach Inn now houses a restaurant. The Texas Museum contains documents and exhibits displaying antiques, guns, and other articles of local historical interest. Open Monday through Saturday 10–6, Sunday 1–6. Nominal charge.

SAN ANGELO The *Fort Concho Preservation and Museum,* at 213 East Avenue D, consists of a group of twenty-one original or reconstructed buildings, most of which date from the late nineteenth century. The museum itself is in an original headquarters building (1876) and two reconstructed enlisted men's barracks. There is also a schoolhouse/chapel and two restored officers' quarters that are entirely original. Some of the surviving buildings are currently occupied by private groups but may be viewed from the exterior. Many consider the fort to be the best-preserved frontier fort in the state. The museum collection includes military memorabilia from the Indian Wars period (1869–89) and many items dealing with early San Angelo and Tom Green County. Open daily 9–5, Sunday 1–5. Closed Christmas and New Year's. Nominal charge. 915-655-9121.

SAN ANTONIO This area, long a favorite of Native Americans, attracted the interest of Spanish officials in the early eighteenth century. Today it is a booming metropolis with a festive Texas-Mexican flair. Tourists wishing to capture all the city has to offer—which is quite extensive and exciting—should visit the *San Antonio Chamber of Commerce,* on the corner of Commerce and South Alamo Streets, or the *Convention and Visitors Bureau,* at 210 South Alamo and 321 Alamo Plaza.

The Alamo—on Alamo Plaza—probably the most famous historic site in Texas, holds the undisputed title of "Cradle of Texas Liberty." It was the focal point of a heroic struggle in which outnumbered Texans, including Jim Bowie, Davy Crockett, and William Travis, held out against Santa Anna's Mexican army for thirteen days in 1836. In the end the defenders were all killed, and the battle cry "Remember the Alamo" later led the Texans to victory. Open Monday through Saturday 9:30–5, Sunday 10–5:30. Free. The names of the Alamo heroes are etched in marble on a monument that dominates the plaza. A state park surrounds the Alamo, and a museum on the grounds contains relics of the famous Battle of the Alamo and many exhibits pertaining to the colonization and the days of the Republic of Texas. Open Monday through Saturday 9–5. Opposite the plaza is a museum-theater presenting a slide show of the siege and battle. It is shown every half hour, and a fee is charged. Open daily 9–5:30. For information on Alamo Historic Site and the park, call 512-222-1693.

In the early eighteenth century there was intense rivalry between Spain and France for domivavce in the northern Mexico and Texas territories. To maintain a hold on this region, Spain built numerous settlements, fortresses, and missions throughout the Southwest. One such complex consisted of the Mission San Antonio de Valero (later rebuilt and renamed the Alamo) and the nearby Presidio de San Antonio de Bejar, constructed to protect the mission. The Presidio was rebuilt in its present location in 1722 and included a *Commandancia* that later became the *Spanish Governor's Palace* (105 Plaza de Armas). The seat of Texas government was here when San Antonio became the capital of the

Spanish province of Texas. In the years following the transition from Spanish rule to United States control, the palace served as a second-hand clothing store, barroom, restaurant, and a schoolhouse. In 1929 the city of San Antonio purchased the building, now largely a ruin, and fully restored it, using authentic building methods and materials. Palace furnishings include antique pieces from the early eighteenth century. Open daily Monday through Saturday 9–5, Sunday 10–5. Closed Christmas Day. Nominal charge. 512-224-0601.

The *Buckhorn Hall of Horns,* at 600 Lone Star Boulevard, is in the new Lone Star Brewery. The hall, originally part of the Buckhorn Saloon in the heart of San Antonio, has an enormous collection of animal horns and mounted animal trophies gathered over the years, beginning in 1881, by Albert Freidrich. The brewery preserved the collection, and the museum now houses the horns plus a Hall of Fins, which has a variety of unusual and rare marine animals. There are many exotic birds in the Hall of Feathers, and additional collections feature rare and early firearms and memorabilia. Open daily 9:30–5, except winter holidays. Nominal charge. 512-226-8301.

Mission Nuestra Señora de la Purísima Concepción, on 807 Mission Road, was established in 1731 and was under construction for more than twenty years. It is the oldest unrestored church in the country. Nominal charge.

Mission San Francisco de la Espada, on Espada Road South, was established in 1731. The church is very popular with tourists and photographers. It has been restored many times and is still in use. Nominal charge.

River Walk is the *Paseo del Rio,* which meanders for several miles through the heart of San Antonio following the river. There are tropical foliage, lovely shade trees, and many sidewalk cafés and little colorful boutiques along the way. The street is below the city's main level.

The José Antonio Navarro State Historic Site, just a block northeast of the governor's mansion, at 228 South Laredo Street, features three limestone buildings from the 1850s restored and operated by the Texas Parks and Wildlife Department. The three structures—the home, office, and kitchen of Navarro, a patriot and signer of the Texas Declaration of Independence—are furnished appropriately with period antiques. Open daily 10 to 4. Nominal charge.

HemisFair Plaza, the site of the 1968 Texas World's Fair, is now an entertainment and recreation area for downtown San Antonio. There are many restaurants, amusement rides, the Hall of Texas History, boutiques, monorails, tramways, and the 750-foot Tower of the Americas, which has an observation deck and several restaurants. Tower open daily. Fee charged.

The *Hertzberg Circus Collection,* 210 West Market Street, depicts the evolution of the "Greatest Show on Earth" with paintings, a mechanized antique clown, pieces from Mr. and Mrs. Tom Thumb's collection, and more. All exhibits are in miniature. Open daily 9–5:30, except Sunday.

The *Pearl Brewery's Jersey Lily Hospitality Center,* in the Pearl Brewery, off the 1700 block of Broadway, is a replica of Roy Bean's establishment. The 1886 room has memorabilia of the brewery's beginnings and early days. There are period furnishings and a large stein collection. Open Monday through Saturday 10–5, June through August; Monday through Friday 10–5, September through May.

The *Mexican Market,* Santa Rosa and Commerce streets, is a colorful collection of shops and stalls offering Mexican goods and local craftwork. Fresh produce is also sold here.

The *McNay Art Institute,* 6000 North New Braunsfels Street, has a fine collection of post-Impressionistic paintings by such notable artists as Cézanne, Toulouse-Lautrec, Van Gogh, Gauguin, and the Americans Homer and Marin. Galleries are devoted to Indian arts and crafts of New Mexico. Open Tuesday through Saturday 9–5; Sunday 2–5. Free.

The *Institute of Texan Cultures,* on Durango Boulevard and Commerce Street, off I-35, was set up in HemisFair Plaza by the University of Texas's Texana department. Twenty-five ethnic areas make up the Institute's main exhibit floor, tracing Texas history through its pioneers. The successes and adventures of farmers, ranchers, shopkeepers, soldiers, and others who populate the state's history are detailed through old photographs, text panels, and many "touch and feel" artifacts. Interpreters help bring history to life by teaching such pioneer crafts as Mexican tortilla-making, weaving, spinning, and pioneer instrument-making. The institute is an excellent place to start a visit to Texas, whose ethnic diversity surprises many—Texans and non-Texans alike. The multimedia show takes place three times daily in the central dome. Open daily Tuesday through Sunday 9–5. Closed Monday, Thanksgiving, and Christmas. Donation. 512-226-7651.

The *San Antonio Museum Association* presently consists of two major municipal museums operated by the city of San Antonio. *The Witte Memorial Museum,* at 3801 Broadway, first opened in 1926 and

Above: NASA exhibits at the Lyndon B. Johnson Space Center in Houston. *Below:* Diorama of the prehistoric ocean floor in the Permian Basin Petroleum Museum in Midland.

Above: An old-time train at the Texas State Railroad Historical Park in Rusk.
Below: Lewis House at the Winedale Historical Center in Round Top.

History comes vividly to life in San Antonio. *Above:* The Alamo. *Below:* The Spanish governor's palace.

Above left: San Jose Mission in San Antonio. *Above right:* Inside the Railroad and Pioneer Museum in Temple. *Below:* A vintage automobile at the San Antonio Museum of Transportation.

comprises a major collection of art and natural history and science material. It includes Art of the Americas from the colonial period to the present; Masters of American Photography from 1920 until today; Southwest Regional Art; natural history and science displays including dioramas, gems, and minerals; American Indian, Oceanic, African, and Oriental culture displays; and examples of decorative arts and other historical items from the San Antonio region. The *San Antonio Museum of Transportation,* in HemisFair Plaza, contains historic carriages, aircraft and automobiles, and the Herff model railroad. Work is nearing completion in transforming the historic Lone Star Brewery buildings into the San Antonio Museum of Art, to be located at 200 West Jones Avenue. When completed in late 1980, the newly restored building, listed on the National Register of Historic Places, will house all of the art collections mentioned above. Museum open weekdays 9–5, weekends and holidays 10–6. Closed Christmas, New Year's, and Fiesta Friday. Donation (nominal amounts suggested). 512-826-0647.

La Villita Historic Complex, bounded by Paseo de la Villita, South Presca, South Alamo, and Nueva streets, is a group of eleven very early buildings that were restored by the city of San Antonio and now house a variety of arts and crafts shops, restaurants, and museums. La Villita, Spanish for "Little City," has been occupied since the early sixteenth century, when it was a village of Cohuiltecan Indians. However, most of the buildings now in the restored district date from the nineteenth century. Crafts represented include pottery and glass-blowing, and there are a number of boutiques within the confines of the early structures. Open all year except Christmas and New Year's. For more information, contact the San Antonio Convention Facilities, 512-299-8610.

To reach *San Jose Mission,* at 6539 San Jose Drive, take I-37 from the downtown area and exit on New Braunfels Avenue South; turn right and go one block to Southcross; turn right onto Southcross and continue to Roosevelt Avenue, then turn left onto Roosevelt; turn left on Mission Road, then left again into the site parking lot. Founded in 1720 by Franciscan Friar Antonio Margil de Jesus, it is one of the outstanding examples of the mission system established in the Southwest by the Catholic Church during Spain's colonial period. The present church was completed in 1777, at which time the mission was described as "the finest mission in this part of America, . . . a model for all others." One of the outstanding parts of the Baroque mission is Rosa's Window, considered one of the finest pieces of Spanish-colonial ornamental sculpture in the nation. The mission, a state and national historic site, consists today of the restored mission compound, the church, a granary, a partially restored convento, and a restored mill. Open every day 9–6; June through August, to 8. Nominal charge. 512-922-2731.

The *San Antonio Zoo,* 3903 North St. Mary's Street, is one of the largest in the Southwest and one of the top zoos in the United States. Its extensive animal collection is within the zoo's natural rock cliffs, which provide a backdrop for displaying animals among natural settings in barless, open-moated exhibits. An outstanding bird collection features flamingos, rare cranes including the endangered whooping crane, waterfowl, and parrots, and other tropical birds. The zoo has one of the largest collections of African antelope in the world. It houses the first white rhino born in captivity outside Africa, a rare and beautiful golden lion tamarin, a monkey island with gelada baboons, and aoudad sheep. There are elephant shows and rides in season. Open daily all year, in winter 9:30–5:30; in summer to 6:30. Nominal charge. 512-734-7183.

Brooks Air Force Base, qouth of San Antonio on I-37, is the site of the headquarters for the Aerospace Medical Division of the Air Force Systems Command. One function of the division has been the establishment of the *Museum of Flight Medicine* in the old Hangar No. 9, the last of the old wooden hangars constructed at Brooks in 1918. It has recently been included in the Texas State Historical Survey. The museum, which contains exhibits concerning the history of the base, the development of manned flight, and the evolution of aerospace medicine, is dedicated to the memory of Astronaut Edward H. White II, a native San Antonian. Open all year Monday through Friday 8–4. Closed weekends and all holidays. Free. 512-536-2204.

The *History and Traditions Museum* at Lackland Air Force Base is dedicated to the history of aviation, especially early plane engines. On the airfield are about 54 antique and historic planes. The museum is at S.W. Military Drive, off Hwy 90 West; 512-671-3444.

SAN FELIPE DE AUSTIN The village and state park here are named in honor of Stephen F. Austin. He virtually began Texas independence and statehood from this tiny town, one of the state's most historic sites. The original town was destroyed by order of Sam Houston at the time of the invasion by Santa Anna's troops, who occupied it until the Texan victory at San Jacinto. San Felipe was the location of Austin's Texas colony and the colonial capital of Texas 1824–36. Stephen Austin had lived here all his life; held here were the conventions of 1832 and 1833 and the Consultation of 1835, which ultimately led to the Texas Revolution. There are many firsts in this historic place: It is the home of the first Texas newspaper, *The Gazette,* founded in 1829; and of the *Telegraph* and *Register* (1835), the official revolutionary organs; the postal system of Texas originated here; the Texas Rangers were founded as a result of meetings here for public safety. Today the sites are in the 600-acre *Stephen F. Austin State Park,* which contains a replica of Austin's log-cabin home and many monuments and historic markers. The crowning glory of the park is a fine statue of Austin, the "Father of Texas." The *J. J. Josey Store* was built in 1847, after the razing of the town. Fully restored, it now houses a museum containing Austin's desk and some of his papers as well as store merchandise displayed as it would have been in its heyday. Open Saturday, Sunday, and holidays; nominal charge.

Stephen F. Austin State Park, near the Brazos River just north of San Felipe on Park Road 38, has an *Interpretative Center* and nature trails. Open Memorial Day to Labor Day. Nominal charge. The *San Felipe Post Office,* which provides information and literature, has an Information Center operated by the Park Association. Open during normal postal hours.

SAN MARCOS *Wonder World*, just off I-35 via Redwood Road exit (follow the signs), is a four-part family attraction that includes a wildlife park, the Wonder Cave, Tejas Tower, and the Anti-Gravity House. The Wonder Cave, the largest dry-formed cave known, was formed by violent earthquakes about 30 million years ago and discovered by Mark Beevers in 1893. The Anti-Gravity House is filled with optical illusions. The wildlife park contains many species of animals that roam free while visitors watch from their seats in an open-air miniature train. Visitors are permitted to pet and feed the many species of native and imported deer. An elevator takes visitors to the top of the Tejas Tower for a panoramic view of the surrounding countryside. Single-fee entrance ticket covers all activities; separate admission available to cave only. Open daily all year 9–5, in summer 8–8. 512-392-3760/6711.

Aquarena Springs is at the mouth of the San Marcos River where huge springs bubble up to form the river at Spring Lake. The springs are considered to be one of Texas's main tourist attractions. Colorful fish, underwater rock formations, and many aquatic plants may be viewed from glass-bottom boats. In the submarine theater, forty-five-minute-long underwater shows are performed daily, throughout the day, and more frequently in summer and on weekends. On the shore of this aquatic wonderland are many various amusements, such as skyrides, an old mill, the Mexican marketplace, many beautiful gardens, and a nature trail. A re-created frontier village has many authentic structures as well as mission ruins. The Dr. Eli T. Merriman Home, a historic one-room log cabin with antique furnishings, is here at the Texan Village, on Loop 82. It is the oldest house in San Marcos and is open—along with the blacksmith shop, frontier jail, and an operating grist mill—daily 9–5. Nominal charge. 512-392-2481. Park grounds are open in summer weekdays 8 A.M.–9 P.M.; weekends 8 A.M.–10 P.M. In winter, open daily 8:30–6. Closed Christmas. Fees charged. 512-392-2481.

SANTA ANNA The *Old Rock House,* on Route 84, 2 miles out of Santa Anna, may well be one of the smallest museums open to the public in the Southwest. The 1873 structure measures just 18 by 24 feet and has been restored to look as it did when it was first built by a squatter named Brestoe. It is currently furnished with pioneer items from 1900 and before that represent the way it would have looked when it was used. Open on request. Free. 915-348-3283.

SARATOGA *Big Thicket National Preserve*, a convergence of North American flora and fauna, consists of numerous separate parcels of land reflecting the amazing variety of ecological settings in this area. It is best explored after a visit to the *Big Thicket Museum* in Saratoga (on Farm Road 770), which presents slide shows and has numerous displays designed to orient the visitor to Big Thicket's culture and biology. There are herbarium displays, preserved reptiles and amphibians, insect collections, and mounted mammals. Several special nature trails near the museum provide an excellent introduction to the area. Museum open Tuesday through Saturday 9–5, Sunday 1–5. Free; charge for guides, tours, and certain educational programs. 713-274-2971.

SEGUIN *Sebastopol House State Historic Structure* is in a state park approximately a half mile west of downtown Seguin; take Court Street (Route 90A) to Erkel Street; turn right, then left at the park sign on the driveway. One of the few remaining examples of Seguin's unusual building techniques, the Greek Revival–style Sebastopol was built 1854–56 of a material called limecrete. A mixture of lime, sand, and gravel, limecrete was poured into wooden forms, layer on layer. No inner supports were used in the walls. During the antebellum years, Seguin was known as Concrete City because of its many buildings constructed out of limecrete. However, upkeep had to be constant, and the buildings were allowed to deteriorate. Eventually most were demolished, and Sebastopol is one of the few left today. It has all-walnut woodwork inside, and three rooms are furnished with period antiques, lamps, and photos relating to the home's inhabitants. Open in summer Monday through Sunday 9–4, in winter Wednesday through Sunday 10–4. Free. 512-379-8202.

SHERMAN The *Sherman Historical Museum,* at 301 South Walnut, is in the old Carnegie Library built in 1914. A regional-history museum dedicated to preserving materials of Sherman and the surrounding Grayson County, its collections include pictures, letters, documents, furniture, clothing, handwork, porcelain, books, farm and ranch tools, and country-store items. Open all year, Friday 9–12 and 1–5, weekends 2–5. Free. 214-893-7623.

SNYDER The *Scurry County Museum,* in the Learning Resource Center of Western Texas College, was founded in 1972 and has exhibits focusing on the area's history, recalling the days of military and Indian trails, buffalo hunters, cattlemen, farmers, and oil. Open Monday through Thursday 9–12 and 1–4:30, Friday 9–12 and 1–3:30, and Snday 1–4:30. Free. 915-573-6107.

SONORA The *Caverns of Sonora* are about 15 miles from Sonora, southwest on Route 290; go 8 miles west on I-10, then 7 miles south on F.M. 1989. Considered by many spelunkers to be the finest and most beautiful anywhere, they were discovered fairly recently and have many unusual and colorful formations. Tours leave every half hour. Open daily 8–6, April through October; 8–5, November through March. Fees charged. 915-387-3105.

STANTON The *Martin County Historical Museum,* on the corner of Convent and Broadway streets, contains historical artifacts of the county. Exhibits are set up chronologically and follow the county's development. Open Wednesday and Saturday in the afternoon. Free. To open soon most afternoons. Call for times. 915-756-2338.

The *Old Jail Museum,* on the northwest corner of Courthouse Square, is in the town's 1908 jailhouse, which has an interesting cell block and a complete replica of an early sheriff's office. Upstairs is Sheriff Don Saunders' personal collection of guns and "Western stuff." Sheriff opens museum on request. Free. 915-756-2338/2722.

STONEWALL The LBJ Ranch, home of the late President Lyndon Baines Johnson, is in Stonewall. The *Lyndon Baines Johnson National Historic Site,* with a replica of his tiny four-room birthplace, is part of the National Historic Site that includes his boyhood home in Johnson City (which see). The LBJ State Park visitors' center offers free park-service tour buses 10–4; tour includes the birthplace cottage, the big *LBJ Ranch;* a one-room school; and the president's grave site in the Johnson family cemetery. Park road closed to private cars 8:30–5:15.

The *LBJ State Park,* a 710-acre park, has a visitors' center presenting interpretative displays on the historic hill country. There are two dog-run cabins, furnished in the style of the former pioneer owners. Open daylight hours. The *Sauer-Beckman Farmstead* offers visitors a glimpse of farm life as it was at the turn of the century. Park and its historic buildings open daily 8–5. 512-644-2252.

SUNSET The *Old West Museum,* in the old-fashioned, frontier-type Sunset Trading Post in the middle of the old Chisholm Trail, contains a collection of Southwest Americana. Display items relate to the early ranching and homesteading period. The post is also the headquarters of the Barbed Wire Historical Society and prints several publications about barbed wire on its premises. Open daily all year 8–6. Nominal charge. 817-872-2027.

SWEETWATER The *Pioneer Museum,* 610 East Third, is in the partially restored 1906 home of the late Judge and Mrs. R. A. Ragland. The steps to the house are flanked by a series of massive, two-story columns, and the building reflects the area's gracious Southwestern architecture. The museum's many early articles describe the daily life of the Texas settlers at the turn of the century. There is a military display, a pioneer schoolroom, examples of history through art, many Indian artifacts, the wood-paneled district courtroom taken from the Nolan County Courthouse, and the saddlery of S. D. Meyers on display in the Saddle Shop. Open daily 2–5, except Monday and holidays. Free. 915-235-8547.

TEMPLE The *Railroad and Pioneer Museum, Inc.,* 710 Jack Baskin Street, can be reached by taking the H Avenue Exit off I-35 and following Avenue H to Thirty-first Street. It is in the former rural depot building of the Santa Fe Railroad Company. The fine old depot has been painstakingly repaired and restored to its former glory and is now dedicated to preserving railroad and pioneer history of central Texas. The main focus is on the period 1881–1920; among its railroad memorabilia and equipment is an old steam engine. Open Tuesday through Saturday 10–4, Sunday 1–4. Closed Monday and major winter holidays. Nominal charge. 817-778-6873 or 773-4210.

The *SPJST Museum,* 520 North Main Street, is dedicated to preserving historical and pioneer items of Temple and the surrounding area, primarily those of the Czech immigrants. The entire collection is in a modern new building belonging to the Slavonic Benevolent Order of the State of Texas, a fraternal insurance society. The museum's initials derive from the Czech name of the society, *Slovanska Podporujici Jednota Statu Texas.* The museum features a complete frontier country doctor's office; a pioneer blacksmith shop and kitchen; farm and mechanical tools; musical instruments; textiles; books; and Czech Bibles from early times. A popular item here is the "Gambler," a unique mechanized doll that drinkers used to determine who paid for the beers. There are early (A.D. 627, 638, and 658) coins; a Bible printed in 1530; and the pistol that killed John Wesley Hardin. Another excellent reason for visiting the SPJST Museum is to meet and talk with its genial curator, Otto Haus. Open daily Monday through Friday, 8–noon. Free. 817-773-1575/773-5294.

TEXARKANA A *Tourist Bureau,* on I-30, west of Route 59, is one of eleven at key entrances to Texas. It provides visitors with information, maps, and literature on all areas of the state. Open daily. Free.

The *Texarkana Historical Society and Museum,* on 219 State Line Avenue, is in the city's first brick structure. It features displays and exhibits of local historical interest, from prehistoric times, with Caddo Indian artifacts and archaeological displays, down to the pioneer and early medical and farm-tool exhibits. An early kitchen, a parlor, and an office are set up here. Open Monday through Friday 10–4, Saturday and Sunday noon–3. 214-793-4831.

TYLER The *Goodman Museum,* at 624 North Broadway, 90 miles west of Shreveport, Louisiana, and 90 miles east of Dallas, is in an 1859 mansion listed in the National Registry of Historic Places. Originally a four-room Greek Revival cottage, it was remodeled by Dr. W. J. Goodman in 1880 into a classic Revival mansion. It features the original period furnishings of the Goodman family and the holdings of the Smith County Historical Society, which is housed here. The society exhibits many items of local interest, including pioneer tools, looms, cradles, and paper artifacts. The Mollie Moore Davis Chapter of the United Daughters of the Confederacy also maintains an exhibit in the Goodman home. The Junior League of Tyler has restored the building to its earlier splendor and strong overtone of Southern grandeur. During the restoration, a unique hand-painted ceiling was discovered in the front parlor. Open daily 1–5; closed major holidays. Free. 214-597-5304.

The *Municipal Rose Garden,* on West Front Street, is one of the largest anywhere, featuring more than 35,000 rosebushes of almost 400 varieties that reach their peak of beauty between April and October. The rose fields surrounding the city supply almost half the field-grown roses in the United States. Free.

The *Tyler Junior College* contains the *Tyler Museum of Art,* in a modern museum building on the campus at 1300 South Mahon Avenue. It offers changing exhibits of single artists and special collections. Open Tuesday through Saturday 10–5, Sunday 1–5.

VICTORIA Victoria was one of the first three towns incorporated by the Republic of Texas. The *McNamara Historical Museum,* at 502 North Liberty Street, has many artifacts from the Spanish, Mexican, and Texan historical eras. It is furnished with Victorian antiques and is located in an 1869 Victorian homestead. Open Tuesday, Wednesday, and Thursday 10–noon and 3–5, Sunday 3–5. Free.

Royston Nave's widow built a Greco-Roman hall to house his paintings. The *Nave Museum,* at 308 Commercial Street, also features changing art exhibits and contemporary art and sculpture. A painter of some note in New York circles in the 1920s, Nave painted a great deal around the Victoria area. Open Wednesday through Sunday 1:30–5:30. Free.

In picturesque Riverside Park, at 110 Memorial Drive, the *Texas Zoo* exhibits only those animals native to the state. More than 150 mammals, birds, reptiles, amphibians, and fish are exhibited in a variety of settings, including outdoor, moat-enclosed areas. Additional animals and natural-history displays are in the Texas Animal Kingdom building. In addition to exhibiting animals, the zoo is also a recognized facility for rehabilitating injured or orphaned wildlife. Major display arcas include hoofed mammals, waterfowl, turtles and alligators, bears, pumas, prairie dogs, small mammals, and a children's zoo. Open daily all year 10–dusk. Nominal charge. Children 6 and under free. 512-573-7681.

WACO The *Texas History Collection,* part of the *Carroll Library* on the Baylor University campus, features relics of early Texas and the Southwestern pioneers. The library has extensive archives on early Texas and surrounding areas. Open Monday through Friday 9–noon and 1–5, Saturday 9–noon. Closed school holidays. Free.

The *Brazos Queen* docks on Lake Brazos, at I-35 Fisher Street exit A replica of an eighteenth-century riverboat, the old paddlewheeler takes guests on a 1½-hour-long scenic excursion on the Brazos River. Excursions daily 2:30, Saturday 9:30 A.M. Closed Monday and winter holidays. Reserve in advance for evening dinner-cruises. 817-752-5800.

Waco has a number of historic homes. Many gracious plantations flourished along the Brazos River before the Civil War destroyed the plantation economy and scattered the population. Many of the historic homes are open by appointment, but several are open all year. *The Fort House,* at 504 South Fourth Street, was built in 1868 in the Greek Revival tradition and features exhibits pertaining to local history as well as period furnishings. *East Terrace,* at 100 Mill Street, is a two-story Italian villa made of local bricks. Built in 1872, it is furnished with period antiques. Both houses are open Saturday and Sunday 2–5. Nominal charge. 817-756-3331.

The *Art Center,* on the campus of McLennon Community College, at 1300 College Drive, is on the crest of a wooded bluff commanding a fine view of the valleys of the Brazos and Bosque rivers. The renovated Mediterranean-style building containing the art center was the summer home of the late lumber-magnate William Waldo Cameron. The center displays the works of Larry Scholder, Vincent Mariani, David Diao, and others, and long-term loans of sculpture by James Surls, Robert Wade, and Herb Rogalla. There are about a dozen temporary exhibitions each year as well as special educational events, classes, and workshops. The art center has a museum shop with pottery, glass, weavings, baskets, sculptures, toys, and jewelry as well as art books. Open Tuesday through Saturday 10–5, Sunday 1–5. Closed Monday, July 4, Christmas, New Year's, and Thanksgiving. Free. 817-752-4371.

The *Central Texas Zoo,* on Route 10 in Waco (use exit 339 off I-35), is a modest-sized zoo with three hundred live animals, including the only breeding pair of bald eagles extant in the southwestern United States. The Reptile House contains fifteen species of rattlesnakes and forty other types of snakes. There is a nursery for baby animals and a continuing program of breeding five species of endangered animals. Open Monday through Friday 9–5, Saturday and Sunday 9–6. Nominal charge. 817-752-0363.

The *Armstrong Browning Library* is south of I-35 on Speight Street between Seventh and Eighth streets, on the Baylor University campus. The world's largest collection of the works and memoirs of Robert and Elizabeth Barrett Browning—more than two thousand original letters and manuscripts written by and to the Brownings—is contained here. It includes most of the books and other publications and work dealing with Robert Browning. Some features of the imposing library structure that appeal to visitors: its huge bronze entrance-doors whose panels depict themes from ten of Browning's poems; and the fifty-one stained-glass windows throughout the hall that illustrate poems and themes by both the Brownings. Open Monday through Friday 9–noon and 2–4, Saturday 9–noon; closed most holidays. Free. 817-755-3566.

The *Strecker Museum* on South Fourth Street, is in the Sid Richardson Science Building at Baylor University. A museum of both science and history, it exhibits material on archaeology, anthropology, biology, geology, and history. Special collections include reptiles and amphibians of Texas and Mexico; fossils of central Texas; and birds' eggs, nests, and skins. There is also a living museum of local amphibians and reptiles. Open Monday through Friday 9–4, Saturday 10–5, Sunday 2–5. Free. 817-755-1110.

The *Texas Ranger Hall of Fame and Museum,* in a 35-acre park on Riverside Drive on Lake Brazos, is the headquarters of Company F Texas Rangers. The park, the site of the original Texas Ranger camp, today features a replica of the original Ranger fort established in 1837. The Texas Rangers were established by Stephen F. Austin in 1823 to help the settlers with the Indians. Displays here commemorate the history and heritage of the Rangers, using dioramas with memorabilia and wax figures. The Hall of Fame recognizes Texas Rangers of note. Open May through August 9–6, September through April 9–5. Fees charged; children under 6 free. 817-754-1433.

WASHINGTON The *Star of the Republic Museum* is in *Washington-on-the-Brazos State Historical Park,* south of Route 105 (between Brenham and Navasota). It honors the site of the signing of the Texas Declaration of Independence and the last capital of the Republic of Texas. The museum presents the history of the Texas Republic through exhibits, publications, and media presentations. Exhibits depict all aspects of the Republic period, including social life, agriculture, transportation, politics, and military affairs. Special programs for groups are available by reservation, and the museum's research library is open to the public. Opened in 1970, the museum is a state-supported institution operated by Blinn College in Brenham. Open Wednesday through Sunday 10–5, September 1 through February 28; same hours daily the rest of the year. Free. 713-878-2461.

The park also contains the *Anson Jones Home,* the residence of the last president of the Republic of Texas. Nominal charge to see interior. 713-878-2214.

WEATHERFORD *Holland Lake Park,* off the Clear Lake Road exit from I-20, is a 10-acre town park with well-marked nature trails exploring three different ecosystems. Also on the grounds is a restored and furnished dog-run cabin, the first built in the county. Free.

The *Texas Railroad Museum,* on East Fort Worth Street, is in the old Santa Fe Depot, two blocks east of Courthouse Square. It features many fine old engines and related railroad articles. In the collection are a San Francisco cable car, a New Orleans streetcar, and a vintage steam engine. The prize of the exhibit is the presidential car once belonging to the president of the Texas and Pacific Line. Open all year Saturday 10–5, Sunday 1:30–5. Nominal charge.

WESLACO The *World's Smallest Telephone Museum,* 535 South Missouri, is a tiny building constructed of hand-set local pebbles. Its roof is of thin-shell concrete construction in the Dutch-barn manner, and it features antique telephones and related articles. Open Monday through Friday 9–5, except holidays. Free.

WEST COLUMBIA The *Varner-Hogg Plantation,* off Route 35, a mile north of West Columbia on the county road, is a *State Historic Park* featuring an elegant Greek Revival plantation home. The land was obtained in a grant from Stephen F. Austin by Martin Varner, a pioneer who established the state's first rum distillery. The last private owner of the plantation was James Hogg, Texas's first native-born governor. The home, built in the 1830s and filled with period furnishings and artifacts, was, along with 53 surrounding acres, donated by a Hogg heir. Open for tours daily 10–noon and 1–5, except Monday and Wednesday. Fee charged.

WHEELER The *Wheeler County Museum,* in the 1908 jailhouse at Fifth and Alan Bean Boulevard, displays items pertaining to the history of Wheeler County. The town requested a post office when the area became "thickly settled" by five families living in dugouts. Open Monday, Wednesday, and Saturday 1–5. Donation.

WICHITA FALLS The *Tourist Bureau,* in the northern part of the city at the junction of U.S. routes 277, 281, and 287, is one of eleven such places provided to visitors. It is staffed by travel counselors and offers free services including maps, literature, and information about tourist areas and sightseeing in Texas. Open daily all year.

The *Wichita Falls Museum and Art Center,* on the Midwestern

Parkway, across from Midwestern State University, presents a series of changing exhibits on the arts, science, and history. It also has a planetarium show for the public every Sunday at 2:30 P.M. Museum open Monday through Saturday 8:30–4:30, Sunday 1–5. Closed national holidays. Free. 817-692-0923.

WIMBERLEY *Pioneer Town,* on River Road south of R.R. 12, is a reproduction of a town of the Old West of about 1880. Created by Raymond Czichos and his family, its buildings are furnished with original and authentic period items. Buildings open to the public include the Silver Spoon Cafe, the stockade, a livery stable and blacksmith shop, the Wagon Museum, the Opera House, the Brass Rail Saloon, the Wells Fargo Company office, the El Dorado Hotel, a pawn shop, and a pioneer chapel. Entertainment at Pioneer Town includes rides on the Pioneer Town Railroad and such shows as the Dr. U. Skinem Medicine Show, a Gay Nineties Review, and an old-time melodrama. Those wishing overnight accommodations may reserve rooms at the nearby 7A Ranch Resort. Open daily June, July, and August, Saturday and Sunday afternoons the rest of the year; closed December and January. Nominal parking charge; separate charges for buildings and entertainments. 512-847-2517.

WINDTHORST The *Old County Jail and Archer County Museum,* on Route 1, a block north and a block east of the courthouse, is in the three-story 1910 jailhouse. The jail's equipment is still in place, and the building is filled with items of local historical interest, including displays of old tools, farm machinery, oil-field machines, a gallows, clothing, glassware, prehistoric fossilized animal bones, and Indian artifacts. Most of the exhibits may be handled, and the curator will answer questions about the items. Open all year Thursday through Monday 9–6, including holidays. Donation.

WOODVILLE *Heritage Garden Village,* a mile west of town on U.S. 190, has more than twenty-five restored early Texas pioneer buildings in an unusual setting created by Clyde E. Gray, who was honored by the Texas Heritage Society for his efforts in historic preservation. There are homes, shops, vehicles, and a restaurant in the village. Of interest is an 1866 log cabin painstakingly restored to its original condition. Exhibits feature buildings, household articles, and photos and documents pertaining to life from pioneer days of the mid-nineteenth century down to the Roaring Twenties. The *Pickett House,* a family-style restaurant in an old schoolhouse, serves meals (weekdays)

11–3, weekends 11–6. Heritage Garden open daily 9–sundown; closed Christmas and New Year's. Nominal charge; children under 6 free.

The *Allan Shivers Library and Museum,* 302 North Charlton, is in the lovely restored Victorian home that the former Texas governor and his wife gave to Woodville. It now contains the governor's papers and memorabilia, as well as early artifacts of the area, and it is furnished with handsome antiques and beautiful rugs. Open Monday through Friday 9–5, Saturday to 3. Closed holidays. Nominal charge.

The *Alabama-Coushatta Indian Reservation,* between Livingston and Woodville on Route 190, is home to two of the Southern Forest tribes. It was created in the 1850s at the insistence of Sam Houston, a staunch friend and ally of the Alabama and Coushatta. It has a Living Indian Village where visitors can watch tribe members making jewelry, baskets, and leather items. The tribes also offer swamp-buggy and miniature railroad rides through the Big Thicket, the dense wooded area in the reservation. Other special attractions are a reptile farm, a petting zoo, a museum and crafts shop, traditional tribal-dance demonstrations, and a restaurant offering typical Native American fare and pit barbecue. Open daily March through November and the first week in December, except Sunday morning. Open weekends only, January and February. Fees charged for activities. From late June through late August, the tribes stage a nightly performance, in the outdoor theater, of *Beyond the Sundown,* which tells the story of the two tribes. Show at 8:30 P.M. Fee charged. 713-563-4391.

ZAVALLA The town of Zavalla, in the Angelina National Forest, is the gateway to several recreation areas. The *Harvard Home Museum,* on F.M. 1270 and Route 69, 2 miles south of town, is in the county's oldest house, an 1853 log cabin complete with pioneer furnishings typical of the period. It also displays local artifacts. Open daily June through August.

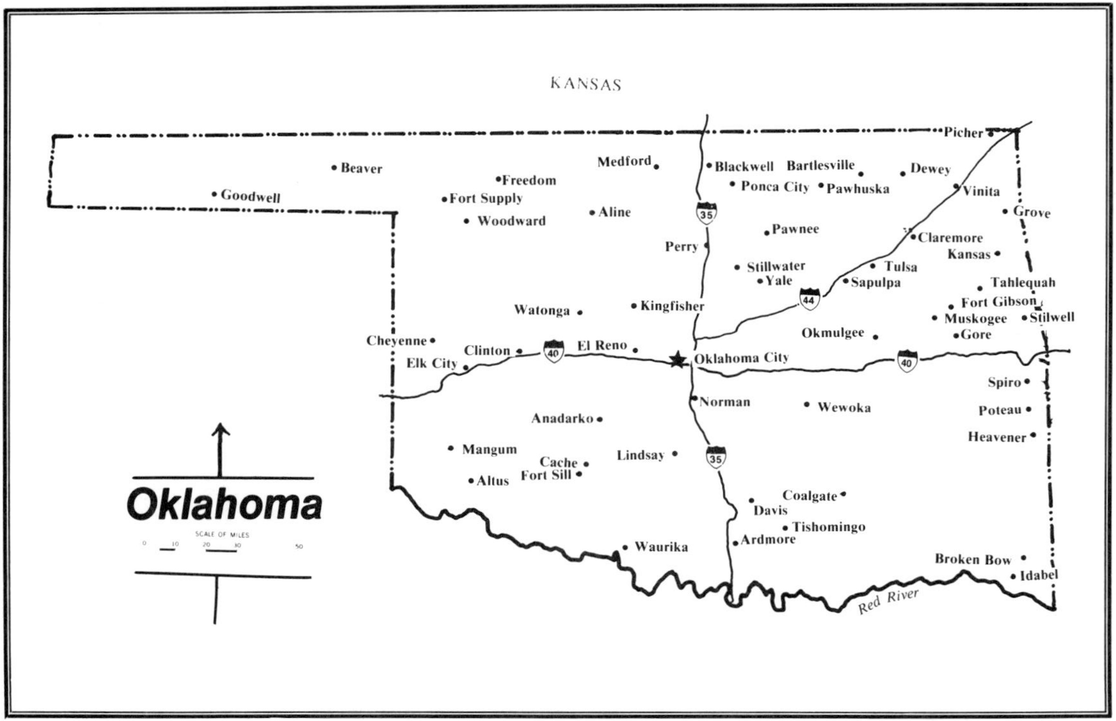
KANSAS
Picher
Beaver
Goodwell
Freedom
Fort Supply
Woodward
Medford
Aline
Blackwell
Bartlesville
Dewey
Ponca City
Pawhuska
Vinita
Grove
35
Pawnee
Perry
Claremore
Kansas
Stillwater
Tulsa
Yale
Sapulpa
44
Tahlequah
Fort Gibson
Muskogee
Stilwell
Gore
Watonga
Kingfisher
Okmulgee
Cheyenne
Clinton
40
El Reno
Oklahoma City
Elk City
Spiro
Norman
Wewoka
Poteau
Anadarko
Heavener
Mangum
Cache
Lindsay
Fort Sill
Altus
Oklahoma
SCALE OF MILES
0
10
20
30
50
Coalgate
Davis
Tishomingo
Ardmore
Waurika
Broken Bow
Idabel
Red River

Oklahoma

THE WORD "OKLAHOMA" is derived from two Choctaw Indian words meaning "red people." The name is a particularly apt one. More than 90 percent of all Native Americans in the United States live west of the Mississippi River, and one-third of these live in Oklahoma. The story of the Native American in the West is inextricably part of the history of this state.

Long before the white man came to Oklahoma, bands of Indians representing eight regional tribes traveled across the prairie hunting vast herds of buffalo. In 1541 the region was explored by both Francisco de Coronado and Hernando de Soto, under the flag of Spain. One hundred and forty-one years later, the French explorer Sieur de La Salle traveled most of the length of the Mississippi River and laid claim to the vast Louisiana Territory, comprising all the lands drained by that river and its tributaries. Although La Salle had not actually stepped on Oklahoma soil, this sweeping statement was taken to include that area within the territorial boundaries. Thus Oklahoma was French land until 1763, when the Treaty of Paris transferred to Spain the Lousiana Territory west of the Misssissippi. Napoleon briefly reclaimed the territory in 1800 but was forced to sell the land to the United States three years later to help finance his costly European campaigns.

Although the initial population of Oklahoma was sparse, the early federal government saw this open prairie region as a likely place to which to transfer many Eastern tribes from their homelands, the better to keep them under control. In 1820 the forced march began along what was to become known as the "Trail of Tears." In twenty-two years most members of the "Five Civilized Tribes"—the Cherokee, Choctaw, Creek, Chickasaw, and Seminole Indians—were forced to trek hundreds of miles to the barren new territory. Hundreds died en route. Although the Indians were promised most of the territory except for the Oklahoma Panhandle, the next fifty years saw treaty after treaty ignored or deliberately broken while land was transferred from tribal ownership to individual-Indian ownership. With the aid of these techniques, white settlers were enabled to take over much of the territory. The most dramatic settlement occurred in 1889: Literally overnight the towns of Guthrie and Oklahoma City went from being unpopulated to having more than 10,000 inhabitants. It was at this time that Oklahoma came to be known as the "Sooner State" because it was said that the settlers arrived "sooner" than the land was open.

Once the territory had been widely settled, its inhabitants set out to help the Indian tribes form townships and obtain U.S. citizenship. In this way, the groundwork was laid for the territory to be granted statehood. By the beginning of the twentieth century, petitions had been submitted by representatives of the Five Civilized Tribes, and by white settlers as well, asking for statehood. Their wish was granted by Congress in 1907, and Oklahoma became the forty-sixth state. Today Oklahoma has a thriving diversified economy and is dependent for about half of its income on manufacturing and for the remainder on agriculture, mining, and petroleum and natural-gas production.

Visitors to the state can obtain a variety of helpful materials by writing to the Oklahoma Tourism and Recreation Department, Division of Tourism Promotion, 500 Will Rogers Building, Oklahoma City, OK 73105. It can be reached by telephone at 405-521-2406. Among the pamphlets it offers, we consider three to be of special interest. They are "Oklahoma Museums and Historic Sites," "Oklahoma and the Cowboy," and "Oklahoma and the Indian." The tourism office also publishes calendars of events.

ALINE Of the approximately a million sod houses that once dotted the vast Plains of North America, the *Sod House* constructed by Marshall McCully in 1894 is one of the few still standing. It is on Route 8, 5 miles north of Cleo Springs. McCully came to the area in that year as one of 100,000 homesteaders flooding into the region. His house was constructed of sod harvested with the traditional sod plow from a half-acre plot about a mile away. Using no metal or wood studding, McCully laid up his sod "bricks" into walls about a yard thick. The roof was laid over rafters of split blackjack logs, and the interior was plastered with a local claylike material. Most sod houses were expected to crumble relatively quickly, but the McCully structure survived and has been restored and furnished in a manner in keeping with its original state. Open Tuesday through Friday 9–5, weekends 2–5. Free. 405-463-2441.

ALTUS The *Museum of the Western Prairie*, 1100 North Hightower, a modern adaptation of the pioneer half-dugout, features the history of the people of the prairies from prehistoric times to the present. Collections and special exhibits relating to farm and ranch life include artifacts from the pioneer prairie dwellers of about 1880–1920, as well as the late George Washington Long's Indian photographs. Displays of antique vehicles and an authentic half-dugout home are in outbuildings. Open Tuesday through Friday 9–5, Saturday and Sunday 2–5; closed Monday. Free. 405-482-1044.

ANADARKO The *Anadarko Philomathic Museum*, 311 East Main Street, is in the Rock Island Depot built in 1912. The brick building, with its terrazzo floors and original lighting fixtures that are still in use, has five rooms containing railroad memorabilia, military equipment and uniforms, an American Indian doll collection, paintings, an early physician's office, and a general store. The museum also features a great deal of local history and a large collection of early photographs. Open daily 1–5. Closed Saturday September through May. Free. 405-247-3240.

At *Indian City U.S.A.*, 2½ miles south of Anadarko on Route 8, Indian guides take visitors through several Plains Indian villages with authentic dwellings of the various tribes. In summer there are short demonstrations of Native American dancing, and a village shop offers local arts and crafts. A museum on the grounds displays Indian art and artifacts and features biographical material on famous Native Americans. Village open daily 9–5; in summer, 9–6. Fee charged. 405-247-5661.

The *National Hall of Fame for American Indians,* on Route 62 next to the Southern Plains Indian Museum, is a sculpture garden honoring Indian leaders, including Hiawatha, Sequoyah, Chief Joseph, and many others. The bronze sculptured portraits are displayed in a beautifully landscaped park. Open during daylight hours. Free. The visitors' center offers descriptive literature on the Hall of Fame and Anadarko's other Indian attractions. Open daily 9–5, except Christmas and New Year's. Free. 405-247-5795.

The *Southern Plains Indian Museum and Crafts Center*, on Route 62 just east of town, is devoted to the creative achievements of Native American artists and craftsmen of the Plains, with a permanent exhibit of diverse historical arts of the tribal peoples of western Oklahoma. A special gallery's changing exhibits promote works by contemporary Native American artists and craftsmen. A shop offering authentic Native American products is operated by the Oklahoma Indian Arts and Crafts Cooperative. Open all year 9–5; Sunday 1–5. Closed most major holidays and Mondays, October to June. Free. 405-247-6221.

ARDMORE The *Charles B. Goddard Center for Visual and Performing Arts*, First Avenue and D Street SW, features traveling art exhibits from galleries around the country. Open daily 9:30–4, except Sunday. 405-226-0909.

The *Eliza Cruce Hall Doll Museum* in the public library on Grand at East Northwest displays three hundred dolls from all over the world, including "Court Dolls" belonging to Marie Antoinette. The exhibits also include many miniature tea sets in pewter, gold, glass, brass, ivory, and so on. Open Monday through Thursday 10–8:30. Friday and Saturday 10–4; closed Sunday. 405-233-8290.

The *Tucker Tower Museum*, in Lake Murray State Park, is housed in a stone copy of an old German castle that was built as part of a WPA project in 1933. Today it contains exhibits of minerals, fossils, Indian and Western artifacts, and a large meteorite. Open daily Monday through Saturday 9–7 in summer, 9–5 in winter; Sunday 1–5. Free. 405-223-2109.

BARTLESVILLE The *Frank Phillips Home,* 1107 Cherokee, is an elaborate twenty-six room mansion built in 1909 by the founder of the Phillips Petroleum Company. The handsome house, which has been painstakingly restored, and its grounds are a memorial to one of Oklahoma's most successful pioneers. Open for tours Monday through Friday, 8–5; closed weekends. Free. 918-336-2491.

The *Nellie Johnstone Oil Well* in Johnstone Park on North Johnstone Avenue is a restoration of Oklahoma's first commercial oil well. Open at all times.

The *Phillips Petroleum Company Exhibit Hall*, on the second floor of the Phillips Building at Fifth and Keeler streets, is devoted to the history of petroleum in Oklahoma, in particular to that of Phillips Petroleum. There are exhibits on oil and gas discovery and processing methods, and on the research and products of the petroleum industry. Open Monday through Friday 8–5; closed weekends and holidays. Free. 918-661-6260.

The *Woolaroc Museum* is on the old Frank Phillips Ranch built in 1929 by the founder of Phillips Petroleum Company in the Osage Hill country of northeastern Oklahoma. The ranch is in a 3,500-acre wildlife preserve where deer, elk, longhorn cattle, buffalo, and many other native Plains species roam free. Visitors drive through the refuge to reach the museum, which exhibits art and artifacts of the Southwest Plains tribes, pioneers, and cowboys. It also contains a large collection of Colt-Paterson guns and many works by such well-known painters of the old West as Frederic Remington, C. M. Russell, and Frank Tenney Johnson. The museum's National Y-Indian Guide Center offers Native American craft demonstrations and a multimedia show portraying the culture and talents of the American Indian. Woolaroc Lodge, built in 1927, is furnished with the original old bark-covered furniture, stuffed animal heads, horn collections, and artwork of the period. Open to tours daily 10–4:30. The Woolaroc complex also has nature trails and facilities for the handicapped. Open daily 10–5, April through October; closed Mondays and holidays, November through March. Free. 918-336-6747.

BEAVER The *Beaver City Museum* on East Main Street exhibits artifacts and memorabilia of the pioneers who came through and settled "No Man's Land." There are displays of glasses worn by the pioneers, as well as household dishes and utensils the Bead Room boasts more than five thousand strings of beads. Open Monday through Saturday 11–5, Sunday 2–5. Donation.

BLACKWELL The *Oklahoma Historical Society's Cherokee Outlet Museum* occupies a large room in an old domed building on South Main. It displays artifacts and household effects of the early pioneers of the Cherokee Outlet. Open Monday through Saturday 9:30–5, Memorial Day through Labor Day; 1–5 the rest of the year. Closed in bad weather and on some holidays. Free. 405-363-0209.

BROKEN BOW The *Chief Gardner Mansion and Museum and Cypress Tree* is 6 miles east of the town on Route 70. The home of Jefferson Gardner, principal chief of the Choctaw Indians, was built in the 1880s and displays prehistoric and historic Choctaw artifacts and historical articles from the early settlers of eastern Oklahoma. The nearby cypress tree, the largest in the state, is about two thousand years old. Open in summer Monday through Saturday 8–6, Sunday 1–6; in winter, on weekends only. Fee charged.

The *Forest Heritage and Education Center of the South*, in Beavers Bend State Park, 11 miles northeast of Broken Bow on Route 259, has displays explaining the history of forestry. Open Monday through Friday 8–4:30; Saturday and Sunday 1–4:30. Free.

CACHE *Eagle Park Old West Ghost Town*, at the intersection of Routes 115 and 62, features eighteen buildings from the area's early history in an old-West setting. Open to visitors are the house of the outlaw Frank James; the Frisco Depot; Saddle Mountain Indian Mission; and the "Star House," home of Quanah Parker, a Comanche Indian chief. Ghost town open daily during daylight hours, May through August; in winter, on weekends only. Fees charged. 405-429-3238.

Quanah Parker Center, named in honor of the Comanche chief, is 5 miles northwest of Cache on Route 115 in the Wichita Mountains Wildlife Refuge. It features "please touch" displays of local Indian history, native wildlife, and information on the mountain range and its ecology. Open daily 9:30–6, May through early September; rest of the year, on weekends only. Free. 405-429-3222.

CHEYENNE The *Black Kettle Museum*, at the intersection of routes 283 and 47, recounts the history of the Battle of Washita. The attack by General George Armstrong Custer on the peaceful encampment of Black Kettle's tribe commenced General P. H. Sheridan's winter campaign against the Indian tribes after they had, in a series of conflicts, protested the breaking of treaties by the U.S. Government. Museum exhibits relate to the cavalry, pioneers, and early Indians. Open Monday through Saturday 9–5, and Sunday 1–5; in daylight savings time, to 7. Free. 405-497-3929.

Washita Battlefield, 2 miles west of town on Routes 47 and 47A, is a historic site with a monument and memorial to the slaughter in 1868 of Chief Black Kettle and his tribe by Custer. Open at all times. Free.

CLAREMORE The *J. M. Davis Gun Museum*, 333 North Lynn Riggs, offers visitors a full mile of gun displays. A large portion of the Davis Collection is dedicated to muzzle-loading firearms, and the complete evolution of the firearm is illustrated in a special display of major developments and changes. There are famous makes and models of guns from all over the world, as well as 70 saddles, hundreds of animal horns and trophy heads, musical instruments, 1,200 steins, swords and knives, pins, buttons, World War I posters, and a comprehensive John Rogers statuary collection. Open Monday through Saturday 8:30–5, Sunday and holidays 1–5. 918-341-5707. Free.

The *Will Rogers Memorial* on West Will Rogers Boulevard is dedicated to keeping alive the memory of Oklahoma's beloved son. The memorial contains dioramas of his life with statuary, show bills, posters, and his saddle collection. Visitors can hear Will's recorded voice spinning yarns and cracking jokes. His tomb is also here. The memorial is open, free of charge, daily 8–5. 918-341-0719.

CLINTON The *Western Trails Museum*, at 2229 Gary Turnpike west of Clinton, has exhibits concerning the settlement of the West and Oklahoma's territorial beginnings. Displays feature articles from early frontier life and such machines as an 1892 printing press as well as dentist's instruments including a primitive X-ray machine. Prehistoric Indian artifacts and fossilized mammoth bones are also exhibited. Open Monday through Saturday 9–5, Sunday 1–5; in daylight savings time, to 7. Free. Closed Christmas. 405-323-1020.

COALGATE The *Coal County Miners Museum and Genealogical Library,* at 118 South Broadway, exhibits collections of mining machinery, equipment, and miners' personal items, as well as pictures and records of early mining days around Coalgate. Outstanding are two models—one of a slope mine and the other of a shaft mine—built by Sam Wells, a former state mine inspector. Their details are authentic down to the tiny mules. Open all year, weekdays 10–5, Saturday and Sunday 10–4. Free. 405-927-3346.

COOKSON *Fort Chickamauga*, on Route 82, ½ mile north of Cookson in the heart of Cherokeeland, is the only fully authorized functional and operational U.S. Cavalry Post in the United States. Although an actual military post, it is tourist-oriented. The fort is constructed to resemble forts of the 1860s and 1870s and at present has fifteen buildings that are either reproductions or have been relocated here. Fort Chickamauga plans eventually to have some fifty frontier buildings, most of them log. The costumed women here are related to the garrison troopers or members of the fort's WAC contingent. Visitors should not expect an entertainment production but may view the cavalry training schedule and observe life in the fort as it was one hundred years ago. Sutler's Store is an early version of the post exchange, and visitors may purchase items here. There are also shops and working blacksmiths at the fort, and many of the crafts and items are for sale. Nominal admission charge; service personnel in uniform free. Open daily except Christmas.

DAVIS The *Davis Museum*, 330 East Main Street, is near Turner Falls, Fort Arbuckle, and the Chickasaw National Recreational area. It incorporates the Arbuckle Historical Society and features collections pertaining to the fort, park, Arbuckle Mountains, and Murray County. Some of the homes in Davis are of historical significance to the Chickasaw Nation. Open Monday, Wednesday, and Friday 2–4. Free. 405-369-2323.

DEWEY The *Dewey Hotel*, directly across the street from the Tom Mix Museum in the original Bartles Store, is one of the oldest buildings in Washington County. Built in 1899 by Jacob Bartles, it is a fine example of a Victorian hotel; early oil-developers and the Dewey Round-up Ropers and Riders stayed here. The hotel has been painstakingly restored and furnished with period antiques by its present owners, the Washington County Historical Society. Open Tuesday through Saturday, 10–5, Sunday 1–5, May through September. Donation. 918-333-0073.

The *Tom Mix Museum*, Eighth and Don Tyler, near the Dewey Hotel, features the personal effects and mementos of the cowboy movie star. There are saddles, trophies, clothing, and many Tom Mix pictures and records. Tuesday through Friday 9–5; Saturday and Sunday 1–5. Closed Monday and holidays. Free. 918-534-1555.

EL RENO The *Canadian County Historical Museum,* in Wade and Grand streets, preserves and maintains the county's history in several old buildings. The Rock Island Depot, built in 1906, houses collections of Indian artifacts, items concerning Fort Reno and Darlington history, and a large group of Rock Island memorabilia. There is an early kitchen, and the Popcorn Theater shows silent films and must be booked in advance. Among other restored buildings in the complex is the Possum Hollar School, a one-room schoolhouse erected in 1906; the Red Cross Canteen dated 1917 (the first in the United States), and the Red Barn filled with farming implements used in the area. Buildings open Tuesday and Friday 10–5, Thursday 10–4, and Sunday 1:30–5. Free. 405-262-5121.

ELK CITY The *Old Town Museum,* Route 66 and Pioneer Road, is in a faithful replica of a turn-of-the-century western Oklahoma gingerbread house. Eleven display-rooms include an Indian Room, the Rock Bluff schoolhouse, a pioneer chapel, a room containing Beutler Brothers rodeo memorabilia, several rooms furnished with period antiques, and others offering changing monthly art exhibits. Open Tuesday through Saturday 10–5, Sunday 2–5. Nominal charge to adults and students; children under 12 free. 405-225-2207.

FORT GIBSON *Fort Gibson Stockade*, in a park and near a National Cemetery, is a National Historic Monument operated by the state of Oklahoma. Fort Gibson was established in 1824, after Osage Indians wiped out a party of Arkansas trappers, as the farthest west military outpost. The fort had riverboat service to New Orleans and was often jammed with caravans of settlers headed for Texas: Jefferson Davis, Lieutenant Colonel Robert E. Lee, General Zachary Taylor, Daniel Boone's son Nathaniel, and many other notables served at the fort. The old stockade has been restored, and many of the original buildings still stand. Six rooms are filled with relics and artifacts of the settlers and the fort. In summer, open weekdays 9–7, Sunday 1–7; in winter, to 5. Free. 918-478-2669.

FORT SILL The *U.S. Army Field Artillery and Fort Sill Museum,* on Routes 277, 281, and 62, 4 miles north of Lawton, contains seven exhibit buildings including Geronimo Guardhouse, Old Stone Corral, and the graves of Geronimo and other Indian chiefs. The museum features the history of the old fort and of field artillery from the Revolutionary War to the present. Open daily 9–4:30; except major winter holidays. Free.

FORT SUPPLY The *Fort Supply Museum* in Fort Supply (set up as a supply base for General George Armstrong Custer's Indian campaign) is a one-family museum established in 1973 by Mary DeWeese to house the many historical items she collected over the years. She and her son, Captain Marion Cooper, renovate the articles and maintain the exhibits, which include early machines and vehicles—many used on the old Miller Brothers 101 Ranch—utensils, photos, articles from old stores and farms, and pioneer artifacts. Open Monday through Saturday 9–5, Sunday 1–5, except major winter holidays. Nominal charge; children under 6 free with adult. 405-766-3081.

FREEDOM *Alabaster Caverns State Park* is on Route 50 south of Freedom and the Cimarron River, then 1 mile east on 50A. The Alabaster Cavern, the world's largest gypsum cave, is a wonderland of pink, white, and multicolored alabaster and transparent crystals of selenite. It can be viewed by visitors on the 2,300-foot-long trail through the underground cavern. The trail leads 80 feet down, and guided tours take tourists through the three sections of the huge cave. Near the cavern entrance is a 150-foot-high natural bridge in Cedar Canyon. Tours leave daily each hour 8–5. Fee charged. 405-621-3381.

GOODWELL *No Man's Land Historical Museum* is on the campus of Panhandle State University on Sewell Street. "No Man's Land," as the Oklahoma Panhandle was called, was the strip of land not included in the territories of Colorado, Kansas, or New Mexico. Before becoming part of Oklahoma, "No Man's Land" was claimed by five nations and the Republic of Texas. The No Man's Land Historical Society was organized in 1934 by "old-timers" for the Cimarron counties that made up the territory. Today its museum houses a collection of local historically significant artifacts and a gallery of art that concentrates on Panhandle artists. There are also historical materials of the region, as well as rocks and minerals, the William E. Baker archaeological collection, and Basket Maker Indian artifacts and materials. Open Tuesday through Friday 9–5, Saturday and Sunday 2–5. Free. 405-349-2670.

GORE *Cherokee Courthouse*, 2½ miles southeast of Gore on Route 64, is a restored log cabin and council house containing Indian artifacts. Open Monday through Saturday 9–5, Sunday 1–5; in daylight savings time, to 7. Free.

GROVE *Har-Ber Village*, overlooking the Grand Lake of the Cherokees west of Route 59 3½ miles down Lake Road, reconstructs and re-creates an early frontier town with some eighty-two different buildings. The Har-Ber reconstruction, sponsored by the Jones Truck Lines, offers extensive collections of dishes, furniture, farm machinery and other early Americana housed in such old buildings as a post office, doctor's office, schoolhouse, and several dwellings. Wheelchair facilities are available. Open daily 9–6, May through October. Free. 918-786-2555.

The *Thunderbird Frontier Museum,* on Route 59 on the way to Sailboat Bridge, exhibits Indian artifacts, guns, saddles, spurs, barbed wire, tools, machines, and antique mounted animals. Open daily except Tuesday 10–5, June through August. Fee charged. 918-786-9590.

HEAVENER *Heavener Runestone* is in *Heavener State Park*, about 2 miles east of Heavener. Several steps lead down to the monolithic 12-foot-high stone in the valley. The slab, which bears an inscription of eight runic carvings believed to date from the year 1012, is considered to be graphic proof that Norse explorers were here, in the continent's interior, some 500 years before Columbus. Open daily 8–8 in summer, and 8–6 in winter. Free. 918-653-2241.

The *Peter Conser House,* on County Road 4 miles south of Heavener, was constructed in 1894 by the Choctaw Indian leader famous for his lighthorse troop, a law-enforcement body in Indian Territory. The house, restored and maintained by the Oklahoma Historical Society, is now much as it was in the early 1900s. Open Tuesday through Friday 9–5, Saturday and Sunday 1–5; closed Mondays and holidays. Free.

IDABEL The *Museum of the Red River,* 812 Southeast Lincoln, on the U.S. 70 bypass, is devoted to the American Indian and has interpretative exhibits of North, Central and South American art and artifacts. Archaeological excavation is being done in the Red River area, and material of the prehistoric Caddo who lived in the region is on display. There are also large collections of fine Caddoan pottery and many examples of stone projectile-points, fine beadwork, basketry, and ceramics of the Plains and Southwest. Open all year Tuesday through Saturday 9–5, Sunday 1–5; closed Monday and holidays. Free. 405-286-3616.

The *Magnolia Mansion*, 601 S.E. Adams Street, is a restored 1910 home complete with period furnishings. Privately owned, it is on the National Register of Historic Places. House shown daily by appointment. Nominal charge. 405-286-3200.

KANSAS *Dripping Springs Antique Horse Drawn Vehicle Museum*, Route 33 about 7 miles east of town, is filled with a very large assortment of such horse-drawn items as bobsleds, surreys, wagons, racing sleighs, and buckboards. Fee charged. Open 8–5 daily.

KINGFISHER The *Chisholm Trail Museum*, 605 Zellers Avenue, contains artifacts from the old Chisholm Trail, which crossed the Red River south of present-day Waurika and extended north to the Kansas border. This famous route was roughly parallel to that followed by the Rock Island Railroad line and, later, U.S. 81. Among the museum's holdings are restorations of Kingfisher's first bank buildings, a log cabin, farm machinery, and a one-room schoolhouse. It also exhibits Indian artifacts, pioneer items, and traces the history of the Chisholm Trail. Open Monday through Saturday 9–5, Sunday 1–5; in daylight saving time, to 7. Closed winter holidays. Free. 405-375-5176.

The *Governor A. J. Seay Mansion,* 11th and Overstreet, is the restored home, built in 1892, of Oklahoma's second territorial governor, Abraham Jefferson Seay. Open Monday through Saturday 9–5, Sunday 1–5; in daylight saving time, to 7. Free. 405-357-5176.

LINDSAY The *Murray-Lindsay Mansion,* 2 miles south of town on Route 76, was built in 1879 by Frank Murray, an early rancher-farmer of the Chicasaw Nation. The handsome, three-story residence was once the center of a 20,000-acre ranch in the rich Washita Valley. It is now restored and furnished with period antiques. Open Tuesday through

Friday 9–5, Saturday and Sunday 1–5; closed Monday. Free.

MANGUM The *Old Greer County Museum and Hall of Fame,* at 222 West Jefferson, half a block from Courthouse Square, occupies three floors and the basement of the town's old hospital building. Its collections, concerning Old Greer County history before Oklahoma achieved statehood in 1907, include reconstructions of old building interiors and exhibits of local items and Indian artifacts. In the Hall of Fame, pictures of pioneers who came here before 1907 are carved into pink granite on the east lawn of the museum. On the south side of the building, from a half-dugout furnished and stocked with home-canned fruits and vegetables, meals are served to groups; a working windmill lends atmosphere to the scene. The hospital interior has room after room filled with period furniture and equipment. Open all year Tuesday through Friday, 9–5, Saturday 2–5. Free. 405-782-2851.

MEDFORD The *Grant County Historical Society and Museum,* 124 North Main Street, houses collections and exhibits of local historical interest, including farm machinery and household appliances, maps, pictures, china, furniture, toys, and clothing. One unusual item is a miniature of a watermelon seeder. Open in summer Monday through Friday 1:30–5:30, in winter 2–4. Donation. 405-395-2888.

MUSKOGEE *Antiques, Inc., Horseless Carriages Unlimited*, 2215 West Shawnee, near U.S. 62, features a large collection of antique automobiles and airplanes. The highlight is the Maharajah of Mysore's 1911 Rolls-Royce, one of many pre- and post-war Rollses and Bentleys in the museum, which also exhibits early furniture. Open in summer 10–6, in winter 10–5. Closed major winter holidays. Fee charged.

The *U.S.S. Batfish*, in the War Memorial Park, ¾ mile off the Muskogee Turnpike, Hyde Park exit, is a highly decorated, record-holding World War II submarine. Open to the public for tours offered continuously weekdays 9–5, Saturday 9–6, Sunday noon–6. Closed November through March 12. Fee charged. 918-687-9466.

The *Five Civilized Tribes Museum* in the old Union Agency building on Agency Hill, Honor Heights Drive, preserves the heritage of the Cherokee, Chickasaw, Choctaw, Seminole, and Creek tribes. The Agency was set up in 1875 to consolidate the affairs of the five Indian nations. The museum houses one of the country's largest collections of traditional Indian art. Extensive collections of art and artifacts document the tribes' stories, and there is a tribal photo gallery, reference library, and a trading post where visitors may purchase works by the Five

Oklahoma's widely varied building styles. *Above:* Caddo Indian houses in Norman's Indian City. *Below:* The Myriad Convention Center.

Above left: An okapi at the Oklahoma City Zoo. *Above right:* A certain Rodgers and Hammerstein musical is very popular in Oklahoma. *Below:* The National Cowboy Hall of Fame in Oklahoma City.

Tribes' members. Throughout the year there are several student, competitive, and one-man art shows in which all work and artifacts are by Five Tribes members or descendants. Open Monday through Saturday 10–5, Sunday 1–5. Closed Thanksgiving and Christmas. Fee charged. 918-683-1701.

The *Grant Foreman Home,* 1419 West Okmulgee, a mile east of Route 69, was built by Judge John R. Thomas, Mrs. Carolyn Foreman's father. The Foremans, Grant and Carolyn, two of Oklahoma's outstanding historians, lived and wrote in this home, which remains today much as it was in their lifetimes. The prolific writers produced more than twenty volumes and many articles between them; their subject, the histories of Indians and pioneers of the West. The house today contains the original furnishings and a collection of mementos they gathered from foreign travels. The caretaker began to work for the Foremans in 1916 and continues to care for the flowers and grounds after their deaths. In his eighties, he often shares stories of long ago with interested visitors. Open Tuesday through Friday 9–5, Saturday and Sunday 1–5; closed Monday. Free. 918-682-0133.

NORMAN The *Stovall Museum of Science and History,* on the campus of the University of Oklahoma at 1335 Asp Avenue, has permanent exhibits including paleontology, natural history, and ethnology, with emphasis on materials from Oklahoma and adjacent regions. Among the distinctive items in the collections are the Permian reptiles and amphibians, and Oklahoma archaeological materials, including specimens from Spiro Mounds and Oklahoma Indian materials. A museum shop offers Indian arts and crafts, jewelry, books, and science games. Open Monday through Friday 9–5, weekends and holidays 1–5. Closed Christmas, Easter, and Thanksgiving. Free. 405-325-4711.

OKLAHOMA CITY The *National Softball Hall of Fame and Museum,* 2801 N.E. Fiftieth Street off I-35, houses the national headquarters of the Amateur Softball Association, the sole governing body of amateur softball in the United States. There are exhibits of the history and memorabilia of the game, as well as displays concerning every aspect of the sport including question-and-answer machines, methods of manufacturing softballs and bats, and turn-of-the-century uniforms, gloves, and equipment. Open Monday through Friday 9–5, Saturday and Sunday noon–5, May through September. Nominal charge. 405-424-5266.

The *Oklahoma Heritage Center*, 201 N.W. Fourteenth Street, is in a mansion filled with classical paintings and furniture from Europe and America. The beautifully landscaped gardens contain tributes to many famous Oklahomans in the form of a Hall of Fame. Open Monday through Saturday 9–5, Sunday 1–5. Closed major winter holidays. Fee charged. 405-235-4458.

The *Oklahoma Historical Society Museum*, 2100 North Lincoln Boulevard, displays the history and growth of Oklahoma from prehistoric times to the present through an excellent series of three-dimensional exhibits and authentic artifacts. There are permanent and special showings of art, and many artifacts and history of the Plains Indians and the Five Civilized Tribes. Open Monday through Friday 8 A.M.–9 P.M.; Saturday 8–6; Sunday 1:30–4:30. Closed state holidays. Free.

The *Oklahoma State Capitol Building,* N.E. Twenty-third and Lincoln Boulevard, is one of the very few state capitols without a dome and the only one with a giant oil-well rig in its front yard and working oil wells on its grounds. The building contains murals and other works of art, including some by Indian artist Charles Banks Wilson. The government provides guided tours of the legislative chambers and halls to interested visitors. Open daily 8–5. Free.

The *Oklahoma Museum of Art*, 7316 Nichols Road, in the 1937 Buttram mansion, features a permanent collection of eighteenth- to twentieth-century European and American art as well as some furniture. There are also changing exhibits in all media. Fee charged. 405-840-2759.

The *Oklahoma Center for Science and Arts (Kirkpatrick Center)*, at 2100 Northeast Fifty-second Street, houses Omniplex, the Kirkpatrick Planetarium, and the Aviation and Space Hall of Fame and Museum. The center features exhibits of artwork from around the world including an Oriental and European ivory collection; Japanese woodblock prints; contemporary African arts and crafts; and reproductions of Korean folk paintings. Open Monday through Saturday 10–5, Sunday noon–5; in summer to 6. Closed major winter holidays. Free. 405-424-6005.

The *Aviation and Space Museum* in the Oklahoma Center near the zoo complex features information and memorabilia concerning aviation greats, from the earliest flyers through the space program. Fee charged. 405-424-5564.

The *Omniplex* and the *Kirkpatrick Planetarium* are in the same building of the Oklahoma Center, near Zoo Lake. Omniplex, a science museum, features a wide variety of informative science displays and collections of historic significance. Exhibits include holograms, 3-D moving pictures; Gravitiam 2, a maze of traveling steel balls; a weather station with tornado films and weather displays; models of a nuclear reactor and an Apollo space capsule; and a model railroad. The Kirkpatrick Planetarium has a 40-foot dome that simulates the night sky with special effects and factual sequences for all ages. Shows change monthly. Open all year Monday through Saturday 10–5, Sunday noon to 5, except Christmas and New Year's. Planetarium admission charge. 405-424-5564.

The *National Cowboy Hall of Fame and Western Heritage Center*, 1700 N.E. Sixty-third Street, was established to preserve Western heritage accurately and authentically and to pay tribute to those who have made outstanding contributions to the West. Honorees are inducted into the Hall of Fame of Great Westerners, Hall of Fame of Great Western Performers, and the Rodeo Hall of Fame. Visitors can walk through a life-sized frontier town with an Indian village, a gold mine, a chuckwagon, and a sod house. The museum's lower level is devoted to Western settlement, culture and industry. A major art collection includes works by many well-known Western painters and sculptors. In a botanical garden at the site is the focal point of the Laura Fraser Studio Collection, the famous *End of the Trail*, a 33-foot-high-statue of Buffalo Bill. A museum shop sells art and artifacts of the West. Open daily 8:30–6 Memorial day to Labor Day, 9:30–5:30 the rest of the year, except major winter holidays. Nominal charge; children under 6 free. 405-478-2251.

The *Oklahoma City Zoo*, two blocks from the Fiftieth Street exit off I-35 West, one of the largest in the country, has more than 1,800 specimens of animals representing 600 species. Its special attractions are the Condor Cliffs; Patagonian Panorama, a walk-through exhibit with free-flying birds; the Children's Zoo with petting and "touch and learn" sections; and a large collection of snakes, including an exhibit of Oklahoma reptiles. Because of its excellent reputation among zoos for its breeding program, it supplies many other zoos with hooved animals. There are isolated breeding areas for endangered species, and 400 acres are available for "Africana," the future wild animal park. Open all year. In summer Monday through Friday 9–6, Saturday, Sunday, and holidays 9–7. September to May, weekdays 9–5 and weekends 9–6. Nominal charge; free on holidays September to May. 405-424-3344.

The *Oklahoma Firefighters Museum*, 2716 N.E. Fiftieth Street, in Lincoln Memorial Park near the Oklahoma City Zoo, has an extensive collection of old pumpers and firefighting equipment primarily from Oklahoma and the surrounding regions. The Oklahoma State Firefighter's Association owns and maintains the museum. Open daily 10–5; closed major winter holidays. Fee charged. 405-424-3440.

The *45th Infantry Division Museum*, in the southwest corner of Lincoln Memorial Park near the Oklahoma City Zoo, is in the former division headquarters of the 1934 WPA Armory. Dedicated to the story of Oklahoma's citizen-soldier, it is considered by generals who have visited it to be one of the country's outstanding military museums. The old Lincoln Park Armory has been nominated for inclusion in the National Registry of Historic Places. It houses memorabilia concerning the history of the Oklahoma National Guard; citizen-soldiers from Indian Territory days to the present (1831–1979); items from Hitler's Munich apartment; weapons used by the militia, 1870 to the present; vehicles; and artillery pieces; and much more. An extensive collection of Bill Mauldin's original cartoons from World War II is on display. Open Tuesday through Friday 9–5, Saturday and Sunday 1–5. Open summer holidays; closed winter holidays. Free. 405-424-5313.

The *1889ers Museum at the William Freemont Harn Homestead* is on N.E. Sixteenth and Stiles in the southeast corner of a 10-acre park, the remaining portion of a homestead made in the Oklahoma Land Run of 1889. The farmhouse, in the National Register of Historic Places, is a typical prestatehood home furnished with historic heirlooms by the descendants of the run. It is much as it was ninety years ago, complete with a vegetable cellar and gardens. The barn is an exact replica of the original barn that burned in the 1950s. Volunteers from the 1889ers Society—made up of descendants of pioneers who made the run in eighty-nine—dress in old-fashioned period clothes to guide tours through the home. The Oklahoma State Capitol building stands on homestead land. Museum open Monday through Saturday 10–4, Sunday 1–4. Free. Children must be accompanied by an adult. 405-235-4058.

OKMULGEE The *Creek Council House and Museum*, Town Square, is an American Indian Museum telling the visual story of the Creek Indians, who were uprooted from their homeland in Alabama and Georgia and trekked over the "Trail of Tears" to reestablish a home in the Indian Territory, now part of Oklahoma. The Creek Council chose a new capital called Okmulgee, or Boiling Springs, and built a log council house in 1868. The museum is in the native stone house built ten years later to replace the log structure. Inside are displays of American Indian art, including items from Creek and other cultures. Pottery, baskets, and wearing apparel are exhibited, as are artifacts collected at Eufaula Mound, a prehistoric Caddoan burial mound. Two rooms show local nineteenth-century pioneer life. Open Tuesday through Saturday 9–5, except national legal holidays. Free. 918-756-2324.

OOLOGAH The *Will Rogers Birthplace*, 1 mile north and 2 miles east of Oologah and Route 169 on Route 1, is a tribute to one of Oklahoma's most beloved sons. The old ranch home contains furnishings and memorabilia of the Rogers family. Open, free of charge, daily 9–5 and until 7 during daylight saving time.

PAWHUSKA The *Osage Tribal Museum*, which belongs to the Osage Tribe, is on a reserve that includes the tribal agency and buildings. It features Osage Indian artifacts and art. Open Monday through Friday 8–4:30; closed weekends and holidays. Free.

PAWNEE The *Pawnee Bill Museum and Mansion*, a mile west of town on Route 64, is a tribute to Gordon William Lilly, one of the West's most colorful characters. He was a great friend of the Pawnees, who made him their "white chief," naming him Pawnee Bill. He later traveled with Buffalo Bill's Wild West Show and left to form "Pawnee Bill's Wild West Show," which was famous and successful throughout the United States and Europe. In the winters, Bill lived in a handsome hand-built log home on a 2,000-acre ranch. Guided tours include fourteen rooms filled with his personal effects and mementos from the show and his life, and with the original furniture. The museum has displays of Bill's life; an Old Town and Indian Trading Post, which he built, at the age of seventy, on the ranch grounds, are replicas of those that once dotted the prairie frontier. Museum and ranch open daily 9–7 in daylight saving time, 9–5 the rest of the year. Free. 405-762-2513.

PERRY The *Cherokee Strip Museum* preserves the history of the Cherokee Strip during and after the 1893 land run. The Cherokee Strip Run was the largest of them all, with some 100,000 people out to stake a claim in the last great frontier opened for settlement in this country. Among the museum's exhibits are an 1890s dentist's office, an old-time gambling machine, and artifacts and keepsakes from the pioneers of the run. Important in the collections are the country schoolhouse and a horse-drawn farm-implement exhibit. Open all year Tuesday through Friday 9–5, Saturday and Sunday 1–5. Closed Monday and holidays.

PICHER The *Tongaha Mining Company*, 2 miles south of town on Route 69, is an operating lead-zinc mine, and there are continuous underground tours of its facilities. Open daily 11–5 May through Labor Day. In winter, open on weekends only, 11–5. Nominal charge.

PONCA CITY The *Cultural Center Museum* at 1000 East Grand, consists of five separate museum rooms and the historic home of oilman-philanthropist E. W. Marland, in which they are located. The house, built in 1914, has twenty-two rooms, a free-floating staircase, an indoor pool, and many very "modern" conveniences that were ahead of their time. The Indian Museum features ethnological and archaeological material of Ponca City's five neighboring tribes as well as items from tribes throughout the country. 101 Ranch Room contains memorabilia from the Miller Brothers ranch, which sat on 101,000 acres south of Ponca City in the early 1900s and was best known for its 101 Wild West Show that toured the United States and Europe. Bryant Baker Studio is a re-creation of the New York studio of the artist commissioned by Marland to sculpt the Pioneer Woman statue. (Pioneer Woman, the third largest bronze statue in the world, can be seen on Monument Road, at the corner of Fourteenth Street and Lake Road, just a mile from the Center.) The other museum room is the DAR Memorial Museum. Center open weekdays all year 10–5, Sunday and holidays 1–5. Closed Tuesday and major winter holidays. Free (fee for out-of-town adults being considered). 405-762-6123.

Pioneer Woman Statue and Museum, 701 Monument Road, are tributes to the American pioneer woman. The large bronze statue was donated to the state by the oil man and philanthropist E. W. Marland, who invited competition among the nation's leading sculptors. The winner, Bryant Baker, was selected by public ballot. Marland's estate and the Baker studio are just minutes away. The statue is in a landscaped park with rose gardens and exotic trees. The museum there contains artifacts of the pioneer period of the state. The statue can be seen at any time. The museum is open, free of charge, Monday through Saturday 9–5 and Sunday 1–5—until 7 during daylight saving time. 405-765-6108.

POTEAU The *Kerr Museum*, 6 miles southwest of town, is in the home of the late Senator, Robert Kerr. The museum is devoted to the history of eastern Oklahoma and has displays of geology, Indian and pioneer artifacts, runestones, and local historical items. The backyard of the house offers a fine view of the area. Open daily 1–5. Nominal charge. 918-647-2284.

SAPULPA The *Sapulpa Historical Society Museum*, 100 East Lee, in the old YWCA building that was the hub of early social and business life in Sapulpa, preserves the history of Sapulpa and early Oklahoma with collections dealing with the pioneer settlers, Indian Territory, early railroading, and the oil boom. Open Tuesday through Sunday 1–4; Saturday 9–4. Closed Monday. Free. 918-224-4871 or 0357.

SPIRO *Spiro Mounds State Park,* just east of Route 59 on Route 9 in Spiro, encompasses 138 acres containing nine earthen mounds, remnants of an Indian culture that flourished from 1200 to 1350. An important center for trade, it was also the scene of religious ceremonials. The Spiro Mounds offer visitors an interpretative center designed to foster understanding of the religious, trade, and symbolic significance of the mounds and sites. Grave-goods that have been uncovered are on display in the center. Park open daily in summer 8–8, in winter 8–6. Free. 918-962-2062.

STILLWATER The *Gardiner Art Gallery,* on Knoblock and Morrill avenues at the eastern edge of the Oklahoma State University campus, features monthly changing exhibits of contemporary art in many and various media. Open Monday through Friday 8–5, Sunday 2–5; closed Saturday and holidays. Free. 405-372-6073.

The *National Wrestling Hall of Fame*, 405 West Hall of Fame Avenue at the northeast corner of the Oklahoma State University campus, is owned and operated by the U.S. Wrestling Federation. In the Honors Court, tribute is paid to the nation's finest wrestlers, coaches, and contributors to the sport. The museum displays wrestling memorabilia, trophies, pictures, gear, Olympic uniforms, medals, and sculpture. There is a Wall of Champions and, the feature of the building, a three-quarter-ton green marble statue, *The Wrestlers*. Nominal charge. Open Monday through Friday 9:30–4:30; weekends by request. 405-377-5242.

STILWELL *Golda's Bitting Springs Mill*, 12 miles west of town, south of Route 51, is an 1838 watermill. It is the only one left in the state that is still in operation and its owner lives here. Open daily. Fee charged.

TAHLEQUAH *Tsa-Le-Gi Village and the Cherokee National Museum* are both 2½ miles south of town and 1 mile east off route 82. In the village, an exact replica of a Cherokee Indian settlement of the 1600s, Cherokees live today much as their ancestors did three hundred years ago. They prepare food, weave, make baskets, and participate in games and ceremonies. The Cherokee National Museum is devoted to Cherokee history from its earliest beginnings through the "Trail of Tears" to the present. There is an amphitheater where the "Trail of Tears" drama is performed in summer months. Village open Tuesday through Sunday 10–5, early May through early September. Museum open Monday through Saturday 10–8, Sunday 1–5, mid-June through mid-August. Fee charged. 918-456-6195.

The *Murrell Home*, the 1845 mansion home of George Murrell, was a center of social activity, and young officers stationed nearby were entertained here. Once one of many antebellum homes in the area, it was the only one to survive the Civil War. The state bought it and restored it to its former elegance with many of its original furnishings. On the mansion grounds are nature trails especially designed to suit the elderly and handicapped, and there are two loops with audio recordings and signs along the way. House and grounds open Monday through Saturday 9–5, Sunday 1–5; in daylight saving time to 7. Closed Christmas. Free. 918-456-2751.

TISHOMINGO The *Chickasaw Council House Museum*, next to the Court House in the center of town, displays artifacts of the Chickasaw culture and is the only Chickasaw Indian museum in the United States. The first Chickasaw Council house built in the new territory is preserved and displayed here. When the Chickasaws established their new nation in 1856, they erected the small log house as the seat of the government at Good Springs on the Pennington Creek (present-day Tishomingo). Open Tuesday through Friday 9–5, Saturday and Sunday 2–5. Closed Monday and legal holidays. Free. 405-371-3351.

TULSA The *World Museum and Art Center,* 1400 Skelly Drive, off the Peoria exit on I-44, features more than a dozen galleries with art and artifacts from more than one hundred countries. The large collections include buggies, classical cars, shrunken heads, porcelain and ceramic, music boxes, ivory, and jade. There are wooden, bronze, and marble statuary, and enormous parchment books. Open daily 8–8 in summer, 8–4:30 the rest of the year. Fee charged. 918-743-6231.

The *Philbrook Art Center*, 2727 South Rockford, in an elegant mansion on perfectly landscaped grounds with fountains and ponds, features permanent collections of Italian Renaissance paintings and sculpture, American and European paintings, English and American miniatures, and a great deal of American Indian pottery, baskets, costumes, and artifacts. There are also monthly changing exhibits and an interesting array of art and sculpture from around the world. Open Monday – Saturday 10–5, Sunday 1–5. Fee charged. 918-749-7941.

Discoveryland Outdoor Musical Dramas are held in the summers in *Discoveryland Amphitheatre*, 10 miles west of Tulsa on West Forty-first Street. Two of Oklahoma's musical stories are presented here out of doors in a wooded setting, mid-June through August: Richard Rodgers and Oscar Hammerstein's *Oklahoma!* and Kermit Hunter's *Dust on Her Petticoats*, the story of Oklahoma's first Congresswoman, Alice M. Robertson. *Dust,* covering the late 1800s to 1930s, concerns Robertson's fight for equal rights and her election to Congress. These shows' proceeds go to provide scholarship funds for children through the World Changers International, the sponsoring organization. Barbecue dinners, served from the barn and a chuckwagon, are offered before shows, and the preshow entertainment begins at 8. *Oklahoma!* plays Monday, Wednesday, Friday, and Saturday, and *Dust* plays Tuesday and Thursday. Dinners are served in the picnic grounds 6:30–7:45. At intermission "Oklahoma mud pies," "Buffalo Chip" cookies, and lemonade are sold. After the shows there are house tours of the set where visitors meet the cast. 918-587-4486. Fees charged for all performances on a reservations-only basis.

Gilcrease Institute of American History and Art, 2300 West Newton Street, contains more than 5,000 articles of American artwork and more than 200,000 artifacts pertaining to American culture. Devoted primarily to the art and history of the frontier West, including the pioneer and Native Americans, the Institute claims to have one of the largest collections of Remington, Russell, and Catlin anywhere. Open Monday through Saturday 9–5, Sunday and legal holidays 1–5. Free. 918-581-5311.

Tulsa Zoological Park, in Mohawk Park, a 2800-acre tract of natural woodland—one of the largest city-owned parks in the United States—is easily reached from I-244 by taking Yale or Sheridan avenues north to 5701 East Thirty-sixth Street. It exhibits more than six hundred animals of more than 200 different species. Barless grottoes house bears, lions, and tigers, providing an unobstructed view of the animals in natural surroundings. The new North American Living Museum displays live animals, plants, Indian artifacts, minerals, and a life-size dinosaur model in four regional buildings labeled Arctic, Desert, Eastern Forests, and Southern Lowlands. There are educational presentations in an outdoor amphitheater in warm weather and an animal-contact area in the Children's Zoo. In good weather visitors can see the elephant-training sessions daily at 11 and 3. Park open daily 10 A.M.—dusk, except

Christmas. Nominal charge. Free Mondays and Saturdays 10–noon, except holidays, and for children 6 or under. 918-835-8471.

VINITA The *Eastern Trails Historical Museum*, 215 West Illinois, traces the area's history from its early years as the Cherokee Nation Indian Territory with displays of Cherokee Indian artifacts, old tools, and pioneering equipment. There are exhibits of leather-working tools, printing equipment, early photographs, and memorabilia of Vinita's early times. One section of the museum depicts a country store, a justice-of-the-peace's office, a dentist's office, a drugstore, and early pioneer rooms. Of special interest is the collection of articles once belonging to Vinnie Ream, a famous sculptress for whom Vinita is named. Open Monday through Saturday 1:30–4:30, except major holidays. Free. 918-256-6731.

WATONGA The *T. B. Ferguson Home Museum*, 519 North Weigel, is a fine 1901 Victorian prairie home sitting behind a white picket fence. It was built by Mr. Ferguson, who was appointed Governor of the Oklahoma Territory by President Teddy Roosevelt and served 1901 to 1906, and its furnishings are typical of the period. While staying in the Ferguson home, Edna Ferber began her novel *Cimarron*, basing the book's main character on Mrs. Ferguson's experiences. At the back of the house is Watonga's first city jail, built in 1892, and a log cabin called the "Way" or "Halfway Station," built about 1870 by the U.S. Cavalry. House and back buildings open all year Monday through Saturday 9–5, Sunday 1–5; in daylight saving time, museum open to 7. Free. 405-623-5069.

WAURIKA The *Chisholm Trail Historical Museum*, just east of the intersection of routes 81 and 70, features the story of the development of the Chisholm Trail from 1867 to 1889. Displays of artifacts show the early settlement of the area and include a pioneer room. A slide presentation, *The Chisholm Trail*, is offered. Open all year Tuesday through Friday 9–5, Saturday and Sunday 2–5; closed Monday and major winter holidays. Free. 405-228-2166.

WEWOKA The *Seminole Nation Museum*, 524 South Wewoka, traces the history of the Seminoles from their beginnings in Florida through their removal over the "Trail of Tears" to Wewoka, capital of the Seminole Indian Nation. The museum, in a native sandstone and cedar building constructed in 1937 as a WPA project, presents Seminole history through various displays and dioramas using Seminole art and artifacts and reconstructions. Dioramas include Stick Ball Game, the

Whipping Tree, and a life-size Chickee, a Florida Seminole house. A section of the museum is devoted to the area's pioneer history, from early times through the oil boom of the 1920s. A museum shop features only local craft items. Museum open daily 1–5, except Christmas and January. Free. 405-257-5580.

WOODWARD The *Plains Indians and Pioneer Historical Foundation,* 2009 Williams Avenue, exhibits early pioneer and Indian artifacts from its many collections, as well as several large historical murals, including those by Paul Laune in the rotunda. Diverse displays include a bank from Fargo, Oklahoma; one of the original buildings from old Fort Supply; a room and artifacts from Woodward's "red light" district; broom-makers; balers; and many art exhibits. Open daily except Monday noon–5, Sunday 2–5; closed holidays. Free. 405-256-6136.

YALE The *Jim Thorpe Home*, 706 East Boston, is the restored and furnished home of one of the world's greatest athletes, Jim Thorpe, a Native American who lived here from 1916 to 1923. Open Tuesday through Friday 9–5, Saturday and Sunday 2–5; closed Monday. Free.

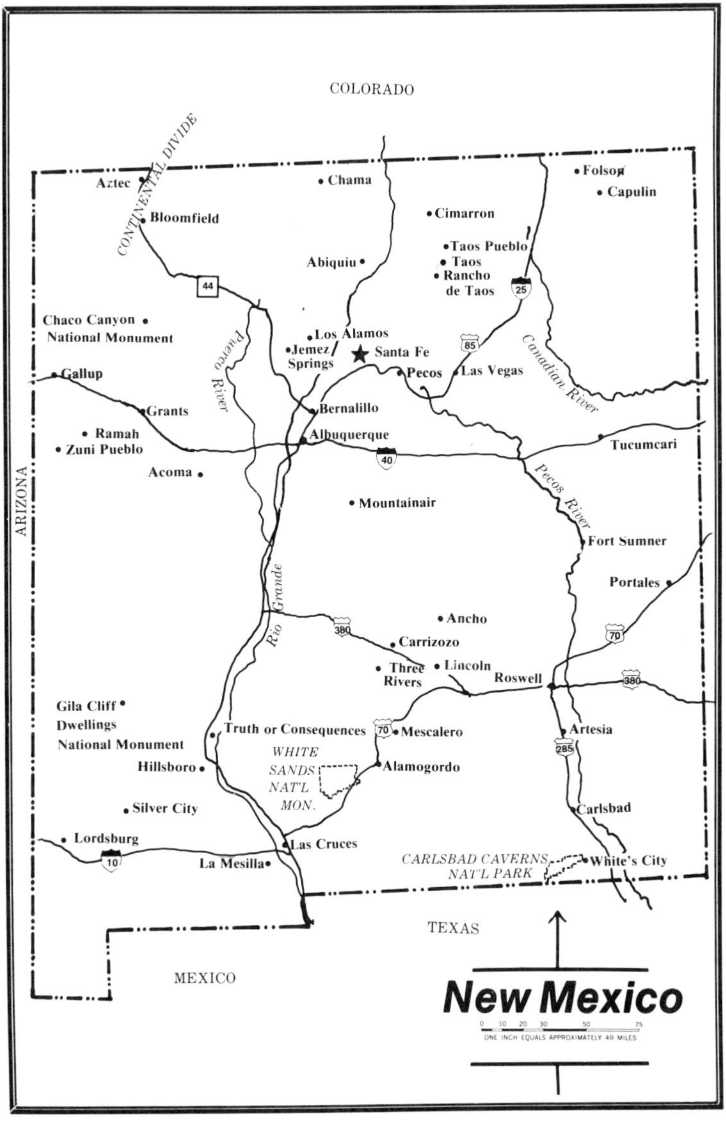

COLORADO
CONTINENTAL DIVIDE
Aztec
Bloomfield
Chama
Cimarron
Folsom
Capulin
Taos Pueblo
Taos
Rancho de Taos
Abiquiu
44
25
Chaco Canyon National Monument
Los Alamos
Jemez Springs
Santa Fe
Pecos
Las Vegas
85
Canadian River
Puerco River
Gallup
Grants
Bernalillo
Ramah
Zuni Pueblo
Albuquerque
40
Tucumcari
Acoma
ARIZONA
Pecos River
Mountainair
Fort Sumner
Portales
Rio Grande
Ancho
380
Carrizozo
70
Three Rivers
Lincoln
Roswell
380
Gila Cliff Dwellings National Monument
Truth or Consequences
70
Mescalero
Artesia
285
WHITE SANDS NAT'L MON.
Alamogordo
Hillsboro
Carlsbad
Silver City
Lordsburg
Las Cruces
10
La Mesilla
CARLSBAD CAVERNS NAT'L PARK
White's City
TEXAS
MEXICO
New Mexico
0 10 20 30 50 75
ONE INCH EQUALS APPROXIMATELY 49 MILES

New Mexico

NEW MEXICO bears evidence of human habitation dating back more than 20,000 years. When white explorers came to the area they were greeted by the Pueblo Indians as well as Navajo, Apache, Ute, and Comanche tribesmen. The explorers came to New Mexico hoping to find the treasure-laden Seven Cities of Cibola. Stories of the cities, never found, were perpetrated by the explorer Cabeza de Vaca, who had been shipwrecked near the Texas coast and had wandered across the southern territories, finally reaching the Pacific Coast. His tales led to dozens of exploratory parties including several to New Mexico. The first formal Spanish colony was settled in 1598 at Pueblo San Juan de los Caballeros. The governing offices were moved to Santa Fe in 1610, making that city the oldest seat of government in the country.

Over the next eighty years there were periodic wars with the Pueblo Indians, and peace in 1692 was followed by a long period of uneventful Spanish rule. Mexico took control of New Mexico following Mexican independence in 1822, but its control ended in 1848, after its defeat in the Mexican War. During the Civil War the region fell initially to the Confederacy but was quickly recaptured by the Union forces in 1862. Kit Carson and others led the effort to restrain the Navajos and Apaches and peace was gradually established. New Mexico attained statehood in 1912.

New Mexico, the Land of Enchantment, is the fifth largest state in the Union but has a population of only slightly more than one million. Tourism is a major source of revenue, and the state offers helpful travel information, including a color brochure "New Mexico," a state road map, the "New Mexico Calendar of Events," and a list of "State Parks and Monuments of New Mexico." Write its Tourist Division, Department of Development, 113 Washington Avenue, Santa Fe, NM 87503. Call toll-free 800-545-9876.

ABIQUIU The *Ghost Ranch Museum*, on Route 84, 14 miles north of Abiquiu, features live southwestern animals and plants, including salamanders, toads, lizards, snakes, and mammals, and also displays a number of predatory and other birds. An entire building in its American Bird Museum section is devoted to early local exploration related to beaver trapping and the importance of the beaver. A quarter-acre Beaver National Forest outlines in miniature the function of a national forest, with half-size models of people, wildlife, livestock, a fire tower, and a mechanized bilingual beaver that tells of conservation in national forests. Ghost Ranch also has outdoor trails and the Echo Amphitheater campground. The area is open 8–4:30 daily in the off-season; closed Sundays January and February. The museum is open daily 8–6 June through September. Donation. 505-685-4312.

ACOMA Acoma, or Sky City, 28 miles east of Grants and 11 miles south of Route 66 (watch for the turnoff marker at the Paraje Trading Post), is probably the oldest continuously occupied city in the United States. The pueblo, inhabited by pre-Columbian Keresan-speaking people, perches dramatically on top of a mesa several hundred feet above the surrounding plain. The first white man to enter the pueblo was Francisco Coronado during his search for the Seven Cities of Gold. Although he and his men had to use toeholds and finger-grips, there is now a roadway to the top (nominal charge). A jeep used in the filming of the movie *Sundown* was the first motor vehicle ever driven to the top of Acoma, where there is a row of dwellings 100 feet long and 40 feet high. Each structure consists of three terraces built in the usual pueblo style. Ladders provide a stairway to the second floor, and narrow steps lead to the top story. The major building at Acoma is the San Esteban Rey Mission. Built in sections beginning in 1629, it is 150 feet long and 40 feet high, and its woodwork is all hand-carved. The adobe used in the construction, the soil for the burial ground, and every piece of wood had to be carried to the top of the mesa on the backs of the Acoma people. Open all year, except for a few religious holidays. Nominal charge. Separate fee for photography.

ALAMOGORDO A good first stop in Alamogordo is the Chamber of Commerce, at 1301 White Sands Boulevard. It offers brochures and assistance in touring the region. 505-437-6120. Next door is the *Tularosa*

Basin Historical Society Museum with displays on the history and cultural heritage of the region. Contact the chamber for its current opening hours.

The *International Space Hall of Fame* is devoted to the recognition of the works of men of all nations who have contributed to the exploration of outer space. More than forty space scientists and explorers from twelve nations have already been inducted into the Hall of Fame. The five-story "golden cube of glass" features exhibits relating to outer space, including permanent displays of moon rocks and satellites, and a simulated ride into outer space and back in the Mercury Module. On the grounds is the "Sonic Wind" sled, which was used to test human endurance up to speeds of 600 mph prior to space travel. Skies permitting, telescope demonstrations are offered for solar and stellar observations. Open daily 8–5, to 6 in summer. Nominal charge. 505-437-5770.

There are many desert regions in the Southwest, but visitors fail to recognize them as such because they do not resemble the topography depicted in countless desert films. This is not the case at *White Sands*, on Route 70-82, 15 miles west of Alamogordo. Here, vast expanses of white gypsum sand dunes stretch as far as the eye can see. The dunes occupy a vast ecological "island" 10 miles wide and 30 miles long, and the monument maintains a 16-mile scenic loop drive designed to acquaint the visitor with the features of the region. Stop for orientation at the visitors center, a fine example of Spanish pueblo-adobe architecture, completed during the Depression with the help of the WPA. With the exception of its modern tar and gravel roof, the center was built using centuries-old construction techniques. Its furniture is also representative of Spanish-Indian design. After visiting the center, proceed along the loop drive and stop at the numbered spots referred to in the guide leaflet about the monument. Visitors' center open daily 8:30–5, except Christmas. Hours extended in warmer months. Nominal charge for entrance to the park. 505-437-1058.

ALBUQUERQUE The *Indian Pueblo Cultural Center*, at 2401 Twelfth Street N.W., between Menaul and I-40, is a modern, horseshoe-shaped building owned by the nineteen pueblos found in the surrounding countryside. The goals of providing cultural and economic benefit to the entire community and bringing the people of the pueblos closer together have resulted in the development of a multipurpose facility. It contains a museum that exhibits details of each of the pueblos represented. Its Arts and Crafts Market is a wholesale and retail outlet for authenticated, hand-crafted Indian objects including jewelry, ceramics, paintings, baskets, beadwork, drums, and other craftwork items. The Living Arts Program presents daily pueblo life through programs of dance, drama, and film as well as guided pueblo tours. A restaurant in the center offers typical pueblo meals. The architecture of the building itself was patterned after the Pueblo Bonito in Chaco Canyon, occupied about 1,200 years ago. Open Monday through Saturday 10–6, Sunday from 12. Open to 7 in summer. Free. 505-843-7270.

The *National Atomic Museum* is on Kirkland Air Force Base, East, south of Central Avenue (Route 66). To reach the base, turn south off Central onto Wyoming. The museum was originally organized to present the history of atomic-weaponry development leading to the production of the "Little Boy" and "Fat Man" atomic bombs against Japan at the end of World War II. Recent nuclear-arms development is also described, and the museum was recently enlarged to include displays on the future of energy, including new uses of coal, nuclear energy, solar energy, and fission and fusion. Open all week 9–5. Free. 505-264-4223.

Jonson Gallery, at the University of New Mexico, exhibits the extensive collection of works in various media by Raymond Jonson, emeritus professor at the university and director of the gallery. There is also a collection of works by contemporary American artists and Jonson students. Open daily 12–6, except Monday. Free.

The *Albuquerque Museum of Art, History and Science* has been in its quarters on Yale Boulevard, S.E. for many years, but starting late June, 1979, it will occupy new quarters in Historic Old Town. The museum displays items relating to the art, history, and science of the Rio Grande Valley. The new 63,000-square-foot building will be the first major cultural institution of its kind to include solar heating as part of the aesthetic design. Open Tuesday through Friday 10–5, weekends 1–5. Closed Monday, Easter, Washington's Birthday, Thanksgiving, and Christmas. Donation. 505-766-7878.

Old Town is the region of Albuquerque where the first settlement occurred. Located one block north of Central Avenue (Route 66), the Old Town Plaza is dominated by San Felipe Church, which has held services continuously since 1706. Art galleries, craft shops, and restaurants surround the gaslit plaza.

The *Telephone Pioneer Museum*, at 201 Third Street, N.W., recounts the history of communications in the southwest from the 1870s to the present. There is a large display of antique telephones and other related material. Open 8–5 Monday through Friday. Free. 505-765-6106.

Sandia Laboratories, a prime contractor to the U.S. Department of Energy, plays a leading role in the development and evaluation of solar-energy systems. Tours of the solar research and development projects include a 17-meter vertical axis wind turbine and a 200-foot "power-tower," the largest in the world. Open Monday through Friday, 8–4:30. Free. 505-264-3268.

ANCHO In the small town of Ancho, 3 miles east of Route 54, north of Carrizozo, is *My House of Old Things*, a museum of antiquities arranged in an eight-room railroad depot dating from 1902. The rooms contain thousands of items, from wrought-iron nails and early kitchen supplies to silver, china, and glassware. There are a number of railroad relics and an operating telegraph key from the days when Ancho was a rail and shipping center for mining and brick and plaster manufacturing. The museum, the lifetime work of its creator, Mrs. Jackie Silvers, is now in the care of her daughter. Open daily May through October 15, 8:30–6. Nominal charge.

ARTESIA The *Artesia Museum and Art Center* exhibits arrowheads, pottery, artifacts, pioneer medical instruments, items from Artesia's oil industry, a mineral collection, an early newspaper press, cooking utensils, and a pictorial history of the town. The art center displays the work of local artists. Open daily 8–5 except Monday. 505-748-2390.

AZTEC The *Aztec Ruins National Monument*, about ¾ mile off U.S. 550 on Ruins Road, is the scene of the ruins of a 500-room Anasazi Indian pueblo. Descendants of the basketmaker Indians who had lived on the site since A.D. 100, the Anasazi ("ancient ones") reached their height in this area between A.D. 1100 and 1300. Then suddenly, and perhaps in response to severe droughts over twenty-five years, the pueblo was abandoned forever (as was the one at Mesa Verde, Colorado). The ruins were first described in detail in the 1870s, and the site was declared a National Monument in 1927, having been donated to the U.S. Government by the American Museum of Natural History. Visitors to the 27-acre site are urged to stop first at the visitors' center, where pottery, baskets, and other items made by the Anasazi are on display. Self-guiding trails lead through the west pueblo, its great kiva (ceremonial rooms), and the Hubbard ruin (a tri-walled structure). Open daily 8–5, longer in summer. Closed Christmas and New Year's. Nominal entrance charge for vehicles. 505-334-6754.

BERNALILLO The region of the *Coronado State Monument* was first visited by the famed Spanish explorer during his search for the Seven Cities of Gold. When he reached the site, the pueblo of Kuaua was the northernmost in a series of Indian villages in the area. When the Spanish returned forty-eight years later, the pueblo had been abandoned. Today, the roofless pueblo ruins, underground ceremonial kivas, and a museum may be visited. The park is open Friday through Tuesday and holidays 9–5. Closed Thanksgiving, Christmas and New Year's. Nominal charge. 505-867-5351.

BLOOMFIELD *Salmon Ruins* is one of the largest of the pre-Columbian "apartment house" dwellings to have been unearthed to date. Built more than eight hundred years ago by Pueblo Indians in the form of a great C extending 500 feet along the back and 200 feet along the arms, the ruins contain more than six hundred rooms. There are a number of underground ceremonial kivas throughout the structure and its courtyard. Visitors should stop first at the San Juan County Archaeological Research Center for information about the site. All artifacts taken from Salmon Ruins will be kept at the center, and many are on display. There is also a gift shop that handles authenticated Navajo rugs and jewelry. Conducted tours of the site originate at the research center, and visitors may watch excavation work in progress during the summer months. Open all year 9–5 daily. 505-632-2013.

CAPULIN *Capulin Mountain National Monument,* entered from Route 325, 3 miles north of Capulin, preserves the cone of an ancient volcano—a harsh reminder of the volcanic activity that was once widespread throughout western North and South America. The mountain's cone rises more than 1,000 feet from its base to an elevation of 8,182 feet. Inactive for about 10,000 years, the mountain consists of loose cinders, ash, and other volcanic debris. From the summit, it is possible to see parts of four states. The visitors' center offers displays explaining the geology of volcanoes and an audiovisual presentation of eruptions by contemporary volcanoes like Capulin Mountain. Open 8–4:30, to 6 in summer. 505-278-2781.

CARLSBAD More than fifty caves are preserved within the boundaries of *Carlsbad Caverns National Park*, reached by a paved road from White's City, 18 miles south of Carlsbad. Carlsbad Caverns are the largest cave system and, indeed, are considered the largest underground attraction in the world. About 250 million years ago, this region was covered by a great sea. The caves formed at the site of a fossil limestone reef at the sea's edge. Later, the reef silted in and was buried, and water seeped through and dissolved the limestone, forming the cave systems. Visitors to the cavern may select two different self-guiding tours. The three-hour tour starts at the natural entrance to the cave, descends 800 feet in an hour and a half of walking, and then continues for another hour and a half, ending at elevators that return all visitors to the surface. Those desiring a shorter trip may take the elevators to the mid-point, join the walk for the second half of the trip, leave by the elevators. Snacks and box lunches are available underground at the halfway point. Because all trips are self-guiding, visitors are welcome to stay as long as they wish belowground until final closing time. A visitors' center on the surface provides material about the caverns and about the area's geology, biology, and human history. Every evening from May through October, countless thousands of bats fly out of the main entrance to seek their meals of insects. Open daily 8–2 (walk-in) or 8–3:30 (elevator entrance) in the winter. Longer hours in other seasons, with summer hours 7–4:30 (walk-in) or 7–6 (elevator entrance). Fee charged for each vehicle entering park grounds. 505-885-8884.

The *Living Desert Zoological and Botanical State Park* was designed to preserve a remnant of the original Chihuahuan desert and present displays of the region's living plants and animals. Included at the park is the entry museum with its mineral and archaeological displays, an aviary, a walk-through Sonoran Desert exhibit, desert botanical gardens, a Nocturnal House with many desert mammals active only in the darker hours, a reptile exhibit, a hoofed-animal exhibit, a display of Mexican wolves, and a propagation house with many desert plants. Open 9–5 daily, 8 A.M. –10 P.M. in summer. Nominal charge. 505-887-5516.

The *Carlsbad Municipal Museum,* at 101 South Halagueno, has exhibits covering asteroid craters, the history of life on earth, the Indians of the Southwest, the conquistadores, local history, and New Mexican artists. The exhibit on the history of asteroid bombardment of the earth is of special interest to those planning to visit the Sierra Madera Asteroid Crater, 160 miles south of Carlsbad on U.S. 385. The crater is the eroded remains of an 8-mile-diameter dish formed about 65 million years ago. Museum open all year Monday through Saturday 1–7:40. Free. 505-885-6676.

Presidents Park within the city limits offers rides on the "Abe Lincoln," an 1880-vintage narrow-gauge steam train that has views of Lake Carlsbad and the municipal golf course. Visitors may walk across the pontoon footbridge and enjoy a cruise down Lake Carlsbad on the "George Washington," a paddlewheel boat powered by an 1858 coal-fired steam engine. Lake Carlsbad offers free swimming, picnicking, and boat-launch sites. Amusement rides are available, including a 1903 carousel.

CARRIZOZO Carrizozo is at the junction of Routes 54 and 380. Both roads pass the *malpais* ("badlands") to the southwest of town, which is one of the youngest and best-preserved lava flows in the country, with miles and miles of thick, writhing lava. The desert around the lava flow is white and gray sands, creating a startling contrast, and its 250 square miles of land had to be bypassed by Indians and pioneers. The *Valley of the Fires State Park* is 3 miles out of town on Route 380 in the lava badlands. The fantastic shapes of the black mass are amazing. Mice living here are black—the only black mice in the world—but the same species living not far away in the White Sands are light gray and white.

CHACO CANYON NATIONAL MONUMENT *Chaco Canyon National Monument* is 60 miles from the nearest town and is reached by Route 57. The 2-mile-wide, 8-mile-long canyon contains the ruins of a prehistoric Indian farming community. Chaco Canyon was a major center of Pueblo Indian culture, and the monument, established to preserve the remains of this 1,300-year-old agricultural society, contains twelve large and more than four hundred smaller ruins. The visitors' center 7 miles beyond the north entrance to the monument has a museum with interpretative exhibits of the canyon and its early inhabitants, as well as information, maps, and tours. Self-guiding trails to the Pueblo Bonito, Chetro Ketl, and the Casa Rinconada complex take about one hour each. Monument always open; visitors' center open 8–5 daily, except Christmas and New Year's. *Pueblo Bonito* is the ruin of the largest house built in America before 1887, housing a thousand people. *Casa Rinconada* is the largest excavated kiva in the state. Free. 505-786-5384.

CHAMA The *Cumbres and Toltec Scenic Railroad* was constructed by the Denver and Rio Grande Railroad in 1880. The 64-mile line climbs the 10,000-foot Cumbres Pass and snakes through Toltec Gorge. The steam-train ride lasts for 6½ hours, and there is a 1½-hour bus ride at one end. The train has a snack bar and restroom facilities in addition to the passenger facilities in converted boxcars. The railroad's operating season is from early June through mid-October. Departures from Chama are at 10 A.M. Saturday and Tuesday and 8 A.M. Sunday and Wednesday.

8 A.M. departures have the bus trip first. Departures also available from Antonito, Colorado. Fee charged for all-day trips. For more information write the train at P.O. Box 789, Chama, NM 87520. 505-756-2151.

CIMARRON The *Old Aztec Mill*, on Route 21, was built by Lucien Maxwell in 1864. Maxwell had the largest land grant ever given by Spain to an individual owner. His three-story stone mill, which ground grain for the local Apaches and Utes, houses items relating to Indian history and the early development of Cimarron. Most of the building is original; the only parts restored are the new roof, the floor, and the stairs. Open daily except Thursdays May 1 to October 1. Nominal charge for persons over 10. 505-376-2516.

The *Philmont Scout Ranch* is 6 miles south of Cimarron on Route 21, in the area of historic Rayado Village, which was a farming village early in the nineteenth century and is listed on the State Historical Register. Lucien Maxwell, owner of the largest land grant ever given to a single person by Spain, built his home here on the Rayado River, and Kit Carson, his friend from their trapping days, joined him for a few years in suppressing the Indian raids. Large barns accommodated freight wagons, and there was a trading post and a small chapel in the village. A number of years ago the Maxwell Ranch was given by Waite Phillips to the Boy Scouts, and it now serves twenty thousand scouts each summer. The *Ernest Thompson Seton Memorial Library and Museum* at the Scout ranch headquarters was built in traditional Pueblo Indian style and houses several thousand drawings and paintings, bird and mammal skins, and hundreds of Indian artifacts including Plains Indian beadwork, Southwestern pottery and basketry, and Navajo weaving and silver. Open daily. Closed weekends September to June. Free. 505-376-2281, ext. 44. The *Kit Carson Museum*, 7 miles farther south on Route 21, has exhibits on the Rayado settlement and the Santa Fe Trail. General exhibits depict the lives of the mountain man, the cowboy, and the Anglo and Mexican settler. A working forge has been restored, and during the summer months curators in historical clothing demonstrate adobe making, muzzle-loading, rifle shooting, and bread baking in Indian ovens called *hornos*. Open daily in summer. Call the above number for current winter schedules and appointments. Free.

FOLSOM The *Folsom Museum,* on Route 325, is primarily a pioneer and historical museum, with exhibits concerning Folsom man, an inhabitant of the region about 8000–9000 B.C. The first evidence of the prehistoric man was the discovery in 1911 of a fossil bison in the area by

George McJunkin, a black cowboy. Fifteen years later his find led archaeologists to the discovery of nineteen projectile points and twenty-three skeletons of the extinct bison. It is certain that the Folsom man hunted these creatures during prehistoric times.

FORT SUMNER In 1854, Major James Carleton first visited a grove of cottonwoods known as the Bosque Rodundo and recommended establishing a military post there. Eight years later his dreams were fulfilled with the construction of *Fort Sumner*, named for Carleton's former commander. The outpost, whose ruins are 2 miles east of the town of Fort Sumner on Route 60, quickly grew to house as many as seven hundred men, and the initial tents and log huts were replaced by adobe structures. A series of catastrophes soon thwarted Carleton's dreams. Timber was scarce, the soil became unproductive, and the Indians who were being trained to farm the local soil became ill from drinking the Pecos River water. In 1868, the garrison was finally abandoned, and the buildings were sold after being stripped of useful wood and allowed slowly to crumble. A major flood in 1941 hastened the destruction of the adobe walls. The ruins were declared a state monument in 1968.

GALLUP The *Gallup Museum of Indian Arts and Crafts,* at 103 West Sixty-sixth Street, contains a major collection of Indian artifacts, especially those of the Zuni, Hopi, and Navajo tribes. Included are pottery, basketry, weaving, jewelry, Kachina dolls, and other handcrafts. Open weekdays 9–12 and 1–5. Summer evening hours weekdays 7–9. Free. 505-863-6849.

GILA CLIFF DWELLINGS NATONAL MONUMENT The *Gila Cliff Dwellings National Monument* 44 miles north of Silver City at the end of Route 15, a steep, winding, two-lane paved road, is in the *Gila National Forest* surrounded by the Gila Wilderness with many well-marked trails. Permits must be obtained to walk or ride horseback in the wilderness or primitive areas of the forest. The monument has well-preserved cliff dwellings in natural cavities on the face of overhanging bluffs, and five caves contain about forty rooms. The dwellings were inhabited for about 150 years from A.D. 1200 to 1350. The Gila Visitors' Center has exhibits and information on the dwellings and forest areas. Permits may be obtained here for wilderness trips. A self-guiding trail leads to the dwellings; it is a steep mile long, and the trip takes about one hour. Monument open 8–6 June to Labor Day, 9–4 the rest of the year. The Gila Visitors' Center open 8–5 daily, except Christmas and New

Year's. Free. 505-534-9344.

GRANTS The *Perpetual Ice Caves* are on the Zuni-Cibola Trail (Route 53) that leads from Grants southwestward to El Morro National Monument and the Zuni Pueblo. The caves, with their display of green ice, were seen in 1540 by the Spanish explorer Francisco Coronado, who was led there by Zuni guides. At the present time, only one of the underground caves is open to the public. Even though surface temperatures often soar above 100°F, the caves remain a cool 30°. Open daily (weather permitting) during daylight hours. Nominal charge. Guided tours, for those wishing to explore the caves in further detail, include several other caves, lava craters, Indian trails, and ruins. Additional charge for tours. 505-783-5194.

HILLSBORO The *Black Range Museum* is in the former Ocean Grove Hotel building, which dates from the rich mining days nearly a century ago. It contains photographs, artifacts, and memorabilia of the area's past, including kitchen tools of an early restaurant operated by Tom Ying, who lived to be 104 years old.

INDIAN RESERVATIONS There are many Indian reservations in New Mexico, and some encourage visitors, at least at their cultural centers where craft and art work are often displayed. Many of the reservations are quite modern in appearance; others, like the Taos Pueblo, have remained virtually unchanged for the last four hundred years. Travelers planning to visit a reservation should remember that the Indian experience with the white man has been almost universally unsatisfactory. Even in recent times the presence of white visitors at Indian ceremonies has been considered intrusive in many cases, and ancient rituals have not been respected. For these reasons, it is wise to inquire in advance if your visit will be welcome. Many reservations are happy to have visitors at most times but not during religious ceremonies. Some reservations charge parking, entrance, or photography fees. The major reservations in the state belong to the Apache, Navajo, and Pueblo tribes, and a few are mentioned in this section of the book. However, the state prints a complete list of reservations, with addresses and telephone numbers, in the "New Mexico Calendar of Events" available at the address shown in the New Mexico introduction.

JEMEZ SPRINGS The *Jemez State Monument*, on Route 4, about 30 miles southwest of Los Alamos, contains the ruins of a large Spanish mission and the mostly unexcavated ruins of the early Giusewa Pueblo. The Mission San Jose de Los Jemez was founded by Father Geronimo

Zarate Salmeron in the winter of 1621. It was rebuilt in 1625 and 1628 and finally abandoned in 1630. The sandstone walls are 6 to 8 feet thick and the church over all is 111 feet long and 33 feet wide. In 1922, a number of murals were discovered that had been done in the al fresco method (painted while the plaster was still wet), a technique rarely used in the Southwestern missons.

LA MESILLA La Mesilla, a quiet, sun-baked adobe village of great charm, was a stopping place for Billy the Kid and the Butterfield stage. Its plaza is surrounded by interesting little shops, historic old buildings, and museums. The town, a State Historic Monument, was a social center for troops from the nearby forts in the 1860s and 1870s, but lawlessness and bloodshed went unchecked. Rustlers and outlaws, even the Democrats and Republicans, fought bloody battles; one such fight left nine politicians dead and many wounded.

The *Gadsden Museum,* on Barker Road, is in a hundred-year-old private home and is owned and operated by the granddaughter and great-granddaughter of Albert J. Fountain, a colorful and prominent early inhabitant of La Mesilla. He was well known as an engineer, architect, lawyer (and defense attorney for Billy the Kid), historian, artist, newspaperman, and New Mexico politician. Fountain disappeared along with his young son in 1896, and the mystery has never been solved. The museum contains family articles and memorabilia, as well as many items of local history. A painting by Fountain portrays the signing of the Gadsden Purchase, which took place in the plaza here in 1854. Open daily 9–11 and 1–5, except New Year's. Nominal charge. 505-526-6293.

LAS CRUCES *Fort Selden* was established in April, 1865, on the banks of the Rio Grande. With the exception of the administration building, it consisted of one-story adobe buildings with cottonwood roof beams covered with peeled willows and dirt. The post was in operation until 1891, when it was closed permanently. The coming of the railroad brought about the demise of many of the expensive and inefficient smaller forts, because a single central fort could now deploy troops over a wider area more rapidly. The ruins of the fort have been declared a State Historic Monument, and an interpretative trail leads through the crumbling barracks and other buildings.

LAS VEGAS The *Rough Rider and City Museum*, at 727 Grand Avenue, was created by the Historical Society of Las Vegas using memorabilia of the Spanish American War. (Many local men rode with Teddy Roosevelt.) Since its formation, the museum has grown to display

Above: White Sands National Monument near Alamogordo deserves its name.
Below: Albuquerque.

Right: Chaco Canyon National Monument. *Below:* El Morro National Monument in Ramah.

Above: Remains of a seventeenth-century Indian village at Gran Quivira National Monument in Mountainair. *Below:* Students touring the Los Alamos Scientific Laboratory.

Above: An exhibit at the Silver City Museum. *Below:* An inviting plaza in Santa Fe.

items dealing with local heritage and frontier life. Exhibits depict life from the Indian period (10,000 years ago to the present) through the Spanish rule, the transition to Mexican jurisdiction, and the establishment of the U.S. Government. Open 9–12 and 1–4, Monday through Saturday. Donation. 505-454-1401.

Fort Union National Monument, 8 miles west of I-25 on Route 477, is the site of three historic forts, with ruins of the third, which was built in 1869. The final fort, constructed of adobe, was divided into two sections, the Post of Fort Union and the Fort Union Depot, and these buildings served as the major quartermaster for all of the Southwest, receiving supplies from the East and dispersing them throughout the region. Visitors may explore the fort at leisure—there is no fixed route. Maps of the ruins are available at the visitors' center, and several audio-visual stations provide additional interpretation. In the summer, tours are given by rangers. Open daily during daylight hours, except Christmas and New Year's. 505-783-5132.

LINCOLN The *Lincoln County Heritage Trust* is a complex of sixteen sites built from about 1850 to 1900. Billy the Kid gained fame here. There are many shops, a church, and houses, all outfitted with appropriate period furnishings and equipment. The courthouse was in operation until 1913 and is a favorite museum now. In addition to the historic clothing, furnishings, tools, and utensils of the period, there are Indian artifacts from early pueblo sites and basketry and beadwork of the Mescalero Apaches. The *Courthouse Museum* is open daily except Thanksgiving and Christmas, and the *Torreon and Wortley Hotels* are open all year. The rest of the museums are open May through September, 9–4:30 off season and 9–5 in summer. Nominal charge. 505-653-4025.

Every year the people of Lincoln and environs present a play, *The Last Escape of Billy the Kid*, held the first full weekend in August. The first show is Friday at 8 P.M. Saturday morning there is a Pony Express race from White Oaks to Lincoln. An old fiddler's contest is held at 3 P.M. and the second show is at 8 on Saturday. Sunday features a parade to the pageant grounds at 1:30, and a matinee is performed at 3:30.

LORDSBURG The ghost town of *Shakespeare,* now a working ranch, is 2½ miles south of Lordsburg. They used to call Shakespeare the town "too mean to die," but die it did in the 1930s after a colorful life and a population of about three thousand during the peak silver-mining days in the 1870s. Today, visitors can see the Stratford Hotel and its adjacent adobe corral, the old mail station, the Grant House stage station and saloon, and the building that housed the general merchandise store, post office, telegraph office, and arsenal, as well as the foundations of many other buildings.

LOS ALAMOS The *Bradbury Science Museum* was designed to portray the history and research efforts of the Los Alamos Scientific Laboratory. About half the research effort is directed toward developing nuclear weapons, and many original weapons developed for use during World War II are on display. Other research includes solar, geothermal, and fusion energy; health and environmental research; computer applications; nuclear waste disposal; isotope generation; and the treatment of cancer by radiation techniques. Guided tours are available. Once a month, public tours are given of the laboratory's half-mile-long atom smasher, the solar-home research area, and the geothermal energy site on the edge of a nearby volcanic crater. Open all year except legal holidays: Monday through Friday 5–5, Saturday 9–5, Sunday 1–5. Free. 505-667-4444.

Bandelier National Monument, on Route 4, which goes west off U.S. 285 at Pojoaque, south of Los Alamos, is in the Upper Rio Grande Valley in north-central New Mexico. Most of the 32,000-acre monument is a rugged, scenic wilderness area. The monument was established in 1916 to preserve the area's many prehistoric Pueblo Indian ruins. More than four hundred identified ruins are accessible, but only on foot. A self-guiding trail leads from the visitors' center in the Frijoles Canyon through the main group of ruins that date from the fifteenth century. The center's museum contains exhibits relating to the life of the prehistoric and present-day Pueblo Indians, and there is a ten-minute orientation program. In summer the many interpretative activities include nightly lectures at the campground and daily ranger walks, which are excellent. A curio shop, snack bar and campground are open only in summer. Center open daily all year, except Christmas, 8–5 (in summer to 6). Nominal parking charge. 505-672-3861.

The *Los Alamos Historical Museum*, at 1921 Juniper Street, is in the oldest building in the town, which was built in 1922 as a guest house for the Los Alamos Ranch School and is made of logs and native stone. In 1943, the Manhattan Project for development of the atom bomb bought out the Ranch School for "undisclosed secret war-time purposes," and several physicists were housed there. The local historical society organized in 1968 has created a museum in the building that exhibits artifacts from early Indian dwellers, the homesteaders of the 1850s, the

Ranch School period, and the secret war-years, and that contains archives and a library, as well as a small fine arts center. Exhibits open Monday through Friday 10–4, Saturday 9–5. Free. 505-662-6272.

MESCALERO The town of Mescalero is in the heart of the Mescalero Apache Indian Reservation. The *Apache Cultural Center,* on Route 70, is open to the public daily. 505-671-4494.

MOUNTAINAIR Atop the Chupadera Mesa lies *Gran Quivira National Monument*, preserving the crumbling ruins of two early Spanish churches and a number of Indian pueblos, most of which remain unexcavated. The first of the churches, San Isidro, was built *ca.* 1626 to serve the one pueblo that remains uncovered. Excavations around and under the exposed pueblo indicate that this village was occupied from about A.D. 800 until the time of Spanish colonization. Visitors to Gran Quivira may walk among the remains of the church walls, the pueblo and its below-ground ceremonial kivas, and the ruins of the outbuildings that supported the church. A visitors' center at the entrance provides orientation to the ruins. Monument open daily 8–5, except Christmas. Free. 505-847-2770.

La Purisima Concepcion de Cuarac was the mission church for the Quarai Pueblo, 8 miles north of Mountainair on Route 14. The mission was started in 1620, and a second church was erected a few years later. The mission and pueblo were thought to be part of a plan to concentrate the Pueblo Indians into fewer settlements so that they could be governed more readily. Like many mission settlements in New Mexico, this one was the scene of continual conflict between the colonial government and church officials. Almost always the Pueblo Indians were the losers in the conflicts and were often reduced to a servile relationship to the priests. Quarai was the seat of the Inquisition in the mid-seventeenth century, and here people were charged with witchcraft and blasphemy and were excommunicated in large numbers. A series of catastrophic Apache raids against the settlement were followed in the early 1670s by pestilence and famine, and the mission and pueblo were finally abandoned in 1675. Quarai was declared a State Historic Monument in 1935, after excavations and stabilization of the church to prevent further deterioration. In 1970, a visitors' center and museum was constructed that portrays life at the pueblo and mission. An interpretative trail explains the historic features of the site. Open daily 9–4:30, except Tuesday and Wednesday. Closed all state holidays.

The Pueblo of Abo, now preserved in the *Abo State Monument*, 10 miles west of Mountainair on Route 60, was occupied for at least four hundred years before the first Spanish exploration. The pueblo's wealth was based on its proximity to the nearby salt beds, and it was on the principal trade route from the Rio Grande to the salt country. The *Mission San Gregorio de Abo*, established in 1620, was one of the most sophisticated in the area; and a report in 1641 stated that it had both an organ and a choir for a congregation of almost sixteen hundred. The church was reported to have been sacked by the Apaches in 1672, and it was completely abandoned by 1680. The site became a state monument in 1938, and much of the excavation of the church, convento, and parts of the pueblo were undertaken as a WPA project. The church and convento have been fenced to protect visitors from the dangerous, unstable high sandstone walls.

PECOS Indians lived in the Pecos region as early as A.D. 1100, but lived in multistoried pueblos only after about 1450. When Francisco Coronado was exploring the region searching for the Seven Cities of Gold, his scouts encountered the pueblo of Cicuye, now known as Pecos Pueblo. A later exploration in 1590 by Castano de Sosa found pueblos "of four and five stories [the Indians] go up little ladders that can be pulled up by hand through the hatchways.... from top to bottom, each house has 15 or 16 rooms. The rooms are worthy of note, being well whitewashed." Soon thereafter, a "splendid temple of distinguished workmanship and beauty" was erected. This, however, was destroyed in the Pueblo rebellion of 1680 and was replaced by a second church, whose ruins are visible at the *Pecos National Monument*, easily reached from either the Rowe or the Glorieta Interchange on I-25, between Las Vegas, New Mexico, and Santa Fe. Also available for exploration by visitors are the ruins of both the North Pueblo (visible only as mounds) and the more recent South Pueblo, constructed by Christian Indians who wished to be closer to mission church. Open daily 8–4:30 (to 7 in summer), except Christmas. Free. 505-757-6414.

PORTALES A complex of museums on and off the campus of Eastern New Mexico University includes the *Miles Museum* and the *General Anthropology Museum*, which feature exhibits related to the Southwest and northern Mexico. The *Roosevelt County Museum*, the home of the Roosevelt County Historical Society, has collections from the 1890s to the present that include printing and publishing and antique office equipment, as well as exhibits of barbed wire, medical and dental equipment, and Indian and pioneer related artifacts. Museums open daily. Free. Seven miles off campus on Route 70 is the *Blackwater Draw Museum* dedicated to the Paleo-Indian, the first people to discover and inhabit the New World. The date of their arrival is unclear but was more than twelve thousand years ago. The museum is in Blackwater Draw, the site of the earliest research on the Paleo-Indian. Open Sunday through Friday 1–4, Donation. 505-562-2592.

RAMAH El Morro National Monument is the site of Inscription Rock, the collected graffiti of three centuries of exploration by the white man. El Morro, "the headland" in Spanish, was probably first visited by Coronado in 1540, but it has been well known for centuries to Indians, who came here to drink water trapped in a natural reservoir holding about 200,000 gallons. As Spanish and American explorers passed the rock during the next three hundred years, about two thousand names were inscribed in the soft sandstone. The first was that of Don Juan de Onate, in April, 1605. There is a trail leading to the top of El Morro as well as literature pointing out the most important inscriptions. At the top are ruins of Indian pueblos that were abandoned long before the first Spaniards entered the region and that remain largely unexcavated. Open daily 8–5, in summer to 8. Closed Christmas. Nominal charge per carload to enter the monument, another charge to walk the trails. 505-783-5132.

RANCHOS DE TAOS *St. Francis of Assisi Church*, in Ranchos de Taos, was built in 1710 by the Franciscans and is the home of the *Mystery Painting*, a picture done by Henri Ault in 1896 that changes in total darkness. The picture's background becomes luminous, outlining the figure of Christ while a shadow of the cross appears over his left shoulder—but the cross was not painted in the picture. The church also exhibits numerous sixteenth-century items. Open June to September daily 9–6; nightly tours at 9 include a showing of the picture. Open September through May daily 10–4, nightly tours Saturday at 9. Free. 505-758-2754.

ROSWELL In the *Roswell Museum and Art Center,* at 100 West Eleventh, a museum of science displaying artifacts of southwestern Indian culture, the Goddard rocket collection, and a small planetarium combine with a museum of art. The focus is on twentieth-century American paintings and sculpture, especially Roswell's artist Peter Hurd, but there are examples of works from other regions as well. Open Monday through Saturday 9–5, Sunday 1–5. Closed Christmas and New Year's. Free. 505-622-4700.

SANTA FE Founded in 1610, Santa Fe has been the capital city under the flags of Spain, Mexico, the Confederacy, and the United States. It is situated in the foothills of the beautiful Sangre de Cristo Mountains, whose peaks rise to more than 13,000 feet. The design of the *Capitol*, one of the newest in the country, was inspired by Indian kivas, the circular underground ceremonial chambers. The Capitol, three blocks south of the Plaza on the Santa Fe Trail, is open to the public for guided tours and historic and cultural displays.

The *Plaza*, at the end of the famous Santa Fe Trail from Missouri, has been the setting for many major historic events. Today, Pueblo Indians sell pottery, jewelry, and other wares in the shadow of the Palace of Governors.

St. Francis Cathedral, one block east of the southeast corner of the Plaza, is a French Romanesque church begun in 1869. Its north chapel contains the oldest representation of the Madonna in the United States, the beloved image of *La Conquistadora* brought by Spanish explorers.

San Miguel Mission, 401 Old Santa Fe Trail, one block from the Plaza, is the oldest church still in use in the United States, dating from 1610. The remains of the early church are sealed beneath the floors of the mission, which contains many religious artifacts of the 1700s, including an early reredos and oil paintings and religious paintings on deer and buffalo hides (*c.* 1630). The Christian Brothers welcome visitors and conduct short tours daily 9–11:30 and 1–5. Free. Next door to the mission at 215 East De Vargas Street, is the *Oldest House* in the United States, the last remnant of the Pueblo of Analco, built around A.D. 1200. The lower walls remain from that time; the ceilings and lower rooms are contemporary with the adjoining 1610 mission. The ancient dwelling now houses a shop, the Atkinson's Trading Company.

The *Museum of New Mexico*, an agency of the state government, administers several state monuments and the Museum of Fine Arts, the Palace of the Governors, and the Museum of International Folk Art. The *Palace of the Governors* was built in 1610, when New Mexico was part of the Spanish empire, and is the oldest public building still in use in this country and its only surviving example of Spanish *casas reales*. Situated in the historic Plaza, it serves as the exhibit building for the state's history division, which was designed to further understanding of New Mexico and the Southwest and has collections of southwestern anthropology, ethnology, and archaeology. The *Museum of Fine Arts,* at the corner of Palace and Lincoln avenues, site of the old army barracks at Fort Marcy, houses almost four thousand works of art, much of the collection emphasizing regional and New Mexico tastes and a large portion of it representing works by Southwestern Indians. The museum building is a reproduction of the historic mission church at Acoma Pueblo. The *Museum of International Folk Art*, on gently rolling land 2 miles south of the Plaza on Camino Lejo, contains enormous collections of folk art objects from around the world. The museum and portions of the collection were gifts from Florence Dibell Bartlett, and recently the museum acquired the Girard Foundation Collection, the largest known private collection of folk art objects in the world. There are changing exhibits throughout the year and excellent lectures and workshops. All above-mentioned museums open daily 9–4:45; closed Monday in the off season. Free. 505-827-2454.

The *Laboratory of Anthropology*, opposite the Museum of International Folk Art, is dedicated to preserving cultural resources—objects, records, and sites—of prehistoric and contemporary people in New Mexico and the Southwest and began as a private research center, funded by John D. Rockefeller. In addition to the acquisition, preservation, and documentation of anthropological collections throughout the state, the lab prepares exhibits interpreting the diverse prehistoric and historic Indian cultures of New Mexico.

The *Christo Rey Church*, on *Canyon Road*, was built in 1939 to commemorate the four-hundredth anniversary of Coronado's conquest. It contains a beautiful reredos, considered to be one of the finest in this country and carved from native stone in 1760 by artisans from Mexico. In the military chapel in Santa Fe in the 1700s, it was moved here after the site was abandoned. The reredos measures 18 by 32 feet and weighs 450,000 pounds. The church is the largest adobe structure in the country, with walls up to 7 feet thick. Canyon Road is an old thoroughfare where artists live and work today and where there is a colorful array of art galleries, studios, and craft shops. *La Fonda Hotel,* at 100 East San Francisco Street on the Plaza, is a reconstructed early adobe hotel still in operation today; it was once the meeting place of many frontier pioneers and was known as "The Inn at the End of the Trail." The *Santa Fe Chamber of Commerce* has offices here and furnishes visitors with excellent maps and tour guides of the area.

Loretto Chapel, on the Old Santa Fe Trail just a block from La Fonda Hotel and the Plaza, is a gothic chapel constructed in 1873–78. It contains the famous *Miracle Staircase* built by an unknown carpenter who arrived on a donkey and erected elegantly beautiful stairs where others had said it was impossible. Built with wooden pegs and no nails, the staircase is circular and has thirty-three steps and two complete 360° turns with no visible means of support. Open daily 9–6 in summer, 9–4 the rest of the year. Very nominal charge; children under 12 free.

Old Cienega Village Museum, El Rancho de las Golondrinas is a living museum of Spanish colonial village culture and history. On Route 2, El Rancho de las Golondrinas (the Ranch of the Sparrows), a historic stopping place on El Camino Real (the King's Highway of the Spanish Empire in America) that led from Old Santa Fe to Mexico City, is one of the most historic ranches in the Southwest. Spread over some 350 rural acres are reconstructed compounds or assemblages of authentic northern New Mexican architecture, agricultural areas, religious edifices, and such commercial enterprises as a village store, blacksmith shop, wheelwright shop, and four of the earliest gristmills in the territory. These complexes date from 1650 to the late 1800s. Most of the rooms and areas are accurately furnished or equipped with original artifacts, many obtained from descendants of the original Hispanic families who pioneered in this area. Because the museum has a very small staff and is a "living and working museum" with farming work, they cannot accommodate drop-ins. Visitors must call or write for an appointment at least three weeks in advance, but all areas are open during open house and festivals. The season is April through October, with tours daily on weekdays. Open to the public the first Sunday of April through September 1–4. Festivals are in early May and late September, with costumed demonstrators in all areas and music, dancing, plays, and food authentic to the period. Fee charged. 505-471-2261.

The *Wheelwright Museum of the American Indian*, 704 Camino Lejo, was chartered in 1937 by Mary Cabot Wheelwright as the Navajo Museum of Ceremonial Art and contains the ceremonial objects left by a Navajo medicine man, Hosteen Klah, including his sand-painting tapestries. In addition to protecting the ceremonial heritage of the Navajo people, the museum focuses on exhibitions honoring contemporary Indian artists. Open Tuesday through Saturday 10–5, Sunday noon–5. Donation. 505-982-4636.

The *Institute of American Indian Arts Museum*, on Cerrillos Road, is a junior college museum housing a large collection of Native American arts and crafts. It is a showplace for work produced by the college students and a national repository of Indian work from Native American groups from Alaska, Maine, Florida, and California. Annual powwows are held the second weekends of May and September at the museum. Open daily in summer 9–5; open in winter Monday through Friday, 9–5. Free.

SILVER CITY Silver City, south of the vast Gila National Forest at the junction of Routes 180, 90, and 15, was first an Apache campsite and later a booming gold, silver, and zinc mining town. The *Silver City Museum* features collections of frontier Victoriana, many articles from an early-twentieth-century mining town, antique vehicles, and Southwest Indian artifacts. There are extensive holdings of historic photos and documents including the John Harlan Collection of eight hundred area photographs. The museum, in the historic H.B. Ailman House (1881), which is on the National Register of Historic Places, has changing exhibits on such diverse subjects as Nigerian craft articles, historic sheet music, and an extensive underwear collection from 1870 to 1920. Open Tues. to Fri. 9–4:30, Sat. 10–1, Sun. 1–4. Free. 505-538-5921.

The *Western New Mexico University Museum*, in Fleming Hall on the central campus of the university, preserves and interprets the history of the diverse cultures represented in the student body and the southwestern New Mexico region. There is a fine collection of Mimbres pottery, a valuable group of American Indian ware, and other exhibits deal with Hispanic history, early stores and offices, mining, as well as a giant model-railroad layout. The museum sells publications dealing with the history of local ancient Indian cultures. Open 8:30–5 weekdays, 1–5 Sunday. Closed Saturday and holidays. Free. 505-538-6386.

TAOS The *Kit Carson Home and Museum*, on East Kit Carson Road on Route 64, is the restored and furnished home of the famed frontier scout, who is buried in the nearby *Kit Carson Memorial State Park*. The house and museum contain mementoes of this early settler, fur and trapping articles, relics from Spanish colonial times, and Indian artifacts. The house was built in 1825 for fur trappers, Kit Carson among them. He later bought the house and lived here with his wife until their deaths in 1868. Open 7:30–7:30 June through September; 8–6 in spring and fall; 8–5 the rest of the year. Closed major winter holidays. Nominal charge; children under 6 free.

The *Stable Gallery* of the *Taos Art Association* is on North Pueblo Road and exhibits the work of nationally prominent Taos resident artists. Throughout the year, numerous one-person shows and special exhibitions are presented. The different galleries of the Stable are all situated in the heart of Taos in the historic *Manby House*, one of the grand estates dating from the turn of the century. The Stable Gallery, the largest and oldest in Taos, has eight exhibition galleries and an outdoor sculpture garden. Open daily 10–5. Free. 505-758-2036.

The *Millicent A. Rogers Memorial Museum,* on Route 3, about 4 miles north of Taos, was established as a living memorial to Ms. Rogers. Its primary aim is to acquire, exhibit, restore, and preserve American Indian and Spanish colonial art, with exhibitions and collections housed in a pueblo-style building surrounded by lovely gardens and patios. Open 9–5 daily May through October, 10–4 the rest of the year. Nominal charge. 505-758-2462.

The *Governor Bent Museum*, a block north of the plaza on Bent Street, is in the Bent House, home of Charles Bent, New Mexico's first territorial governor in 1846. The next year, during an uprising over American rule, Bent was killed in the home, and his family dug through the adobe wall in an attempt to escape. The house, a historical landmark, contains items of the Bent family, Indian artifacts, old Americana, and a gallery of western art featuring old Taos artwork as well as contemporary artists' work. The place where the family dug and the tools they used to dig with are still in evidence. Open 9–5 daily April through November, 10–4 December through March. Nominal charge. 505-758-3096.

TAOS PUEBLO The *Taos Pueblo* contains four- and five-story dwellings that look much as they did when they were first visited by the Spanish in the early seventeenth century. The pueblo permits visitors, who are charged fees for parking and photography. Like all the pueblos of the Southwest, Taos is a village that has survived in its current form because it has not embraced contemporary white culture. A visitor should not expect to feel welcome but is free to inspect a culture relatively free from the intrusions of the twentieth century. Write the pueblo at Box 1846, Taos Pueblo, NM 87571. 505-758-4146.

THREE RIVERS The *Three Rivers Petroglyph Site*, at the end of a 5-mile gravel road east of U.S. 54 in Three Rivers, contains about five hundred carvings made between A.D. 900 and 1300 by the Jornada branch of the Mogollon Indian culture. The designs are similar to the Mimbres style found throughout southwestern New Mexico. The tribespeople lived in houses made of mud and tree limbs; some rooms were made by digging into the surrounding earth. One multiroom dwelling and a single-room house have been partially reconstructed at the site as close to their original locations as possible. Free.

TRUTH OR CONSEQUENCES The town was formerly called Hot Springs but changed its name officially in 1950, thanks to the interest in it by television game host Ralph Edwards. The *Geronimo Springs Museum*, at 325 Main Street, includes the Ralph Edwards Wing and houses Indian artifacts, military items, rocks and minerals of the region, pioneer articles, and art work that includes contemporary murals and sculpture depicting Geronimo, Pancho Villa, Juan de Onate, and others. The Ralph Edwards Fiesta is held the first weekend in May each year. Open daily 9–5, except Sunday. Closed Christmas and Thanksgiving. Nominal charge. 505-894-6600.

TUCUMCARI The *Tucumcari Historical Museum*, at 416 South Adams Street, includes artifacts from Indian cultures extending back twelve thousand years, an early Sheriff's office, an authentic western school room, an early western hospital, a 1900 windmill, and gems and minerals. 505-461-3451, ext. 48.

WHITE'S CITY The *Million Dollar Museum* in White's City, on Route 62–180, southwest of Carlsbad, has eleven rooms of displays representing more than fifty different collections. Included are dolls and doll houses, a six-thousand-year-old mummified Indian, the Whittling Cowboys ranch, guns, chinaware, old vehicles, music boxes, and many more items from the old West.

ZUNI PUEBLO The *Zuni Pueblo*, said to be the largest inhabited pueblo in the United States, was built on the ruins of the ancient site of Halone, one of the fabled "Seven Golden Cities of Cibola" that lured Francisco Coronado into exploring most of the southwest before he discovered there were no secret storehouses of wealth in the Indian nation. Halone was destroyed during Apache and Navajo uprisings in the fifteenth and sixteenth centuries. The Zunis fled Halone but returned later to build the present pueblo. The new village was built around the Spanish mission of Our Lady of Guadalupe, which was destroyed by Apaches then rebuilt and then destroyed during the Pueblo rebellion against the Spanish in 1680. The mission was rebuilt for a third time, only to be destroyed again in 1849. It was restored in 1968. The Zuni pueblo consists of individual dwellings made of adobe and native stone. About six thousand persons live here, farming and producing outstanding Zuni silver, turquoise, shell, and coral handcrafted jewelry. Visitors may enter the pueblo; a fee is charged for each person photographed. Camping is available for a fee. Write the pueblo at Box 339. Zuni, NM 87327. 505-782-4481.

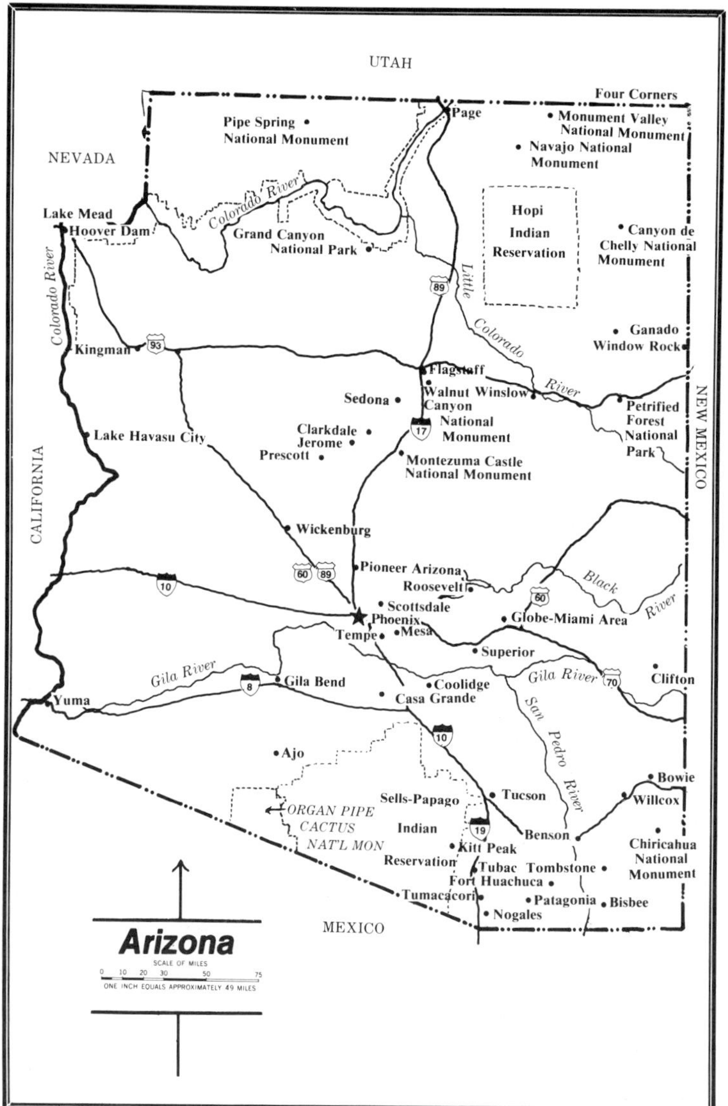
UTAH
NEVADA
CALIFORNIA
NEW MEXICO
MEXICO
Four Corners
Page
Pipe Spring National Monument
Monument Valley National Monument
Navajo National Monument
Colorado River
Lake Mead
Hoover Dam
Grand Canyon National Park
Hopi Indian Reservation
Canyon de Chelly National Monument
Little Colorado River
89
Kingman
93
Ganado
Window Rock
Flagstaff
Walnut Canyon National Monument
Winslow
Sedona
Petrified Forest National Park
Clarkdale
Jerome
Prescott
17
Lake Havasu City
Montezuma Castle National Monument
Wickenburg
60
89
Pioneer Arizona
Roosevelt
Black River
10
Scottsdale
Phoenix
Globe-Miami Area
Tempe
Mesa
Superior
Gila River
8
Gila Bend
Coolidge
Clifton
70
Yuma
Casa Grande
San Pedro River
Ajo
Sells-Papago Indian Reservation
Tucson
Bowie
Willcox
ORGAN PIPE CACTUS NAT'L MON
19
Benson
Chiricahua National Monument
Kitt Peak
Tubac
Tombstone
Fort Huachuca
Tumacacori
Patagonia
Bisbee
Nogales
Arizona
SCALE OF MILES
0 10 20 30 50 75
ONE INCH EQUALS APPROXIMATELY 49 MILES

Arizona

SEVERAL THOUSAND YEARS before the first Spanish exploration of this area, Indians had settled widely in Arizona. Over the centuries, the early tribes gave way to the Papago and the Pima, which survive today and were joined centuries ago by the Apache and the Navajo. The first Spanish explorers stumbled on the region after they had been shipwrecked near the Texas coast. The few survivors who managed to reach a small Spanish settlement near the Pacific Coast brought with them tales of incredible wealth in what they called the Seven Cities of Cibola. This led to many expeditions through much of the southwest in a vain search for the treasure cities.

The first party to reach what is now Arizona was led by Marcos de Niza in 1539. He was followed almost immediately by Francisco Vasquez de Coronado. Not until the late seventeenth century, however, was there any development of the area by Europeans. This was a consequence of the establishment of twenty-four missions by the Roman Catholic Church. The first permanent white settlement outside the mission system was at Tubac in 1752. Tucson followed as an early fortress in 1776. When Mexico gained independence from Spain in 1822, the Arizona territory became a part of the new country. Later, after the treaties ending the Mexican War in 1848, the United States took control of New Mexico, which then included parts of Arizona.

As the conflict over slavery grew in the Eastern states, so did conflict within Arizona as to which side to espouse. In the end, the Union prevailed, and Congress established a separate Arizona Territory governed by a representative of the Union. The first government seat was at Fort Whipple, around which emerged the town of Prescott. For the next twenty years, the Apache were a source of fear among the settlers. Numerous raiding parties were led by fierce warriors, including the famed Cochise and Geronimo. In 1886, peace with the Indians was finally achieved with the surrender of Geronimo. Statehood followed in 1912.

Arizona has great appeal to tourists. For instance, the Grand Canyon is visited by more tourists than practically any other natural attraction in the country. In addition, the tremendous variety of terrain—from desert to mountain—gives dimension to the state. Much of the old West lives on in towns like Tombstone and Jerome. Even a piece of old London, London Bridge, was recently transplanted to Lake Havusa City. The state has a particularly helpful travel-promotion department, which will gladly send prospective visitors a wealth of useful information. Write to the State of Arizona, Office of Tourism, 1700 West Washington, Phoenix, AZ 85007. The telephone number is 602-271-3618.

AJO *Organ Pipe Cactus National Monument*, south of Ajo on Route 86, is named for a cactus species rarely found in the United States, and it includes stark mountains and canyons and the Sonoran Desert, with unusual varieties of plants and animals. The visitors' center provides information and tour maps for hikers, backpackers, and those who wish to take scenic drives. It also has exhibits of desert life forms. Lectures, films, campfire talks, and guided walks are available all year. The Monument is always open, but temperatures are extremely high in the summer. Route 85 goes through the Monument to the Mexican border and continues on to *Rocky Point*, a picturesque fishing village on the Gulf of Mexico in Sonora.

ARCOSANTI Reached by a marked dirt road east of Route 17 at Cordes Junction above Pioneer and Phoenix, *Arcosanti* is a prototype of a small city planned and designed by Paolo Soleri and the Cosanti Foundation (see **Scottsdale**). Hundreds of students and professionals have come here each year since 1970 to work on the city and attend lectures by Soleri. Public performances by visiting artists are held here, where ecology is combined with innovative architecture. When completed, the city will house and provide working facilities for five thousand people within one structure. Guided tours daily except Christmas at 11 and 2. Open 9–5 daily. Nominal charge. 602-948-6145.

BENSON *The San Pedro Valley Historical Society*, in the old (*ca.* 1880) Southern Pacific Railroad depot in the City Park, has some interesting local historical items, and the building is popular with railroad buffs. Open daily except Sunday 9:30–4. Free. 602-586-4632.

BISBEE A mile high on the historic Cochise Trail in the southeastern corner of the state, Bisbee is a colorful old-West town of the 1880s, known as Arizona's "Queen of the Mining Camps." Its old homes sit precariously on steep hillsides, and many of its businesses offer visitors walking-tour maps of the town.

The *Copper Queen Mine Tour* offers an underground journey into one of the West's most famous copper mines on U.S. 80. Visitors can see how men and machines worked at the turn of the century deep in the rocks, where the mine temperature is a constant 47° F. Open daily 10–5. Fees charged; children under 6 free. *The Lavender Pit*, one of the largest open-pit copper mines in the world, is traversed by U.S. 80. The area is open twenty-four hours a day. Free (tours for a nominal charge at noon daily; children under 6 free). 602-432-2071.

Every July 4 the town celebrates with "old-time miners" contests, a rodeo, and other sporting events. The miners compete in hard-rock drilling, mucking, and other mine activities from the past.

The *Bisbee Historical Museum and Restoration Association,* at 37 Main Street, offers exhibits of local pioneer and Indian history and artifacts. Open 10–3 daily except Sunday and major holidays. Donation.

The *Bisbee Mining and Historical Museum*, Queen Plaza, has a permanent mining exhibit including a simulated mine tunnel for walking through. There are archives and a library for research, and tours of real mines are available. Open 10–4 daily but 1–4 Sunday. Donation. 602-432-7071.

Bisbee retains the old "wild and woolly" section of town called *Brewery Gulch*, with its saloons and quaint shops. On Labor Day weekend, the town celebrates *Brewery Gulch Days* with lots of food, drink, and old-fashioned entertainment.

BOWIE In Cochise County in the southeast corner of the state, Bowie is surrounded by mountains and is known as the "Garden of the Sun." *Fort Bowie National Historic Site*, about 12 miles south of town, is dedicated to preserving the Butterfield Overland Mail Route, Apache Pass Station, Apache Spring, and Fort Bowie complex. The fort was established in 1862 as headquarters for military operations against Cochise, Geronimo, and the Chiricahua Indians. The site's small museum is open all year 8–5.

CANYON DE CHELLY NATIONAL MONUMENT Chinle, headquarters of *Canyon de Chelly National Monument*, can be reached by driving east from Route 8 on Routes 7 and 64. The visitors' center here is a good place to start a tour of the canyon and its prehistoric ruins. The canyon sheltered Pueblo Indians for a thousand years beginning in A.D. 306. Some of the ruins of their dwellings nestle below towering cliffs, and others are perched high on canyon ledges. The visitors' center has archaeological exhibits concerning the canyon's occupation by the ancient Anazai and present-day Navajo. Open daily (except Christmas and New Year's) 8–5 in winter and 8–7 in summer. Free. Trips into the canyon are permitted only with authorized guides or park rangers, as the area is hazardous, with quicksand, loose rocks, high canyon walls, and deep, soft sand. There is a 20-mile scenic drive along the canyon's rim with spectacular overlooks. One self-guiding trail to the White House Ruin is the exception to the mandatory-guide rule.

CASA GRANDE The *Casa Grande Valley Historical Society and Museum*, at 110 West Florence Boulevard, includes the "Casa Grande Old Stone Church," an auditorium for the Society and a state and national historic place. There are collections of objects of local historical importance, such as household furnishings, ranching equipment, clothing, and law-enforcement articles. Open daily 1–5 except Mondays and holidays. Sometimes closed in July and August. Donation. 602-836-2223.

"O'odham Tash" Celebration (Indian Days) is a festival held throughout the city the third weekend in February. The museum then extends its hours and offers old-time crafts demonstrations.

CHIRICAHUA NATIONAL MONUMENT *Chiricahua National Monument* is in the southeast corner of the state in the Chiricahua Mountains, about 36 miles from Willcox on the Dos Cabezas Star Route (Route 186). The mountains, which rise sharply out of the vast desert connecting New Mexico and Arizona, are forested and richly green, a stark contrast to the desert. The high desert valleys have unusual lava and rock formations of slender pinnacles, balanced rocks, and weird lifelike figures. It is sometimes called the Rhyolite Park or the Wonderland of Rocks. The Monument, populated by interesting plants and animals, has a visitors' center and self-guiding walks and hiking trails. June through Labor Day there are evening campfire programs on Thursday, Friday, and Saturday nights. In summer a shuttle bus takes hikers from the visitors' center to the trailhead at 9 A.M. and 2 P.M. daily; in winter the bus operates on weekends only.

CLARKDALE *Tuzigoot National Monument*, just north of Clarkdale off Route 89A, is a remnant of a prehistoric town built by Indians who once farmed the Verde Valley. The stone dwelling boasted 110 rooms when it was inhabited between A.D. 1125 and 1400. The visitors' center and museum contain artifacts unearthed during excavations and have interpretative exhibits. There are self-guiding tours of the knoll overlooking Jerome and Clarkdale nearby. Monument open 7–7 June to September and 8–5 the rest of the year. Nominal charge for cars and for individuals in public vehicles.

CLIFTON The *Greenlee County Historical Society*, 8 Park Avenue, is in the former living quarters of the owners and staff of the Longfellow Copper Mine. The house was built of adobe and cottonwood and willow logs in 1874. The museum contains historical artifacts and pictures of early mining in Clifton, Morenci, and Metcalf, in the nation's leading copper-producing district. Clifton's first jail is here, dug and blasted out of the side of a bluff by a fellow who, after being paid for his work, got drunk and became the first prisoner to be locked in the new facilities. Museum open Tuesday and Thursday 2–4:30. Free.

COOLIDGE *Casa Grande Ruins National Monument*, on Route 87 just north of Coolidge, features a well-preserved, prominent, four-story earthen building, the function of which is unknown today. The Casa Grande, as it is called, was built more than six hundred years ago, and it may have been a ceremonial building or an ancient astronomical observatory. The prehistoric Indians who built it lived and farmed the Gila Valley for thousands of years. Their greatest achievement is still in evidence today—an irrigation system with more than 600 miles of canals, 2–6 feet wide and 3 feet deep. The visitors' center offers explanatory material, history, and a representative collection of artifacts of the Hohokam Indians who lived here. Monument open daily 7–6. Nominal charge for vehicles and individuals on tours. Children under 17 and adults over 62 free.

FLAGSTAFF A large educational and cultural center of more than 32,000 population, Flagstaff is completely surrounded by the *Coconino National Forest* with its towering mountains, including the state's highest, *Humphreys Peak* (12,670 feet), just north of the city.

Northern Arizona Pioneers' Historical Society, on Route 180 North, contains artifacts and photos from Flagstaff and Coconino County, covering the area's history from the 1850s to the present. The museum, in the Coconino County Poor Farm, in summer demonstrates pioneer crafts and sells some of the finished products. Open all year, except major winter holidays, Monday through Saturday 9–5, Sunday 1:30–5; closes an hour earlier in winter. Donation. 602-774-6272.

The Museum of Northern Arizona, on Route 180 3 miles out of town, has exhibits relating to the area's present-day Native American cultures and showing the biology, geology, archaeology, and paleontology of the Colorado Plateau. Open all year, except major winter holidays, 9–5 Monday through Saturday and 1:30–5 Sunday. Free.

The Museum of Northern Arizona sponsors the *Hopi Craftsman Show* very early in July and the *Navajo Craftsman Show* at the end of July. Many Indian tribes attend the big *Southwest Indian Powwow* held in Flagstaff over the July 4 weekend, with dancing, exhibits, Native American foods, and parades. The Chamber of Commerce (602-774-4505) has information on these activities.

Throughout the year, the *Museum of Northern Arizona* offers instructive outdoor expeditions encompassing a back-country area of the Colorado Plateau. Interpretative guides lead groups of up to twenty-five adults on two- to four-day backpacking trips for a set fee. There are Grand Canyon Hiking Trips, Verde Valley Archaeological Tours, and many more. Write Box 720, Flagstaff, AZ 86001.

Sunset Crater National Monument is north of Flagstaff about 2 miles off Route 89. The paved road leading to the volcanic cone is surrounded on all sides by the volcanic cinders. About A.D. 1065 the volcano erupted, spewing ash and lava over the countryside, and the terrain looks much the same today as it did just after the eruption. The park service's visitors' center is open daily except major holidays 8–6. Free.

Wupatki National Monument is 18 miles north of Sunset Crater, about 30 miles from Flagstaff. Both monuments can be reached by a paved road through the volcanic cinders with unusual plant and animal communities along the way in the Coconino National Forest. The Wupatki Monument is also reached by paved road about 14 miles east off Route 89. Here more than eight hundred prehistoric ruins, dating from A.D. 1075 to about 1250, cover some 35,000 acres. The Wupatki Ruin, largest on the monument, contained more than a hundred rooms and was three stories tall. There are self-guiding trails and guided tours are available in summer. The visitors' center is open daily 8–5, except Christmas and New Year's; closes later in summer. Free. 602-774-7000.

FORT HUACHUCA *Fort Huachuca Historical Museum*, on Boyd and Grierson streets, has period rooms complete with lifelike figures that add to the realistic interpretation of a Western Army outpost of the late nineteenth century. The old post, a National Historic Landmark, is at the mouth of the Huachuca Canyon, west of the modern post, and its 1890s buildings contain military artifacts from the Indian Wars to the present. Open weekdays 9–4, weekends 1–4, except on federal holidays. Free. 602-538-5736.

FOUR CORNERS Just off Route 160, *Four Corners* is where Arizona, New Mexico, Utah, and Colorado meet. Trading posts and Navajo arts and crafts centers dot the route to the Four Corners, which is on Navajo land.

GANADO *Hubbell Trading Post National Historic Site*, just off Route 264 west of Window Rock, is a historic building devoted to the way of life and role of traders, in particular John Lorenzo Hubbell, who established this trading post in the 1870s. His home has Indian artifacts, rugs, and art work, and a Navajo trading post also still operates here. Open daily 8–5, later in warmer months. Closed winter holidays. Free. 602-755-3254.

Kinlichee, about 8 miles northeast of Ganado, contains an interesting collection of prehistoric Indian ruins maintained by the Navajo tribe.

GILA BEND *Painted Rocks State Historic Park*, about 25 miles northwest of Gila Bend, north off I-8 in the Painted Rocks Mountains, is a collection of Indian rock-art drawings of lizards, men, geometric figures, and strange, unidentifiable depictions dating back to prehistoric times. The park lies along the historic Gila Trail traveled by scores of pioneers and "49ers." The picnic area here has rest rooms but no water.

GLOBE-MIAMI AREA *Salt River Canyon*, on Route 88 between Globe and Apache Junction, is a gorge called the mini–Grand Canyon because of its colors and rock formations. Route 60 North out of Globe winds into and out of the canyon, permitting visitors a close-up view. *Apache Trail*, one of the most beautiful drives in Arizona, is 120 miles long, starting from Globe and Miami and continuing through the Apache Mountains and past Roosevelt, Apache, and Canyon lakes.

Miami, a picturesque canyon town, is in the midst of America's richest copper fields, and the open-pit workings can be seen from Route 60. Free mine tours are conducted daily Monday through Friday at 1 from the *Inspiration Copper Company*'s main gate.

The *Clara T. Woody Museum*, 1300 North Broad Street, Globe, contains artifacts found in the Besh-ba-Gowah Indian Ruin, as well as mining and early pioneer artifacts. Open Tuesday through Saturday 10–5. Free. 602-425-7385.

The *Besh-ba-Gowan Indian Ruin* between Miami and Globe, south of Route 60, is a two-hundred-room prehistoric Pueblo village excavated near Miami. The village was constructed of adobe around A.D. 1225 by the Salado Indians.

GRAND CANYON NATIONAL PARK The *Grand Canyon* is probably the most popular tourist attraction in this country. The enormous natural wonder offers many services to visitors; the *South Rim Visitor's Center* provides information and maps and has a small, informative museum. Open daily 8–5; summer hours usually 7 A.M.–9 P.M. Free. The *South Rim*, reached by Route 64, offers scenic drives, sightseeing buses, boat trips, hiking into the canyon, and mule trips. The boating is available from private concessions and usually takes several days. Mule trips into the canyon take two days and require reservations several months in advance. There are two small museums in the park. *Yavapai Museum* deals with the geology of the Grand Canyon; the *Tusyan Museum*, on the east rim, at an excavated Pueblo ruin, offers exhibits of the prehistory and ethnology of Native American groups in the Grand Canyon area. The museums are open 9–5 in summer; hours vary the rest of the year. Free. The park admission charge is nominal. The *North Rim*, reached by Route 67, is open in the summer only, due to weather conditions, and offers some of the best views in the park. Mule trips into the canyon are available here, with advance reservations, and there are horseback rides along the rim as well as lectures and hikes. Nominal charge for park admission. For reservations and information write the park supervisor, Grand Canyon National Park, Grand Canyon, AZ 86023.

HEREFORD *Coronado National Memorial* is in the scenic Montezuma Canyon of the Huachuca Mountains. The memorial lies along the international boundary where Coronado first entered what is now the United States, in 1540. Memorial headquarters, with a small museum telling of the Coronado expedition, is 5 miles up the canyon road from the junction with Route 92. A ranger is on duty daily 8–5. There are foot trails to the Coronado Peak, and exhibits along the trail give additional information. The annual *Coronado International Historical Pageant*, with Spanish folk dancing, music, crafts, and foods, is held each spring near the ranger headquarters. For further information, write the Memorial, Box 125, Hereford, AZ 85615; or call the park service in Bisbee, 602-366-5515.

HOPI INDIAN RESERVATION The *Hopi Indian Reservation* crossed by Route 264, running east-west from Window Rock to Tuba City, and by Route 87, which runs north-south, contains several villages, either in the canyon valleys or atop high mesas. The Hopis are famed for their twined basketry, Kachina dolls, and ceremonial dances, and they have laid down hard and fast rules for tourists that must be obeyed: no cameras, tape recorders, or sketching materials of any kind are permitted. To avoid temptation, it is advisable to lock such belongings in the car trunk. There are several areas where visitors are not allowed, and warning signs should be heeded. One such area is Oraibi, the oldest continually inhabited community in America, situated on top of a mesa with terraced pueblos and ancient ceremonial chambers. *New Oraibi*, at the foot of the mesa, is the tribal headquarters. The *Hopi Cultural Center*, near the junction of Routes 87 and 264, contains artifacts of Hopi history, an arts and crafts shop, and a motel and restaurant offering local Indian foods. The entire route offers fine scenery and many Hopi arts and crafts shops, outlets, and trading posts where visitors are welcome. The most impressive Hopi village, *Walpi*, is on top of First Mesa and has panoramic views of the area and cliffside kivas.

JEROME On Route 89A, midway between Phoenix and the Grand Canyon, is the historic mining town of Jerome. Situated on steep mountainsides overlooking the Verde Valley, the lively ghost town, once known as the "Billion Dollar Copper Camp" or the "City in the Sky," was famed for its wickedness and violence. *Jerome State Historic Park* consists primarily of a mining museum in the former home of James Douglas, owner of the Little Daisy Mine in Jerome. The museum covers history of the town, mining, and mineral displays, and its setting offers a good view of the town and mountains beyond. Open daily 8:30–5:30, except Christmas. Nominal charge for adults; children under 18 free.

The third weekend in May each year the town sponsors an open-house tour, *"Paseo das Casas,"* which includes many historic buildings and unique homes.

KINGMAN The *Mohave Museum of History and Arts*, 400 West Beale Street, is an outstanding small community museum, whose main exhibit is an interpretative history of Mohave County from prehistoric times to the present. Its Andy Devine Room pays tribute to a native son, with memorabilia of the actor's life and films. The Wallapai Indian Room contains a life-size wickiup and a children's area where they may grind mesquite beans with the old tools. The museum also offers excellent turquoise and silver jewelry collections, an art gallery with work of local and regional artists, and a gift shop that sells local crafts and Indian jewelry. Open Monday through Friday 10–5, Saturday and Sunday 1–5, except major holidays. Donation. 602-753-3195.

In early October each year Kingman celebrates its founding in 1882, as well as Andy Devine's birthday, October 7. There are marathon runs, showings of Andy's films, an arts and crafts show, and often a rodeo. 602-753-3195.

KITT PEAK Kitt Peak is a 6,875-foot mountain in the *Papago Indian Reservation* southwest of Tucson. The huge *Kitt Peak National Observatory* with the world's largest solar telescope is on the peak south of Route 86 on Route 386. The site offers the largest concentration of facilities for stellar, solar, and planetary research in the world, and its visitors' center includes exhibits featuring astronomy and the ongoing Kitt Peak research. Open daily 10–4.

LAKE HAVASU CITY The city is centered around the resort lake, and the main feature is the imported *London Bridge*. It was purchased for almost $2.5 million and cost more than $5 million to disassemble, transport, and rebuild next to an authentic English village owned by the City of London. There is a replica of British royalty's legendary gold coach used for coronations and other state occasions. The *London Bridge Days* festival, usually held the second weekend in October, offers English foods, parades, costumes, and entertainment. London Bridge is open daily from 7 A.M. until late at night, all year. Free.

LAKE MEAD AND THE HOOVER DAM Lake Mead, in the northern corner of Arizona on the Nevada border just east of Las Vegas, can be reached by several routes leading southeast off I-15 in Arizona or Nevada or by Route 93 leading northwest from Kingman. It is a vast National Recreation Area whose main feature is the lake and the *Hoover Dam*. The largest of all federal reclamation projects and an impressive architectural feat, Hoover Dam is the highest concrete dam in the United States (727 feet). It plugs the Black Canyon and Lake Mead reservoir, which is 115 miles long and covers 227 square miles. Interior tours of the dam last about thirty-five minutes, with one leaving every 15 minutes. There is an exhibit of the generating unit and topographical models of the area. Open for tours in summer 7:30–7, the rest of the year 8:30–4:15. Nominal charge; children under 16 free.

MESA Mesa is one of Phoenix's suburbs (see **Scottsdale, Tempe, Rawhide, and Pioneer Arizona**). The *Mesa Museum* at 53 North MacDonald Street features participation exhibitions for visitors of all ages, who can try their hand at panning for gold, using ancient Hohokam tools, and being locked up in an 1890s jail cell. Open 10–4, Tuesday through Saturday. 602-834-2230.

Tours of the area begin at the Mesa Museum, with maps for self-guiding tours of the town's historic sites.

MONTEZUMA CASTLE NATIONAL MONUMENT The National Monument, north of Camp Verde, just east off I-17, includes the *Montezuma Castle*, one of the best preserved prehistoric cliff dwellings in the Southwest, and *Montezuma's Well*, 7 miles to the northeast. Exhibits at the visitors' center show examples of weaving, shell and turquoise jewelry, and pottery tools and fragments and explaining the history of the dwellings and the Indians who lived in them. The ruins—of two five-story apartment houses, one with twenty rooms, the other with forty-five—are reached only by ladders high up to the limestone cliffs. They are quite fragile, and the better preserved of the two can be viewed only from the valley. At Montezuma's Well, another example of prehistoric Indian work, small cliff dwellings and pueblos around a natural limestone-rimmed sink were constructed. Irrigation ditches can still be seen, because limestone deposits from the water cemented their sides. Open daily 8–5; from May to October, open longer. Nominal charge for cars. Well area free.

MONUMENT VALLEY NATIONAL MONUMENT *Monument Valley* can be reached by Route 163 north from Kayent toward Mexican Hat, Utah. This Navajo tribal park is full of eroded buttes and mesas that are like skyscrapers and that dominate the valley scenery. Here, Navajo families tend sheep, and there are many trading posts dotting the area. Monument Valley has rolling sand dunes, natural arches, ancient ruins, and traditional Indian hogans. The visitors' center, east of Route 163, has interesting exhibits and vistas.

NAVAJO NATIONAL MONUMENT The *Navajo National Monument*, on Route 564 off Route 160 between Kayenta and Cow

Springs, consists of three sections: *Inscription House, Betatakin*, and *Keet Seel*, the most extensive pueblo ruins in Arizona. At Betatakin there are a visitors' center, exhibits, trails, and a crafts shop. A trail leads to the Ledge House, a 135-room pueblo ruin in the Tsegi Canyon. Keet Seel's ruins date from A.D. 1250 and are very well preserved.

NOGALES Nogales, south of Tucson on Route 89, is directly across the border from Nogales, Sonora, Mexico, and is a gateway to Mexico and an official port of entry into the United States. The first week of May each year the two Nogaleses hold a joint *Fiesta de Mayo*, featuring dances, parades, entertainment, and, in Mexico, a bullfight. The picturesque Mexican Nogales has shops and open bazaars, and both towns are surrounded by a high mountain range.

Pimeria Alta Historical Museum in the civic building contains exhibits of local historical interest, such as artifacts of Native Americans and pioneers and equipment used by early miners. Open Wednesday through Sunday, 1–5. Free.

PAGE Page, on I-89, is on the east side of the enormous *Glen Canyon Dam* near Arizona's north-central border. The dam is part of the interstate *Glen Canyon Dam and National Recreation* area. The visitors' center at the damsite, on I-89 near the rim of the Glen Canyon, is open for information on self-guiding tours of the dam and Lake Powell, which was formed by damming the Colorado River. It also has exhibits of the area's history and geology. Open daily 8:30–5, longer hours in summer. The *Page/Lake Powell Chamber of Commerce* has more information on the attractions of the area and on opening times. 602-645-2741.

The *John Wesley Powell Memorial Museum*, on Seventh and Navajo streets, is dedicated to the memory of Powell, who explored the Colorado River and its tributaries. There is a replica of his boat and pictures and history of the area then (1869) and now. The Indian Culture Room has many Indian artifacts, as does the Arizona Room, which also has items relating to the early pioneers. The museum arranges tours and has a bookshop. Open daily 9–5, May 16 through September 15. Closed Sundays, September 16 through November 1; open 10–4, November through April, except weekends. Free. 602-645-2741.

PATAGONIA The *Stradling Museum of the Horse*, 350 Third Avenue, in this town northeast of Nogales, has an extensive collection of horse, Indian, and art items collected by Mrs. Stradling, a true horse lover. The museum is the only one of its kind dedicated solely to the horse. The collection contains horse brass and many saddles, coaches, and related artifacts. Open daily 9–5, except Thanksgiving, Christmas, and January 1–4. Nominal charge; children under 12 free. 602-394-2264.

PETRIFIED FOREST NATIONAL PARK *Petrified Forest National Park*, off I-40 between Holbrook, a historic cattle town, and Navajo, is open all year and contains world-famous displays of petrified wood. The most colorful parts of the *Painted Desert*, much of which can be seen from Route 66, are included in this 94,000-acre park. *Puerco Indian Ruin*, an ancient pueblo, and *Newspaper Rock*, a massive sandstone block with petroglyphs (picture writing) on its surface, are among the park's points of interest, and its colored sands and mesas are breathtaking. There is a visitors' center–museum that offers exhibits of the natural and human history of the area, as well as self-guiding hiking and auto tours of the desert, ruins, and petrified trees. Open dawn to sunset.

PHOENIX A large sprawling city, Phoenix is the capital of Arizona. A good place to start a visit is at the *Phoenix and Valley of the Sun Convention and Visitors' Bureau*, 2701 East Camelback Road, which supplies visitors with brochures and information on where to go and what to do in the area. Open 8–6 Monday through Friday. 602-957-0070.

The *Phoenix Art Museum*, at the northeast corner of McDowell and Central avenues, has a permanent collection of painting, sculpture, and decorative arts from the fifteenth through the twentieth centuries. The major strengths are their eighteenth-century French painting, Western American, and contemporary and Oriental art. There are a "hands-on" junior museum, special exhibitions, tours, and a museum shop. Open Tuesday through Saturday 10–5, Sundays 1–5, and Wednesday evenings until 9. Free. 602-257-1222.

The *Sun City–Phoenix Art Museum*, at 9744 West Bell Road, Sun City (a suburb of Phoenix), is a satellite to the Art Museum and draws its exhibitions from the latter's permanent collections, local collections, and national tours. Open Tuesday through Saturday, 10–4; Sundays 1–4, except Mondays, holidays, and July and August. Free parking and admission. 602-974-2583.

The *Arizona History Room,* First Avenue and Washington Street, is privately operated by the First National Bank of Arizona. The museum's main feature is the Territorial Banking Room, which contains furniture, fixtures, and records from territorial banks. Other temporary exhibits, which change frequently, feature local and banking histories. Open all year Monday through Friday, 10–3, except banking holidays. Free.

The *Arizona Historical Society, Phoenix Chapter and Museum*, 1242 North Central Avenue, features the history of Phoenix and central Arizona, including a costume gallery, old-fashioned drugstore, and a Touch Museum for children. There are also many changing historical exhibits. Open daily 10–4, except Sunday and Monday. Donation. 602-255-4479.

The *Heard Museum*, 22 East Monte Vista Road, is a museum of anthropology and primitive art. Its permanent exhibits depict prehistoric and historic Indian cultures of the Southwest. Temporary changing exhibits present Southwestern Indian arts and crafts as well as primitive arts and crafts from around the world. Open Monday through Saturday 10–5 and Sunday 1–5, closed most major holidays. Nominal charge. 602-252-8848.

The *Arizona Mineral Museum*, Arizona Department of Mineral Resources, intersection of McDowell Road, Nineteenth Avenue, and Grand Avenue, is in the Mineral Building at the fairgrounds. The museum's outstanding collections of crystallized minerals and ore samples are of interest to collectors and prospectors. It also displays fossils, Indian artifacts, and mining-industry items, with its fluorescent rocks, stone spheres and stone bowls of particular interest. Museum officials offer tourists and rockhounds information on places in Arizona where minerals and rocks can be collected. Open weekdays 8–5, Saturday and Sunday 1–5. Closed state holidays. Free. 602-255-3791.

The *Pueblo Grande Museum*, 4619 East Washington Street, is a site museum dedicated to the prehistoric Hohokam farmers (300 B.C. to A.D. 1400), who developed the first irrigation project in the southwest. Part of an early Hohokam ruin, the museum has exhibits conserving and interpreting Phoenix's prehistoric heritage. Visitors in June, July, and August may observe archaeology in progress. Open weekdays 9–4:45, Sundays 1–4:45. Free. 602-275-3452.

The *Desert Botanical Garden* can be reached via Fifty-eighth Street and Van Buren Street or Sixty-fourth Street and McDowell Road. In the northeast corner of Papago Park on 150 acres of natural desert, it offers more than a thousand varieties of cacti and other unusual plants from the world's arid lands. More than half of all cacti species are represented. In early March, its eight-day *Annual Cactus Show* gives awards for outstanding exhibits of cacti, leaf succulents, and more. Open every day 9 to sunset. Nominal charge. 602-947-2800.

The *Phoenix Zoo*, considered one of the top ten zoos in this country,

Arizona's future and past. *Above:* Building Arcosanti, which will house five thousand persons in one structure. *Below:* An old stone church in Casa Grande.

The San Francisco Peaks are the highest in Arizona.

Above: A typical Arizona rodeo scene. *Below:* Touring Lake Powell by boat.

Above left: A blacksmith at work in Pioneer Arizona. *Above right:* Giant cacti thrive at the Saguaro National Monument. *Below:* A reconstructed nineteenth-century church in Pioneer Arizona.

is at 6200 East Van Buren Street and Sixtieth Street. Open in summer 9–7 and off season 9–5. Nominal charge; children under 4 free. 602-273-1341.

The *Japanese Flower Gardens*, on East Baseline Road south of town, offer acres of brilliantly colored flowers in bloom from December through May.

The *Judaica Museum of Temple Beth Israel*, Tenth Avenue and Osborne Road, exhibits the art and ceremonial objects of Judaica as well as items created by Jewish artists. Open Monday, Tuesday, and Thursday 12:30–5:30 and Friday, Saturday, and Sunday 9:00–12:30 P.M. Free. 602-264-4428, ext. 28.

The *Hall of Flame* (National Historical Fire Foundation), in the Phoenix Activity Complex at 6101 East Van Buren Street, is one of the largest, most comprehensive exhibitions of antique fire-fighting equipment in America. The collection includes beautifully restored hand pumpers, both hand-drawn and horse-drawn, steamers, and an ornate parade hose-carriage. The antique items represented come from all over the world, and most date from before the turn of the century. Open daily 9–5, except major winter holidays. Nominal charge; children under 6 free. 602-"ASK-FIRE."

PIONEER ARIZONA On I-17 at the Pioneer Road exit just 12 miles north of Phoenix, *Pioneer Arizona* is an outdoor, living-history museum seeking to re-create life in Arizona pioneer towns of the late nineteenth century. It consists of nearly thirty buildings, both original and reconstructions, from all over the state. Craft demonstrations, such as blacksmithing, potterymaking, weaving, and needlework are featured, and the homes and shops are furnished with period antiques and equipment. The buildings include the first frame house in Phoenix (1880s); a one-room schoolhouse and teacherage; an 1879 church; the sheriff's office; a bank; and several pioneer cabins, including a group of farm buildings from northern Arizona. The opera hall holds variety and melodrama performances Wednesday through Sunday. Special events include a Mountain Man Rendezvous in early February and a Harvest Festival around Thanksgiving. Open daily 9–5 in the off season and 9–7 Memorial Day to Labor Day. Closed Christmas. Nominal charge includes a tour of the museum from a horse-drawn wagon. 602-993-0210.

PIPE SPRING NATIONAL MONUMENT *Pipe Spring National Monument* is in the northwestern area of Arizona near the Utah border, just south of Route 389 west of Fredonia. It is a memorial to early cattle ranching and its cowboys, and visitors can view the fortified ranch house, bunkhouses, work sheds, blacksmith shop, and corrals typical of nineteenth-century ranches. An interpretative visitors' center has guide service, and in the summer living history programs portray such pioneer crafts as butter and cheese making, rag-rug making, looming, quilting, and gardening, as well as seasonal cattle round-ups and calf brandings. Open daily 8–5, tours closing at 4:30. Nominal charge; children under 17 free. 602-643-5505.

PRESCOTT The ''mile-high'' city of Prescott was the first capital of territorial Arizona and today is the headquarters of the huge *Prescott National Forest.*

The *Smoki Museum*, in a reproduction of a pueblo building, offers early artifacts of the Smoki Indians, as well as prehistoric displays and exhibits. Open June to September 1 10–4:30. Free. The *Smoki Ceremonials and Snake Dance* are held annually the first or second Saturday in August at the fairgrounds during the dark of the moon. Only one performance is given each year, for which there is a charge. Children under 6 free. The *Prescott Chamber of Commerce* has more information on the ceremonies and museum. 602-445-2000.

The *Sharlot Hall Historical Museum*, 415 West Gurley Street, contains the Governor's Mansion, built on this site in 1864, the Bashford House, and Fremont's home, all with historic items of the old Arizona territory. Restorations were done in the early 1920s under the supervision of poet-historian Sharlot Hall, and the buildings are furnished with authentic period antiques. Open Tuesday through Saturday 9–5, Sunday 1–5; closed major holidays. Donation. 602-445-3122.

The *Frontier Days Rodeo* is held at the fairgrounds on Miller Valley Road in early July each year. Fees charged. 602-445-8113.

Whiskey Row (Montezuma Street) is in downtown Prescott, just across from the courthouse. Its many colorful establishments include the famous *Palace Bar*, a hangout for local ranchers housed in a fine old turn-of-the-century building. *Pioneer Square*, on West Gurley Street near Granite Creek, also has a collection of early pioneer buildings.

ROOSEVELT The *Roosevelt Dam and lake* are situated along the Apache Trail (Route 88). The dam is the largest dam in the world. The *Tonto National Monument* on Route 88 overlooks Roosevelt Lake and features ancient cliff dwellings of the Salado Indians, inhabited in the fourteenth century. The area is rich in Indian artifacts, and the dwellings are well preserved and consist of individual rooms in a natural cave.

SCOTTSDALE Part of this resort suburb of Phoenix is a representation of an old Western town with fake fronts, wooden sidewalks, and old frontier saloons. The *Scottsdale Historical Society* maintains a rotating display of Scottsdale artifacts in the Chamber of Commerce building in the historic Little Red Schoolhouse on the Scottsdale Mall, Main Street and Brown Avenue. Open 8:30–5, Monday through Friday. Free admission and parking. 602-994-2426.

The *Scottsdale Center for the Arts* in the Scottsdale Mall features traveling individual and group exhibits, as well as tours and classes. There are also exhibitions in the center's gallery and atrium areas, film in its cinema, and stage performances in its theater. Open daily 10–5. Admission charge to theaters. 602-994-2315.

The first week in February an Arabian Horse Show and Rodeo is held in the rodeo grounds at Seventy-fourth Street and Osborn Road. Included in the festivities is the Parada del Sol. For more information, contact the Chamber of Commerce. 602-994-2426.

The *Cosanti Foundation*, 6433 Doubletree Road, is an Arizona State Historic Site. The Foundation is the headquarters of Paolo Soleri, an architect, philosopher, and craftsman famed for his innovative urban designs called arcologies, and for his ceramic and metal windbells and sculptures. The Cosanti Complex of earth-formed concrete structures houses his studios, craft workshops, and display areas. The windbells are made in the craft area and the sculpture and bells are sold here and at Arcosanti. Open daily 9–5, except Christmas. 602-948-6145.

Rawhide, on Scottsdale Road 4 miles north of Bell Road, is a commercial 1880s town featuring stagecoach rides out into the desert, cookouts, reconstructed old buildings, museums, and souvenir shops. Open 5 P.M. to midnight Monday through Friday and noon to midnight Saturday and Sunday. Free. 602-992-6111.

SEDONA The town is at the southern entrance to *Oak Creek Canyon*, which extends 16 miles north of Sedona. Its highway, Route 89A northeast toward Flagstaff, climbs to an elevation of 6,000 feet. The canyon with its towering walls boasts the *Slide Rock,* where the rushing waters push visitors down a natural chute.

Tlaquepaque, an arts-and-crafts village in Sedona, is modeled after the Mexican suburbs of Guadalajara. There are many unusual shops and galleries here, as well as an annex of the *Museum of Northern Arizona* that offers changing exhibits of Arizona's plateau history and arts. Free. 602–282–4838.

SELLS—PAPAGO INDIAN RESERVATION Sells is the headquarters of the *Papago Indian Reservation* at the junction of routes 19 and 86. The tribal headquarters, once called the "Place Where the Turtle Sticks in the Mud," offers the *Papago Arts and Crafts Center* and trading posts.

SUPERIOR The *Boyce Thompson Southwestern Arboretum*, just off Route 60 west of Superior, contains gardens of unusual desert plants from all over the world. Its facilities include a visitors' center with bopks, guide pamphlets, and a unique gift shop. There are self-guiding trails, greenhouses with unusual cacti and succulents, and natural Sonoran Desert biological communities. The Picket Post Mountain is reserved for botanical research. Open daily 8–5. 602-689-2811.

TEMPE A suburb of Phoenix, Tempe is the home of *Arizona State University*, on Routes 60, 80, and 89. The *Salt River Project History Center* in Tempe is near the Hall of Flame (see **Phoenix**) on 1521 Project Drive, between Washington and Van Buren avenues. Its prehistoric artifacts, photographs, early electrical equipment, and films illustrate the past, present, and future of the Salt River Valley and the project. Open Monday through Friday 8:30–4. Free. 602-273-5422.

The *University Art Collection*, in Matthews Center on the Arizona State campus, has a large, significant collection of American paintings, prints, sculpture, crafts, and folk art. Two galleries offer temporary displays that change monthly. Open Monday through Friday 10–5, Sunday 1–5. Free. 602-965-2874. *Grady Gammage Auditorium* was designed by Frank Lloyd Wright and is an acoustically perfect masterpiece. Also on campus is the *Matthews Center Gallery* with exhibits of American and Mexican craftsmanship. Open Monday through Friday 10–5, and during school sessions on Sunday 1–5, except summer. Free.

The *Tempe Historical Museum* at the corner of Rural and Southern streets, features historic items from the general period 1870–1930. There are period rooms, a Model-T fire engine, a chuck wagon, farming and carpentry tools, and musical and medical instruments. A gift shop, the New Arizona Mercantile Company, is in an old post office inside the museum and specializes in replicas and handmade items similar to those on display. Open Tuesday through Saturday 9–5; closed August. Free. 602-966-7902.

Legend City, on West Washington Street, is an amusement park featuring some thirty rides, a children's section, entertainment, and food. Open June through August 5–midnight Monday, Wednesday, and Friday. The rest of the year, open Friday, 5–midnight; Saturday, noon-midnight; Sunday, noon–8. Nominal charge.

TOMBSTONE The entire town of *Tombstone* is a National Historic Landmark. Known as the "town too tough to die," it is located in Cochise County just north of Bisbee. Most famous for the notorious *Gunfight at OK Corral*, the old mining town is a noted tourist attraction with several museums, the OK Corral, and *Boothill Cemetery*. Boothill, with its 250 tombstones, is always open and is free. The *Courthouse Museum* has gallows in its yard and exhibits of mining equipment. The *Wells Fargo Museum* is the largest in town, with fourteen rooms of historic exhibits, and the *Bird Cage Theater*, an 1881 dance hall, is also now a museum. Museums open daily 9–5. Nominal charge. There are many special entertainment events on Memorial Day and Labor Day weekends. During *Helldorado Days,* held Friday through Sunday the third weekend in October each year, the town performs historic reenactments in the streets, with fast-draw contests, melodrama, and an 1880s fashion show. Contact the *Chamber of Commerce* for more information. 602–457–3552.

TUBAC The oldest European settlement in Arizona, *Tubac* is located in the Santa Cruz River Valley between two mountain ranges. The town has a large artists' colony, and its more than twenty arts-and-crafts shops and galleries show works by local craftspeople.

Tubac Presidio State Historic Park, at the corner of River Avenue and Wilson Road, was Arizona's first state park. It highlights the contributions of the Spaniards, Mexicans, and Americans in the state's history. The large museum and interpretative center illustrate the area's high and low points in a 250-year span, and includes dioramas and an underground exhibit of the Presidio, or fort. The park sponsors movies and walking tours on Saturday and Sunday 11:30 and 2. Open daily 8–5:30, except Christmas. Nominal charge; children free. 602–398–2252.

The *Tubac Center of the Arts* displays the work of artists and craftspeople living in southern Arizona. Open Tuesday through Sunday 10–4:30, October through May. Free. 602-398-2371.

TUCSON The second largest city in Arizona, Tucson sprawls out surrounded by desert and mountain ranges and has grown up under several flags; those of Spain, Mexico, the Confederacy, and the United States. The best way to begin a visit to the city and its surroundings is at the *Tucson Convention and Visitors Bureau*, 120 West Broadway Box

27210, Tucson, AZ 85726. 602-791-4768. They will provide information on special fairs, rodeos, and festivals, as well as to regular attractions.

The *Saguaro National Monument* is a preserve protecting the stands of giant saguaro cactus. Because of the altitude range of almost 6,550 feet, the park contains a wide diversity of habitats and is especially beautiful in spring, when the cactus blossoms are in bloom. The Monument is divided into two sections, each with miles of nature trails, wilderness hiking, and visitors' centers. The *Rincon Mountain Unit* is the headquarters, 15 miles east of the city on Old Spanish Trail. It is open daily 8–8, and the visitors' center 8–5. Nominal fee for the area's scenic drive. 602-296-8576. The *Tucson Mountain Unit* is located 16 miles west of the city on Kinney Road. The information center is open 8–5; the park is always open. Free. 602-883-6366.

The *Arizona-Sonora Desert Museum* is in the *Tucson Mountain Park*, 14 miles west of Tucson and adjacent to the Saguaro National Monument. It is on Kinney Road and is well-marked. Called the "Living Museum," it features exhibits of desert botany, zoology, geology, and anthropology. Nature trails and live-animal collections are outstanding; visitors are able to see, in a few hours, the results of years of wilderness searching in the Sonora Desert. The Desert Museum, one of the best of its kind, also has an orientation center, a nursery, and natural environments. Open daily 8:30–sundown. Admission charged; children under 6 free. 602-883-1380. *Old Tucson*, on Kinney Road in Tucson Mountain Park, is a reconstructed village showing Tucson as it appeared in the mid-1800s. More than sixty motion pictures and many TV shows have been filmed here. Visitors may watch the filming, see gunfights and tour the soundstage, frontier museums, shops, and High Chaparral Ranch. The many tourist attractions include train, stage, horseback, and antique-car rides. Open Memorial Day through Labor Day, Monday through Thursday, 9–5:30; Friday and Saturday to midnight; Sunday to 10:30. The rest of the year, open daily 9–5:30. Charge for rides and admission; children under 4 free. 602-883-0100.

Mission San-Xavier Del Bac is 9 miles south of Tucson on San Xavier Road, off Route 19. Considered the most beautiful structure of its kind in the Southwest, the mission was established in 1700, 2 miles south of Jesuit Father Kino's first church. The original building was destroyed during the Pima Revolt in 1751, and the present church was built by Franciscans in the late eighteenth century. Here is a blend of architecture, with no surface left unadorned and every nook and cranny meticulously painted. Open every day. Masses held daily at 8:30 A.M.; Sunday at 8:30, 10:30, and 12:30. Lectures offered hourly 9:30–4:30, except Sunday. Donation. 602-294-2624.

The *Tucson Rodeo (La Fiesta de los Vaqueros)*, held annually the last weekend in February at Tucson Rodeo Field, 4801 South Sixth Avenue, starts at 9 A.M. on Thursday with the world's longest non-mechanized parade. All seats reserved. Call 602-884-0065, or write the Tucson Chamber of Commerce Rodeo Committee, Box 991, Tucson, AZ 85702.

The *Fort Lowell Museum*, at 2900 North Craycroft Road in the Fort Lowell County Park, is a branch of the Arizona Historical Society. It is a reconstruction of the commanding officer's quarters and contains period furnishings, uniforms, and equipment of Fort Lowell's frontier soldiers. There is now an outdoor exhibit on the prehistoric Indians who once lived at the historic site. Open daily 10–4; and closed Sundays, Mondays, and most holidays. Free. 602-885-3832.

The *Arizona Historical Society Museum*, 949 East Second Street at Park Avenue, features exhibit items dealing with the state's history from early Spanish days to the present. The collections include manuscripts and a research library. Open Monday through Friday 9–5; Saturday 9–1; and Sunday 1–5. Closed major holidays. Free. 602-885-3832.

The *Tucson Museum of Art*, 235 West Alameda, in the historic district, features a permanent collection of exhibitions of pre-Hispanic, Spanish colonial, Western art, contemporary Southwestern arts, nineteenth- and twentieth-century American and European painting, graphics, sculptures, and decorative arts. Its five buildings in Territorial and Mexican adobe style include the Museum of Mexican Heritage and the library and are on the National Registry of Historic Sites. Open Tuesday through Saturday 10–5, Sunday 1–5. Closed holidays. Free, with free tours. 602-624-2333.

The *University of Arizona,* at University Boulevard and Park Avenue, was founded in 1885. The campus of almost 300 acres contains many museums open to the public. Among the most interesting are: the *Arizona State Museum*, with four interpretative areas on the archaeology, ethnology, and the natural history of Arizona, as well as exhibits of primitive art and Indian cultures. Open Monday through Saturday 9–5, Sunday 3–5. Closed holidays. Free. 602-626-4096. The *Museum of Art* in the Fine Arts Complex at Speedway at Olive, offers a fine collection of art with changing exhibits and traveling shows. Open daily 9–5, Sundays 12–5. Closed holidays. Free. 602-626-2173. *Flandrau*

Planetarium, East Third Street and Cherry Avenue, offers shows, science halls, and displays of astronomical art. The Halls of Science are free, and Starshows are scheduled Tuesday through Sunday afternoons. For times, call 602-884-4556. Nominal fee; children under 5 not admitted to theater. The *Center for Creative Photography*, 843 East University Boulevard, offers changing exhibits of major photographers and an excellent library. Open Monday through Friday, 9–6. Free. The *Mineralogical Museum in the Geology Building* features gems, minerals, and rocks. Open Monday through Friday 8–5. Free.

TUMACACORI Just south of Tubac on Route 19 is the *Tumacacori Mission National Monument*, which preserves the ruins of a historic mission established in 1690 by Jesuit Father Kino. The church illustrates the Spanish colonial endeavor and is indicative of the Spanish influence characteristic of all the frontier historic missions. A museum offers exhibits of early Indian and Spanish life, and self-guiding tours of the church are available. On the first Sunday in December an *All-Day Fiesta* is held on the Monument grounds. Open daily 8–6.

WALNUT CANYON NATIONAL MONUMENT *Walnut Canyon* is situated east of Flagstaff off Route 66. Here, sheltered by the overhang of the enormous limestone canyon walls, are prehistoric cliff dwellings of the "Sinagua." The Indians lived here from the 1150s until the middle of the 1200s, and the ruins were discovered in 1850. There are two self-guided walking trails: the Island Trail and the Rim Trail. The Island Trail is the way to see the dwellings up close. The museum and visitors' center tell the story of the Indians, and the center offers lists of native plants, birds, and mammals found in the canyon area. Open all year except Christmas and New Year's; in winter 8–5; in summer 7–7. Nominal charge for cars.

WICKENBURG The *Desert Caballeros Western Museum*, 20 North Frontier Street, hosts an extensive western art collection, as well as exhibits of prehistoric Indian artifacts, ceramic wares, crafts, and an exceptional mineral collection. The museum contains period rooms, a hall of history, and street scenes of early Wickenburg. Open Tuesday through Saturday 10–4, Sunday 1–4. Nominal charge.

WILLCOX The *Sulphur Springs Valley Historical Society* at 137 East Maley Street, has a large collection of photos taken by Harry Parks, who lived in Willcox during its heyday. The town was once the biggest cattle-shipping area in the state, and the museum contains items of local historic interest including Indian artifacts, cattle-raising and agricultural tools, and mining equipment. Open Monday through Friday 10:30–4:30. Free. 714-384-4261.

WINDOW ROCK Window Rock is the headquarters of the enormous Navajo Indian tribe and their reservation, which encompasses an area larger than the state of Massachusetts. The *Navajo Tribal Museum*, on Route 264 not far from the Mexican border, contains collections representing Navajo ethnology and archaeology, the natural history of the Southwest, and the area's prehistory. In addition the Navajos have a zoo on the Navajo National Fairgrounds, with animals of the Southwest. Both museum and zoo are funded by the Navajo tribe. Open Monday through Friday 9–5; April through November, Saturday 9–5, Sunday 1–5. Closed most major holidays. Free. 602-871-6457.

Window Rock itself is a large, unusual rock formation that forms a "window" through which the town can be seen. For centuries this formation has been important in Navajo ceremonies and myths. *Tse Bonito Tribal Park*, just south of Window Rock on Route 3, encompasses several large sandstone monoliths known as "haystacks."

The *Navajo Arts and Crafts Guild* offers excellent displays of Indian craftsmanship, including rugs and jewelry, which can be purchased. Open Monday through Friday 9–6. Closed major holidays in winter. Free.

The *Navajo Nation Fair*, held the second week of September at the Navajo Nation Fairgrounds, is for and by the Navajos and offers livestock exhibits, dances, ceremonies, a rodeo, crafts exhibits sponsored by the Guild, and Indian foods.

WINSLOW *Great Meteor Crater,* about 20 miles west of Winslow, is 6 miles south of I-40 on a well-marked paved road. The enormous crater, 4,150 feet from rim to rim and 570 feet deep, was formed when a meteor struck the earth with the force of a multimegaton hydrogen bomb, destroying all life within a 100-mile radius. The crater's scarred surface resembles the surface of the moon and is used by American astronaut teams for training. A museum and gift shops on the crater's rim feature minerals, gems, rocks, and Indian artifacts. Crater and interpretative center open daily 8–sunset. Admission charged; children under 8 free.

YUMA Yuma is in the Arizona desert in the far southwestern corner of the state, on Routes 8 and 80. The *Century House Museum*, 240 Madison Avenue, is a branch of the Arizona Historical Society, and was built in 1870. It contains collections of Yuma and Arizona photographs, documents, and period furnishings, and offers interpretative exhibits on Yuma and Arizona history. Its historic gardens and aviaries with exotic birds are open all year, Tuesday through Saturday 10–4. Free.

The *Yuma Fine Arts Association*, 281 Gila Street, is housed in the old Southern Pacific Railroad Center and exhibits works of local and regional artists. Open Tuesday through Sunday, 10–5. Closed Mondays and holidays. Free.

The *Annual Southwestern Invitational* held during May is a major exhibition of state artists in all media. The *Quechan Indian Museum* in Fort Yuma across the Colorado River in California, near the prison, is the headquarters for the Quechan Indian tribe and houses tribal relics. Open Monday through Friday 8–5. Nominal charge. For more information on Yuma's historic attractions, contact the Chamber of Commerce, 714-782-2567.

Yuma Territorial Prison, part of a historic state park on a bluff overlooking the Colorado River, was built in 1875 to house many of the old West's most notorious badmen. Visitors may tour the cell blocks and dungeons carved into the rock hillside, which afford a startling look into a convict's life in the early days of the West. The park's interpretative center has exhibits describing the men, their crimes and punishments. Photographs, documents and objects made and used by the inmates are on display. Nominal charge; children under 18 free.

Yuma Crossing Days is a one-day celebration held the next to last weekend in February. The historic landmarks and museums of Yuma combine to put on pageants, Indian dances, and special exhibits and demonstrations at various buildings and sites in town. There are horse-drawn shuttles and stage-coach, carriage, beer-wagon, and locomotive transportation between major functions. The festival is named for the famed crossing used by the Indians, pioneers, Spaniards, and Mexicans, where trails converged for the easiest passage over the Colorado. For more information, contact the Yuma Chamber of Commerce. 602-782-2567.

Index

Amusement parks (*see* Parks, theme and amusement)
Anthropology (*see also* Indian mounds; Museums, historical; Museums, natural history; Museums, science; Parks, historical; Pueblos; Ruins): Folsom man, 123; General Anthropology Museum, 134; Laboratory of Anthropology, 137
Aquariums: Dallas Aquarium, 19; Sea-Arama Marine World, 40
Arboretums: Aline McAshan Botanical Hall and Arboretum, 46; Boyce Thompson Southwestern Arboretum, 164
Archaeology (*see also* Cliff dwellings; Museums, historical; Museums, natural history; Museums, science; Parks, scenic; Pueblos; Ruins): Canyon de Chelly National Monument, 146; Folsom Museum, 123; Red River area, 99
Architecture (*see also* Historic buildings, reconstructions, and replicas): Arcosanti, 144; Cosanti Foundation, 163
Art centers (*see also* Art galleries; Museums, art): Amarillo Art Center, 4; Oklahoma Heritage Center, 104; Philbrook Art Center, 110; Wichita Falls Museum and Art Center, 85; World Museum and Art Center, 110
Art galleries (*see also* Art centers; Museums, art): Gardiner Art Gallery, 109; Jonson Gallery, 118; Michener Galleries, 8; Stable Gallery, 139
Arts and crafts (*see also* Art centers; Art galleries; Crafts demonstrations; Museums, art; Museums, historical; Museums, Indian; Museums, pioneer): Matthews Center Gallery, 164; Navajo Arts and Crafts Guild, 169; Papago Arts and Crafts Center, 164; Tlaquepaque, 163; Tubac Center of the Arts, 165
Atom bomb (*see also* Museums, military; Museums, science; Nuclear energy): Los Alamos Ranch School (Los Alamos Historical Museum), 132
Automobiles (*see* Museums, conveyance)
Aviation (*see* Halls of fame; Military bases; Museums, conveyance; Museums, military)

Battlefields: Alamo, 68; San Jacinto Battlefield, 51; Washita Battlefield, 94
Black art and culture: Museum of African-American Life and Culture, 27
Boat trips (*see* Sightseeing tours and excursions)
Border towns: Nogales, Arizona, 134; Nuevo Laredo, Texas, 55
Botanical gardens (*see* Arboretums; Gardens)
Boundary markers: Chamizal National Memorial, 31
Boy Scouts: Philmont Scout Ranch, 123
Buildings (*see* Historic buildings, reconstructions, and replicas)
Burial grounds: Boothill Cemetery, 165; Fort Gibson National Cemetery, 96; LBJ grave site, 88

Cactus: Annual Cactus Show, 136; Organ Pipe Cactus National Monument, 144; Saguaro National Monument, 166
Campgrounds: Echo Amphitheater campground, 116; Yesteryear campground, 57
Canyons: Black Canyon, 152; Canyon de Chelly National Monument, 146; Cedar Canyon, 97; Chaco Canyon National Monument, 122; Frijoles Canyon, 132; Glen Canyon, 134; Grand Canyon, 143; Huachuca Canyon, 149; Montezuma Canyon, 150; Oak Creek Canyon, 163; Palo Duro Canyon, 15; Salt River Canyon, 149; Tsegi Canyon, 154; Walnut Canyon, 168
Capitol buildings: Oklahoma State Capitol, 104; Sante Fe Capitol, 136; Texas Capitol, 5

Cattle Ranching: Finch Farm and Ranch Display (Square House Museum), 64; King Ranch, 54; Nita Stewart Haley Memorial Library and J. Evetts Haley Historical Center, 59; 101 Ranch Room (Cultural Center Museum), 108; Pipe Spring National Monument, 161
Caves and caverns: Alabaster Caverns State Park, 97; Carlsbad Caverns, 120; Cascade Caverns, 11; Cave Without a Name, 11; Caverns of Sonora, 79; Longhorn Cavern State Park, 14; Natural Bridge Caverns, 62; Perpetual Ice Caves, 125; Wonder Cave, 77
Churches and chapels: Christo Rey Church 137; Loretto Chapel, 137; St. Francis of Assisi Church, 135; St. Francis Cathedral, 136
Cliff dwellings: Gila cliff dwellings, 124; Montezuma Castle, 153; Tonto National Monument, 162
Copper mining (*see* Mines; Mining towns; Museums, historical)
Cowboys (*see* Cattle ranching; Halls of fame; Museums, historical)
Crafts demonstrations (*see also* Arts and Crafts; Historic buildings, reconstructions, and replicas; Indian art and culture; Museums, historical; Museums, Indian): Alabama-Coushatta Indian Reservation, 87; Casa Grande Valley Historical Society and Museum, 146; Institute of Texan Cultures, 70; Kit Carson Museum, 123; La Villita Historic Complex, 75; Northern Arizona Pioneers' Historical Society, 148; Pioneer Arizona, 161; Pipe Spring National Monument, 161
Craters: Great Meteor Crater, 169

Dams: Glen Canyon Dam, 134; Hoover Dam, 152; Roosevelt Dam, 162
Deserts (*see also* Museums, desert; Parks, desert): Living Desert Zoological and Botanical State Park, 121
Dinosaurs: Dinosaur Valley State Park, 41
Dioramas: Judge Roy Bean Visitor Center, 55; "Pana-Theatre" diorama, 59; Seminole Nation Museum, 112; Texas Ranger Hall of Fame and Museum, 84; Tubac Presidio State Historic Park, 165; Wilderness Park Museum, 32
Dramatic and slide show presentations: Alamo slide show, 68; *Chisholm Trail, The*, 112; Discoveryland Outdoor Musical Dramas, 111; *Last Escape of Billy the Kid, The*, 31; *1900 Storm, The,* 40; *Palo-Duro*, 15; Siglo de Oro Drama Festival, 31; *Texas*, 15; "Trail of Tears" drama, 110
Dunes: Monahans Sandhills State Park, 59; White Sands, 117

Ecology (*see also* Museums, historical; Museums, nature and wildlife; Museums, science; Parks, nature and wildlife): Heard Natural Science Museum and Wildlife Sanctuary, 56; Holland Lake Park, 85

Fairs (*see* Festivals, fairs, and annual events)
Festivals, fairs, and annual events (*see also* Dramatic and slide show presentations): All-day Fiesta (Tumacacori), 168; Andy Devine's Birthday, 152; Annual Cactus Show, 156; Annual Southwestern Invitational art exhibit, 170; Arabian Horse Show and Rodeo, 163; Bisbee rodeo, 145; Brewery Gulch Days, 145; Coronado International Historical Pageant, 151; El Paso-Chamizal Festival of the Arts, 31; Fiesta de Mayo, 154; Frontier Days Rodeo, 162; Helldorado Days, 165; Institute of American Indian Arts Museum powwows, 139; "Live Steam Days," 3; London Bridge Days, 152; Mountain Man Rendezvous, 161; Navajo Nation Fair, 169; *O'odham Tash* Celebration (Indian Days), 146; "Old-time miners" contests, 145; *Paseo das Casas,* 151; Pioneer Arizona Harvest Festival, 161; Pony Express race, 131; Southwest Indian Powwow, 148; Tucson Rodeo (La Fiesta de los Vaqueros),

167; Yuma Crossing Days, 170
Firefighting: Fire Museum of Texas, 43; Hall of Flame, 161; Oklahoma Firefighters Museum, 106; Texas Forestry Museum, 56
Fishing (*see also* Dams; Parks, recreational): Rocky Point Village, 144
Five Civilized Tribes (*see* Indian peoples)
Folk Art (*see also* Indian art and culture; Museums, art; Museums, Indian): Museum of International Folk Art, 137
Forests and forestry (*see also* Parks, nature and wildlife): Beaver National Forest replica, 116; Coconino National Forest, 148; Forest Heritage and Education Center of the South, 93; Gila National Forest, 124; Texas Forestry Museum, 56
Forts: Fort Arbuckle, 95; Fort Bliss, 30; Fort Bowie, 145; Fort Chickamauga, 95; Fort Concho, 67; Fort Croghan, 14; Fort Davis, 33; Fort Duncan, 29; Fort Gibson Stockade, 96; Fort Hood, 54; Fort Huachuca, 149; Fort Lowell, 167; Fort McIntosh, 55; Fort Marcy, 137; Fort Parker, 58; Fort Selden, 126; Fort Sill, 97; Fort Stockton, 34; Fort Sumner, 124; Fort Supply, 97; Fort Union, 131; Fort Whipple, 143; Presidio de San Antonio de Bejar, 68; Presidio La Bahia, 42; Tubac Presidio, 165; Tucson fortress, 143
Fossils (*see also* Museums, historical; Museums, natural history and wildlife): Petrified Forest National Park, 155
Game preserve (*see also* Parks, nature and wildlife; Zoos): International Wildlife, 42
Gardens (*see also* Arboretums): Aquarena Springs, 77; Century House Museum, 169; Desert Botanical Garden, 156; Fort Worth Botanic Gardens, 37; Garden Center (Dallas), 20; Garden of Peace, 37; Japanese Flower Gardens, 161; Judge Roy Bean Visitor Center gardens, 55; Municipal Rose Garden (Tyler), 82; National Cowboy Hall of Fame and Western Heritage Center gardens, 105; Sydnor Powhatan gardens, 39
Ghost towns (*see also* Mining towns): Eagle Park Old West Ghost Town, 94; Shakespeare, 131; Yesteryear, 57

Halls of fame: National Cowboy Hall of Fame, 105; National Cowgirl Hall of Fame, 44; National Hall of Fame for American Indians, 91; National Soft Ball Hall of Fame and Museum, 103; National Wrestling Hall of Fame, 109; Oklahoma Heritage Center Hall of Fame, 104; Old Greer County Museum and Hall of Fame, 100; Texas Ranger Hall of Fame and Museum, 84
Hiking (*see also* Canyons; Caves and caverns; Nature trails; Parks, nature and wildlife; Parks, scenic; Parks, volcanic; Parks, wilderness): Grand Canyon Hiking Trips, 148
Historic buildings, reconstructions, and replicas (*see also* Forts; Ghost towns; Mining towns; Museums, historical; Museums, Indian; Muscums, pioneer; Parks, historical; Pueblos; Ruins; Town districts): Adolpus Sterne house, 60; Alamo (Mission San Antonio de Valero), 68; Allen House Museum, 58; Anson Jones Home, 84; Asenath Weems House, 16; Ashton Villa, 40; Bastrop, Texas, 9; Bates-Sheppard home, 18; Bent House, 140; Bird Cage Theatre, 165; Bishop's Palace, 39; C. Erhard and Sons Drug Store, 9; Carter Log House, 33; Casa Grande Old Stone Church, 146; Cherokee Courthouse, 98; Dewey Hotel, 96; Dr. Eli T. Merriman Home, 78; E. W. Marland House, 108; East Terrace, 83; El Rancho de las Golondrinas, 138; Excelsior House Hotel, 52; Ferdinand Lindheimer Home, 61; Fort Concho Preservation and Museum, 67; Fort House, 83; Frank Phillips Home, 92; Freeman Plantation, 52; Ginocchio Hotel and National Historic District, 58; Governor A. J. Seay Mansion, 99; Governor's Mansion (Austin), 5; Grant Foreman

Home, 103; Greenlee County Historical Society, 147; Grotto of Our Lady of Lourdes, 66; Gruene village, 62; H. B. Ailman House, 139; Har-Ber Village, 98; Harvard Home Museum, 87; Henkel Square, 66; Heritage Garden Village, 86; Highlands Mansion, 52; Honeymoon Cottage, 65; Indian City U.S.A., 91; J. J. Josey Store, 77; Jefferson, Texas, homes, 52; John Neely Bryan Cabin, 27; José Antonio Navarro State Historic Site, 69; Kit Carson Home and Museum, 139; La Fonda Hotel, 137; La Mesilla, 126; La Villita Historic Complex, 75; LBJ Ranch, 79; Lincoln County Heritage Trust, 131; Log Cabin Village, 36; London Bridge, 152; Magnolia Mansion, 99; Magoffin Home, 30; Manby House, 140; Moody-Bradley House, 33; Millard's Crossing, 60; Murray-Lindsay Mansion, 99; Murrell Home, 110; National Cowboy Hall of Fame and Western Heritage Center, 105; Old Aztec Mill, 123; Old City Park (Dallas), 28; Old Pecos Town, 64; "Old Ranch," 53; Old Tucson, 166; Old University Building (Old Nacogdoches University), 61; Oldest House (United States), 136; Orient Hotel and Saloon, 64; Palace of the Governors, 136; Panhandle-Plains Historical Museum Pioneer Village, 15; Pearl Brewery's Jersey Lily Hospitality Center, 74; Peter Conser House, 98; Pioneer Arizona, 161; Pioneer Village, 17; Potter-Watson Cabin, 33; Rayado Village, 123; Sauer-Beckman Farmstead, 80; Sebastopol House State Historic Structure, 78; Sharlot Hall Historical Museum, 162; Sod House, 90; Spanish Governor's Palace, 68; Square House, 63; Stagecoach Inn (Chappell Hill), 15; Stagecoach Inn (Salado), 67; Stephen F. Austin home, 76; Sydnor Powhatan House, 39; T. B. Ferguson Home Museum, 112; Texas Hall of State, 19; Thistle Hill, 35; Tlaquepaque, 163; Tombstone, Arizona, 165; Torreon Hotel, 131; Truehart House, 34; Tsa-Le-Gi Cherokee Village, 109; Varner-Hogg Plantation, 85; William Freemont Harn Homestead, 106; Winedale Historical Center, 66; Wise County (Texas) Courthouse, 28; Wortley Hotel, 131; Yates Hotel, 66

Historic sites (*see also* Historic buildings, reconstructions, and replicas; Parks, historical): Fort Bowie National Historic Site, 145

Historic trails: Apache Trail, 149, 162; Chisholm Trail, 99, 112, 80; Cochise Trail, 145; El Camino Real, 138; Gila Trail, 149; Old Spanish Trail, 166; Sante Fe Trail, 136–37; Zuni-Cibola Trail, 125

Homesteading: Aline, Oklahoma, 90

Ice Caves (*see* Caves and caverns)

Indian art and culture (*see also* Historic buildings, restorations, and replicas; Indian reservations; Missions; Museums, art; Museums, historical; Museums, Indian; Parks, historical; Petroglyphs): Apache Cultural Center, 133; Hopi Cultural Center, 151; Indian Pueblo Cultural Center, 117; National Y-Indian Guide Center, 93

Indian ceremonies and rituals (*see also* Indian reservations): Smoki Ceremonials and Snake Dance, 162

Indian crafts (*see also* Arts and crafts; Crafts demonstrations; Indian art and culture; Museums, historic; Museums, Indian): Hopi Craftsman Show, 148; Navajo Craftsman Show, 148

Indian mounds: Eufaula Mound, 107; Spiro Mounds State Park, 109

Indian peoples: Acoma, 116; Alabama, 87; Anasazi, 119, 146; Apache, 15, 115, 125, 133, 144; Arapaho, 15; Caddoan, 53, 81, 107; Cherokee, 90, 109, 112; Chickasaw, 90, 110; Chiricahua, 146; Choctaw, 90; Cohuiltecan, 75; Comanche, 15, 115; Coushatta, 87; Creek, 90, 106; Hohokam, 156; Hopi, 124; Karaukwa, 39; Kiowa, 15;

Mescalero Apache, 131; Mongollon, 140; Navajo, 115, 124, 125, 143, 144, 148, 155; Paleo-Indian, 132; Papago, 143, 152, 164; Pima, 143, 166; Plains, 104, 123; Pueblo, 120, 122, 125, 132; Quechan, 170; Salado, 162; Seminole, 90, 112–13; Smoki, 162; Tigua, 31; Ute, 115; Zuni, 124–25, 141
Indian reservations: Alabama-Coushatta Indian Reservation, 87; Apache Indian Reservation, 125; Hopi Indian Reservation, 151; Mescalero Apache Indian Reservation, 133; Monument Valley, 153; Navajo Indian Reservation, 125, 169; New Oraibi, 151; Papago Indian Reservation, 152, 164; Pueblo Indian Reservation, 125; Tigua Indian Reservation, 31
Irrigation systems, 127, 153, 156

Jails: Calhoun County "Jail" Museum, 65; Mesa Museum, 153; Old County Jail and Archer County Museum, 86; Old Jail Museum, 79; Yuma Territorial Prison, 170
John Rogers statuary, 94

Lava "badlands" (*see* Parks, scenic)
Libraries: Armstrong Browning Library, 83; Coal County Miners Museum and Genealogical Library, 95; Ernest Thompson Seton Memorial Library and Museum, 123; Fort Worth Public Library, 36; Sam Houston Regional Library and Research Center, 56; Sam Rayburn Library, 11

Markets and shopping districts (*see also* Town districts): Mexican Market (San Antonio), 70; Nuevo Laredo market, 55
Memorials, shrines, and commemorative museums (*see also* Burial grounds): Andy Devine Room (Mohave Museum), 152; Babe Didrickson Zaharias Memorial Museum, 10; Coronado National Memorial, 150; Cultural Center DAR Memorial Museum, 108; Douglas MacArthur Academy of Freedom, 13; Eisenhower Birthplace, 28; Elisabet Ney Studio, 6; Jim Thorpe Home, 113; John Wesley Powell Memorial Museum, 134; Kit Carson Memorial State Park, 139; Lyndon Baines Johnson National Historic sites, 53, 79; Millicent A. Rogers Memorial Museum, 140; Miss Ima Hogg Museum, 65; O. Henry Home, 7; Pawnee Bill Museum and Mansion, 107; Sam Rayburn House Museum, 11; Sophienburg Memorial Museum, 62; Stillman House Museum, 13; Tom Mix Museum, 96
Military bases (*see also* Forts): Brooks Air Force Base, 76; Kirkland Air Force Base, 118
Mines (*see also* Mining towns; Museums, mining): Copper Queen Mine, 145; Inspiration Copper Company, 150; Lavandar Pit, 145; Tongaha Mining Company, 108
Mining towns: Bisbee, Arizona, 145; Jerome, Arizona, 151; Miami, Arizona, 149
Miracle Staircase, 137
Missions: La Purisima Concepción de Cuarac, 133; Mission Espiritu Santo, 42; Mission Nuestra Señora de la Purisima Concepción, 69; Mission San Francisco de la Espada, 69; Mission San Fancisco de los Tejas, 43; Mission San Gregorio de Abo, 134; Mission San Xavier del Bac, 166; Mission Tejas State Park, 42; Our Lady of Guadalupe Mission, 141; San Esteban Rey Mission, 116; San José Mission, 75; San Miguel Mission, 136
Monuments (*see* Battlefields; Parks, historical)
Motion-picture locations: Old Tucson, 166
Museums (*see also* Historic buildings, reconstructions, and replicas; Memorials, shrines, and commemorative museums): Acadian, La Maison des Acadiens French Museum, 61; antiques, My House of Old Things, 119; art (*see*

also Art centers; Art galleries; Museums, Indian), Abilene Fine Arts Museum, 2, Albuquerque Museum of Art, History, and Science, 118, Arizona State University Art Collection, 164, Art League of Houston, 51, Art Museum of South Texas, 17, Artesia Museum and Art Center, 119, Beaumont Art Museum, 10, Chamizal National Memorial Cultural Center, 31, Charles B. Goddard Center for Visual and Performing Arts, 92, Contemporary Arts Museum, 46, Dallas Museum of Fine Arts, 20, El Paso Museum of Art, 31, Fort Worth Art Museum, 35, Galveston Arts Center on the Strand, 40, Gilcrease Institute of American History and Art, 111, Governor Bent Museum, 140, Japanese Art Museum, 17, Kimbell Art Museum, 36, Laguna Gloria Art Museum, 7, McNay Art Institute, 70, Meadows Museum, 27, Museum of Fine Arts (Houston), 44, Museum of Fine Arts (Santa Fe), 136, Nave Museum, 82, Neale House and Brownsville Art League's Museum, 13, Oklahoma Museum of Art, 39, Phoenix Art Museum, 155, Rice Museum, 73, Roswell Museum and Art Center, 27, Scottsdale Center for the Arts, 163, Stark Museum of Art, 81; Sun City-Phoenix Art Museum, 155, Tucson Museum of Art, 167, Tyler Museum of Art, 82, University Art Museum (Austin), 8, University of Arizona Fine Arts Complex, 147, Witte Memorial Museum, 70, Woolaroc Museum, 93, Yuma Fine Arts Association, 170; aviation and space (*see also* Halls of fame; Space exploration), Aviation and Space Museum, 104; banking, Arizona History Room, 155; children's (*see* "Touch" and participation exhibits); circus, Hertzberg Circus Collection, 70; clocks, Old Clock Museum, 64; communications, Telephone Pioneer Museum, 118, World's Smallest Telephone Museum, 85; conveyance, Antiques, Inc., Horseless Carriages Unlimited, 100, Dripping Springs Antique Horse Drawn Vehicle Museum, 99, Pate Museum of Transportation, 37, San Antonio Museum of Transportation, 70; costume, Historic Costumes and Furnishings Collection of the DAR Museum, 28; cowboy, National Cowboy Hall of Fame and Western Heritage Center, 105; decorative arts, Bayou Bend Museum, 44, Museum of American Architecture and Decorative Arts, 46; desert (*see also* Deserts; Parks, scenic), Arizona-Sonora Desert Museum, 166; doll (*see also* Museums, historical), Eliza Cruce Hall Doll Museum, 92, Franks Antique Shop and Doll Museum, 58; forestry (*see* Forests and forestry); geology (*see also* Museums, mining; Museums, natural history and wildlife), Yavapai Museum, 150; historical (*see also* Halls of fame; Missions; Museums, pioneer; Parks, historical), Albuquerque Museum of Art, History, and Science, 118, Allan Shivers Library and Museum, 87, Amon Carter Museum, 35, Annie Riggs Hotel Museum, 34, Arizona Historical Society, 156, Arizona Historical Society Museum (Tucson), 167, Arizona State Museum, 167, Artesia Museum and Art Center, 119, Bastrop County Historical Museum, 9, Bigfoot Wallace Museum, 29, Bisbee Historical Museum and Restoration Association, 145, Black Range Museum, 125, Bosque Memorial Museum, 16, Buckthorn Museum, 41, Canadian County Historical Museum, 96, Carlsbad Municipal Museum, 121, Casa Grande Valley Historical Society and Museum, 146, Central Texas Area Museum, 67, Century House Museum, 169, Cherokee Strip Museum, 107, Chief Gardner Mansion and Museum and Cypress Tree, 93, Chisholm Trail Historical Museum, 112, Chisholm Trail Museum, 99, Clara T. Woody Museum, 150, Coleman County Museum, 16, Corpus

Christi Museum, 17, Davis Museum, 95, Deaf Smith County Museum, 43, Desert Caballeros Western Museum, 168, Douglas MacArthur Academy of Freedom, 13, Eastern Trails Historical Museum, 112, 1889ers Museum, 106, Fort Bend County Historical Museum, 66, Fort Huachuca Historical Museum, 149, Fort Lowell Museum, 167, Fort Supply Museum, 97, Fort Worth Museum of Science and History, 36, Freestone County Museum, 33, Frontier Times Museum, 8, Gadsden Museum, 126, Galveston County Historical Museum, 39, Geronimo Springs Museum, 141, Gilcrease Insitute of American History and Art, 111, Goliad State Park, 42, Goodman Museum, 81, Grant County Historical Society and Museum, 100, Greenlee County Historical Society, 147, Harrison County Historical Museum, 57, Helium Time Column Museum, 4, Heritage Museum, 11, Hidalgo County Historical Museum, 30, Historical Collection at North Texas University, 29, Hoya Memorial Library and Museum, 60, Hutchinson County Museum (Boom Town Revisited), 12, Institute of Texan Cultures, 74, Jefferson Historical Society Museum, 53, John E. Conner Museum, 54, John F. Kennedy Museum, 19, John Jay French Trading Post Museum, 10, Judge Roy Bean Visitor Center, 55, Kerr Museum, 108, Kimble Historical Museum, 53, Kit Carson Museum, 123, Koliba Home Museum, 16, LBJ State Park museum, 80, Ledbetter Picket House Museum, 3, Lee County Museum, 41, Lincoln County Courthouse Museum, 131, Los Alamos Historical Museum, 132, Lyndon B. Johnson Library and Museum, 8, McNamara Historical Museum, 82, Martin County Historical Museum, 79, Matagorda County Historical Museum, 51, Menardville Museum, 58, Miles Museum, 134, Million Dollar Museum, 141, Mohave Museum of History and Arts, 152; Morton Museum of Cooke County, 38, Museum of New Mexico, 136, Museum of Northern Arizona, 148, Museum of Northern Arizona annex (Tlaquepaque), 163, Museum of the Big Bend, 3, Museum of the Republic of the Rio Grande, 55, Museum of the Western Prairie, 91, Neill-Cochran Museum House, 7, Neill Museum, 34, No Man's Land Historical Museum, 97, Northington-Heard Memorial Museum, 30, Nuevo Santander Museum, 55, Oklahoma Historical Society Museum, 104, Old Cienega Village Museum, 138, Old Land Office Building Museum, 6, Old Town Museum, 96, Old West Museum, 80, Panhandle-Plains Historical Museum, 15, Patterson Memorial County Library and Museum, 17, Pimeria Alta Historical Museum, 154, Pioneer Woman Statue and Museum, 108, Polk County Memorial Museum, 56, Port Arthur Historical Museum, 65, Rankin Museum, 65, Roosevelt County Museum, 134, Rough Rider and City Museum, 126, Salt River Project History Center, 164, San Antonio Museum Association, 70, San Jacinto Museum of History, 51, San Pedro Valley Historical Society, 144, Sapulpa Historical Society Museum, 109, Schleicher County Museum, 32, Scottsdale Historical Society, 163, Scurry County Museum, 79, Sherman Historical Museum, 79, Silver City Museum, 139, Somervell County Museum, 41, SPJST Museum, 81, Square House Museum, 63, Star of the Republic Museum, 84, Stone Fort Museum, 61, Stonewall Saloon Museum, 67, Sulphur Springs Valley Historical Society, 168, Tempe Historical Museum, 164, Texarkana Historical Society and Museum, 81, Texas Baptist Historical Center and Museum, 51, Texas Memorial Museum, 8, Thunderbird Frontier Museum, 98,

Tucker Tower Museum, 92, Tucumari Historical Museum, 141, Tularosa Basin Historical Society Museum, 116–17, Washington-on-the-Brazos State Historical Park, 84, Wells Fargo Museum, 165, West of the Pecos Museum, 64, Western New Mexico University Museum, 139, Western Trails Museum, 95, Wheeler County Museum, 85, White Deer Land Museum, 63, Whitehead Memorial Museum, 28, XIT Museum, 18; horse, Stradling Museum of the Horse, 154; Indian (*see also* Halls of Fame; Indian art and culture), Blackwater Draw Museum, 135, Cherokee National Museum, 109, Chickasaw Council House Museum, 110, Creek Council House and Museum, 106, Cultural Center Indian Museum, 108, Ernest Thompson Seton Memorial Library and Museum, 123, Five Civilized Tribes Museum, 100, Gallup Museum of Indian Arts and Crafts, 124, Heard Museum, 156, Indian City U.S.A., 91, Institute of American Indian Arts Museum, 138, Museum of the Red River, 99, Navajo Tribal Museum, 169, Plains Indians and Pioneer Historical Foundation, 113, Pueblo Grande Museum, 156, Quechan Indian Museum, 170, Seminole Nation Museum, 112, Smoki Museum, 162, Southern Plains Indian Museum and Crafts Center, 92, Tusyan Museum, 150, Wheelwright Museum of the American Indian, 138; Jewish, Judaica Museum of Temple Beth Israel, 161; marine (*see* Aquariums); medical science (*see also* Museums, natural history; Museums, science), Museum of Flight Medicine, 76, Museum of Medical Science, 46; Mexican, Museum of Mexican Heritage, 167; military (*see also* Forts; Parks, historical), Admiral Nimitz Center, 37, Black Kettle Museum, 94, Confederate Air Force Flying Museum, 43, El Paso Cavalry Museum, 32, Fort Bliss Replica Museum, 30, Fort Davis Museum, 34, 45th Infantry Division Museum, 106, Museum of the 1st Cavalry Division and the 2d Armored Division, 54, 36th Infantry Division War Museum, 8, U.S. Army Field Artillery and Fort Sill Museum, 97; mineralogy, Arizona Mineral Museum, 156, University of Arizona Mineralogy Museum, 168; mining (*see also* Mining towns; Museums, historic; Parks, historic), Bisbee Mining and Historical Museum, 146, Coal County Miners Museum and Genealogical Library, 95, Courthouse Museum, 165; natural history and wildlife (*see also* Aquariums; Parks, natural history and wildlife; Zoos), American Bird Museum, 116, Big Thicket Museum, 78, Brazos Valley Museum, 14, Brazosport Museum of Natural Science, 12, Buckthorn Hall of Horns, 69, Dallas Museum of Natural History, 20, El Paso Centennial Museum, 32, Ghost Ranch Museum, 116, Lake Meredith Aquatic and Wildlife Museum, 38, Natural Science Center, 6, Quanah Parker Center, 94, Strecker Museum, 84, Wilderness Park Museum, 32, Witte Memorial Museum, 70; oil (*see also* Petroleum), Gladys City Boomtown Museum, 10, Permian Basin Petroleum Museum, 59; pioneer, Beaver City Museum, 93, Callahan County Pioneer Museum, 8, Cherokee Outlet Museum, 93, Firehall Museum, 18, Folsom Museum, 123, Geraldine Humphreys Museum, 55, Hemphill County Pioneer Museum, 14, Northern Arizona Pioneers' Historical Society, 148, Old Rock House, 78, Pioneer Memorial Museum, 18, Pioneer Museum (Sweetwater), 80, Plains Indians and Pioneer Historical Foundation, 113; presidential, Presidential Museum, 62; religious (*see also* Churches; Missions), Biblical Arts Center, 27; science (*see also* Anthropology; Archaeology, Museums, medical science; Museums, natural history and wildlife), Albuquerque Museum of Art, History, and Science, 118, Bradbury Science Museum, 132, Carlsbad Municipal Museum, 121, Dallas Health and Science Museum, 19, Fort Worth Museum of Science and History, 35, Houston Museum of Natural Science, 45, Oklahoma Center for Science and Arts, 104, Omniplex, 105, Roswell Museum and Art Center, 135, Stovall Museum of Science and History, 103, Wichita Falls Museum and Art Center, 85, Witte Memorial Museum, 70; sports (*see* Halls of fame); steam power (*see also* Railroadiana), Live Steam Museum, 3; weapons (*see also* Forts; Museums, historical; Museums, military), Confederate Research Center and Audie Murphy Gun Museum, 44, J. M. Davis Gun Museum, 94, National Atomic Museum, 118, Woolaroc Museum, 93

NASA (*see* Space exploration)
National Monuments (*see* Cactus; Canyons; Cattle ranching; Cliff dwellings; Forts; Parks, scenic; Parks, volcanic; Parks, wilderness; Pueblos; Ruins)
Natural bridge (Cedar Canyon), 97
Nature trails (*see also* Canyons; Deserts; Parks, nature and wildlife; Parks, scenic): Aquarena Springs, 77; Arizona-Sonora Desert Museum, 166; Big Thicket National Preserve, 78; Caddo Lake State Park, 53; Chiricahua National Monument, 144; Heard Natural Science Museum and Wildlife Sanctuary, 56–57; Holland Lake Park, 85; Monahans Sandhills State Park, 59; Saguaro National Monument, 166; Stephen F. Austin State Park, 77; Texas Forestry Museum, 56; Woolaroc complex, 93
Naval vessels: *Texas*, 51; *U.S.S. Batfish*, 100; *U.S.S. Cavalla*, 41; *U.S.S. Stewart*, 41
Nuclear energy (*see also* Atom bomb; Museums, science): National Atomic Museum, 118

Observatories: Kitt Peak National Observatory, 152; McDonald Observatory, 34
Oil (*see also* Museums, oil): Beaumont, Texas, 9; Lucas Gusher, 9; Moorhead derrick, 54; Nellie Johnstone Oil Well, 92; Oklahoma State Capitol Building, 104; Pioneer Park, 54; Spindletop oil field, 9
Old Rip (horned toad), 29
Oriental art (*see* Galleries, art; Museums, art)
Overland routes (*see* Historic trails)

Paintings (*see also* Art galleries; Museums, art; Religious art): *Bluebonnet* (Walker), 7; *Boom Town* (Benton), 12
Parks: Amusement (*see* Parks, theme and amusement); desert (*see also* Fossils), Chiricahua National Monument, 146, Organ Pipe Cactus National Monument, 144; historical (*see also* Indian mounds), Alamo State Park, 68, Alibates Flint Quarries National Monument, 38, Caddo Lake State Park, 53, Coronado State Monument, 120, Governor Hogg Shrine State Historical Park, 65, Heavener State Park, 98, Jerome State Historic Park, 151, Johnstone Park, 92, Jourdan-Bachman Pioneer Settlers Memorial Park and Pioneer Farm, 7, Lincoln Memorial Park, 106, Old Fort Parker State Historic Site, 58, Painted Rocks State Historic Park, 149, Port Isabel Lighthouse, 65, San Felipe de Austin State Park, 76, Texas State Railroad State Historical Park, 67, Tubac Presidio State Historic Park, 165, Yuma Territorial Prison State Park, 170; military (*see also* Forts; Parks, historical; Ruins), Seawolf Park, 41; nature and wildlife (*see also* Deserts; Forests and forestry), Big Bend National Park, 10, Big Thicket National Preserve, 78, Frank Phillips Ranch, 92, Santa Ana National Wildlife Refuge, 3, Wichita Mountains Wildlife Refuge, 94;

recreational (*see also* Parks, theme and amusement), Chickasaw National Recreational Area, 95, Dallas State Fair Park grounds, 19, Glen Canyon Dam and National Recreation Area, 154, Lake Mead and Hoover Dam recreation area, 152; scenic (*see also* Canyons; Caves and Caverns; Dunes; Forests and forestry; Parks, desert; Parks, volcanic; Parks, wilderness), Carlsbad Caverns National Park, 20, Grand Canyon, vii, 143,150, Monument Valley National Monument, 153, Palo Duro Canyon State Park, 15, Petrified Forest National Park, 155, Valley of the Fires State Park, 122; theme and amusement, Alamo Village, 12, Aquarena Springs, 77, Astroworld, 45, HemisFair Plaza, 69, Legend City, 164, Old Abilene Town, 2, Pioneer Town, 86, Presidents Park, 121, Rawhide, 163, Six Flags over Texas, 5, Six Shooter Junction, 43, Wonder World, 77; tribal, Tse Bonito Tribal Park, 169; volcanic, Capulin Mountain National Monument, 120, Sunset Crater National Monument, 148; wilderness (*see also* Forests and forestry; Parks, desert; Parks, volcanic), Bandelier National Monument, 132, Gila Cliff Dwellings National Monument, 124

Petroglyphs (*see also* Indian art and culture): Newspaper Rock, 155; Three Rivers Petroglyph Site, 30

Petroleum (*see also* Oil; Museums, oil): Phillips Petroleum Company Exhibit Hall, 92

Photography (*see also* Museums, art; Museums, historical): Center for Creative Photography, 168; John Harlan photograph collection, 139; George Washington Long photography collection, 91

Planetariums: Burke Baker Planetarium, 45; Don Harrington Discovery Center, 4; Flandrau Planetarium, 167; Kirkpatrick Planetarium, 104

Prehistoric edifices (*see* Pueblos; Ruins)

Prehistoric Indians (*see* Indian peoples; Irrigation systems; Pueblos; Ruins)

Pueblos (*see also* Ruins): Abo State Monument, 133; Acoma (Sky City), 116, 137; Albuquerque region pueblos, 117; Aztec Ruins National Monument, 119; Betatakin, 154; Casa Rinconada, 122; Giusewa Pueblo, 125; Inscription House, 154; Keet Seel, 154; Ledge House, 154; Montezuma's Well, 153; Pecos Pueblo, 134; Pueblo Bonito, 122; Pueblo of Analco, 136; Quarai Pueblo, 133; Taos Pueblo, 140; Zuni Pueblo, 141

Railroadiana: Age of Steam Railroad Museum, 20; Cumbres and Toltec Scenic Railroad, 122; Jay Gould's Private Railroad Car, 52; Railroad and Pioneer Museum, Inc., 80; Southern Pacific Railroad depot, 145; Texas Railroad Museum, 85; Texas State Railroad, 67

Ranching (*see* Cattle ranching)

Religious art (*see also* Art galleries; Churches; Missions; Museums, art): *La Conquistadora*, 136; *Miracle at Pentecost* mural, 27; Mystery Painting (Ault), 135

Research facilities (*see also* Museums, medical science; Museums, natural history and wildlife; Museums, science): King Ranch, 54; Kitt Peak Observatory, 152; San Juan County Archaeological Research Center, 120; Sandia Laboratories, 119

Restored and historic districts (*see* Town districts)

Rockhounding: Arizona Mineral Museum, 136; Woodward Agate Ranch, 4

Rocks and rock formations (*see also* Canyons): Inscription Rock, 135; Rhyolite Park (Wonderland of Rocks), 146; Tse Bonito Tribal Park, 169; Window Rock formation, 169

Rodeos (*see* Festivals, fairs, and annual events)

Ruins (*see also* Forts; Museums, Indian;

Parks, historical; Parks, scenic): Aztec Ruins National Monument, 119; Besh-ba-Gowan Indian Ruin, 150; Casa Grande Ruins National Monument, 147; Chaco Canyon National Monument, 122; Coronado State Monument, 120; El Morro National Monument, 135; Gran Quivira National Monument, 133; Kinlichee ruins, 149; Navajo National Monument, 153; Pecos National Monument, 134, Puerco Indian Ruin, 155; Salmon Ruins, 120; Tumacacori Mission National Monument, 168; Tusyan Museum, 150; Tuzigoot National Monument, 147; White House, 146; Wupatki National Monument, 148
Runestones: Heavener Runestone, 98; Kerr Museum, 108
Scenic Drives (*see also* Parks, scenic; Parks, volcanic): Apache Trail, 149; Arizona Route 60 North, 150; Canyon de Chelly, 146; El Camino del Rio, 55; Painted Desert, 155; South Rim (Grand Canyon) 150; White Sands loop drive, 117
Sculpture: Coleman County Museum horse statue, 16; *End of the Trail* (Buffalo Bill statue), 105; *Pioneer Woman*, 108; Rosa's Window, 75; *Wrestlers, The*, 109
Shopping (*see* Markets and shopping districts; Town districts)
Sightseeing tours and excursions (*see also* Mines): *Brasos Queen* trip, 82; Cumbres and Toltec Scenic Railroad, 122; *Cypress Queen* cruise, 53; Ellen Trout Zoo miniature train ride, 56; Hoover Dam tours, 153; Ranger Peak Aerial Tramway, 30; Rio Grande Float Trips, 54; South Rim (Grand Canyon), 150; Texas State Railroad trip, 67; Treasure Isle Tour Train, 39
Slide shows (*see* Dramatic and slide presentations)
Soft Ball (*see* Halls of fame)
Solar energy (*see also* Museums, science; Research facilities): National Atomic Museum, 118; Sandia Laboratories, 119
Space exploration (*see also* Halls of fame; Museums, aviation and space): Lyndon B. Johnson Space Center, 44
State boundaries: Four Corners, 149; No Man's Land (Oklahoma), 97
Texas Rangers (*see also* Halls of fame): Texas Ranger Museum, 33
"Touch" and participation exhibits: Arizona Historical Society Touch Museum, 156; Dallas Museum of Natural History, 20; Institute of Texan Cultures, 70; Mesa Museum, 153; Mohave Museum of History and Arts, 152; Natural Science Center, 6; Oklahoma City Zoo, 105; Old County Jail and Archer County Museum, 86; Phoenix Art Museum, 155; Quanah Parker Center, 94
Tours (*see* Sightseeing tours and excursions)
Town districts (*see also* Markets and shopping districts): Brewery Gulch (Bisbee), 145; Canyon Road (Santa Fe), 137; Old Town (Albuquerque), 118; Paseo del Rio (San Antonio), 69; Santa Fe Plaza, 136; Whiskey Row (Prescott), 162
Trading posts: Hubbell Trading Post National Historic Site, 149; Lajitas Trading Post, 54; Sunset Trading Post, 80
Trails (*see* Historic trails; Nature trails)
Volcanoes (*see* Parks, volcanic)
Waterfalls: Slide Rock, 163
Watermill: Golda's Bitting Springs Mill, 109
Women (*see* Halls of fame)
Wrestling (*see* Halls of fame)
Zoos: Abilene Zoological Gardens, 2; Central Texas Zoo, 83; Ellen Trout Zoo, 56; Forest Park Zoo, 37; Gladys Porter Zoo, 12; Hermann Park Zoo, 45; Living Desert Zoological and Botanical State Park, 121; Navajo Nation Fairgrounds Zoo, 169; Oklahoma City Zoo, 105; Phoenix Zoo, 156; San Antonio Zoo, 76; Texas Zoo (Victoria), 82; Tulsa Zoological Park, 111